Dr Chris Johnstone is one of the UK's leading resilience trainers, with more than three decades' experience teaching in this field. He graduated in medicine with distinction in 1986, after a first degree specialising in psychology. Experiencing burnout and depression as a junior hospital doctor, he became a leading figure in the campaign to improve working conditions. He trained as a GP before moving into the mental-health field, where for many years he ran groups teaching resilience skills. Influenced much by positive psychology, he trained with Martin Seligman and other leading practitioners in 2005. Since then he has pioneered the role of resilience training in mental-health promotion, coaching practice and the workplace. His previous book *Active Hope* (co-authored with Joanna Macy) has been published in more than eight languages, his video-based online course *Personal Resilience in an Hour* has participants from more than 55 countries. He lives in the north of Scotland, where he teaches online at CollegeofWellbeing.com.

Praise for Seven Ways to Build Resilience

'Practical and clear with strategies that work, this is, by far, the best book I've read on resilience.'
Miriam Akhtar, Author of Positive Psychology for Overcoming Depression

'Chris Johnstone is a writer whose voice is inviting, engaging and to the point.'
Joanna Macy, co-author of Active Hope and Coming Back to Life

'After working through the programme described in this book, I had an emergency admission to hospital. I asked myself 'what would a story of resilience look like here?' and applied my resilience toolkit. Doing that transformed a potentially horrendous situation. These tools really work.'
Heather Thompson, Personal Development Coach, www.positivelycoaching.co.uk

Further praise for *Seven Ways to Build Resilience*

'If you want to strengthen your unique tapestry of personal resilience, this inspiring and far-reaching book weaves in much-needed threads.'
David Peters, Professor Emeritus, The Centre for Resilience, University of Westminster

'If you are dealing with a difficult situation, in a personal or professional capacity, then this book provides a well-researched and practical step-by-step guide to finding a new positive direction. Can't recommend it highly enough!'
Deirdre Murray, Executive Coach, Trainer and Author, PeopleResources.ie

'Chris Johnstone's sparkling insight, playful wisdom and clarity of understanding never fails to inspire and energise.'
Sarah Pugh, Trainer for Practical Sustainability, www.shiftbristol.org.uk

'Chris Johnstone is a gifted trainer who manages to turn complex ideas into clear and practical guiding wisdom.'
Nicola Banning, Editor of BACP Workplace

'There is a wealth of material here for anyone wanting help to nurture their own resilience or anyone wanting to support resilience in other people.'
Lisa Rossetti, academic researcher, executive coach and community writing practitioner

'I find Chris Johnstone's approach to resilience both inspiring and easy to implement. He offers useful tools and practices that get results. A much-needed approach in today's world.'
Lisbet Michelsen, Coach-therapist, Somerset

'Chris Johnstone has assembled a treasure trove of practices, background science and real-life examples of how to build resilience.'
Kathy Sipple, co-Author of Empower Your Life *and other books about sustainable living, kathysipple.com*

Seven Ways to
Build Resilience

Dr Chris Johnstone

ROBINSON

ROBINSON

First published in Great Britain in 2019 by Robinson

1 3 5 7 9 10 8 6 4 2

A CIP catalogue record for this book
is available from the British Library.

ISBN: 978-1-47214-113-2

Typeset in Gentium Basic by Hewer Text UK Ltd, Edinburgh
Printed and bound in Great Britain by Clays Ltd, Elcograf S.p.A.

Papers used by Robinson are from well-managed forests and other responsible sources.

Robinson
An imprint of
Little, Brown Book Group
Carmelite House
50 Victoria Embankment
London EC4Y 0DZ

An Hachette UK Company
www.hachette.co.uk

www.littlebrown.co.uk

Contents

Introduction

For just a moment, I close my eyes. When I open them I'm on the wrong side of the road with a car speeding towards me. Swerving to avoid a collision, my car spins out of control and veers off the road towards a rock face.

This was me in May 1989. My holiday in Scotland had just crashed into a pile of rocks. While I escaped with few injuries, my car was a wreck. Falling asleep at the wheel was just a symptom, though. There was a deeper crisis unfolding in my life.

Only days before, I'd finished a working week of 112 hours. After many months of round-the-clock shifts as a junior doctor, I was suffering from severe exhaustion. I'd become clinically depressed. I was burned out to a cinder.

Resilience is a two-part story

In the chapters ahead, we're going to follow a storyline that is in two parts. There's what happens – that's part one, and it involves bumping into some kind of difficulty. 'Here's me, facing this . . .' is how it begins. For me crashing, it wasn't just the rocks – I was also facing the worst time of my life, when I had felt so depressed I even considered killing myself.

Then we come to the second part of the story, which is what happens next. When we are going through bumpy times, what comes next is still in front of us. It is something we can still influence. We're going to be looking at what helps us develop a better version of how that next bit goes.

There's a key insight here: whatever situation we face, no matter how awful, there are always different ways it can work out. When I train people in resilience, I draw this as a diagram that looks like a spider on its side. From the starting point of where we are now, a range of timelines extend into the future, each leg of the spider representing a different version of how things might go.

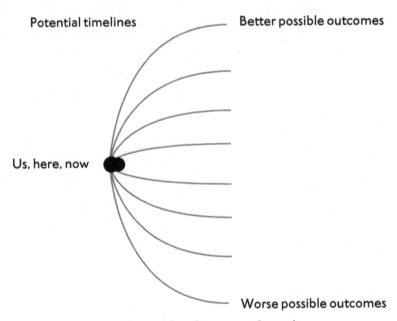

Fig. 1: The spider diagram of timelines

When things take a turn for the worse, and you find yourself on the downward slope of a difficult timeline, think of this as the first part of the story. The spider diagram reminds you that even from the bottom of a pit, there are still different ways it can go. Things could get worse, that's true. Something else is possible too.

In difficult situations, there are times when we surprise ourselves, finding new strengths and rising to the occasion in ways that make the second part of the story turn out better than expected. Resilience is what helps us do this: it is our capacity to cope with adversity, make the best of things and recover from setbacks. In a story of resilience, the first part descends into a dip. The second part is about how we find, and follow, the upslope.

Fig. 2: Resilience as a two-part story

Is resilience learnable?

You might know people who seem naturally thick-skinned, bouncing back from one disaster after another. 'All you have to do is get back up and try again,' said billionaire Richard Branson after he nearly died crashing his bicycle at high speed in 2016.[1] In previous close brushes with death, he'd capsized his speedboat trying to cross the Atlantic, fallen from a great height into the same ocean when a balloon trip went wrong and survived the burning down of his home. What is it that makes some people more resilient than others?

This life-enhancing ability to deal with difficult times is sometimes thought of as a natural quality, like tallness, that some people have, and others don't. Unlike tallness though, research confirms that resilience can be cultivated.[2] It has a lot in common with physical fitness. While some people are naturally in better shape than others, we can all train ourselves to get fitter. Resilience is a form of psychological fitness where, rather than growing muscles, we're building inner strengths. However, even this isn't the whole story.

Have you had an important learning experience years ago that still makes a difference to your life now? The benefits of a physical fitness session might wear off within weeks, but there are lessons I learned about resilience decades ago that still have a positive impact on my life today. Some skills, like being able to swim or ride a bicycle, never really leave you. Once you gain them they are always there somewhere in the background, ready to be used when needed. That's why the focus of this book is on skills – seven particular skills – that strengthen our capacity to face and deal with challenges. Together they can take your resilience to new levels; once learned, they can still be with you years later, in ways that bring long-term improvement to your life.

Over recent decades, there has been a shift in our scientific understanding of what resilience is based on and what helps it grow. Ground-breaking research published in 1995 showed that teaching resilience skills to children reduced their risk of depression, with benefits still present years later.[3] As the training intervention was developed by psychologists at the University of Pennsylvania, it has become known as the Penn Resilience Program. Further studies showed that it helps reduce anxiety and depression in adults too.[4]

General George Casey, US army chief of staff, was so impressed by these findings that he asked Martin Seligman, the psychologist leading this research, to help design resilience training for US service personnel. 'I want to create an army that is just as psychologically fit,' he said, 'as it is physically fit.'[5] Outcome studies show the programme they developed helps reduce levels of depression, anxiety, drug and alcohol problems and post-traumatic stress disorder.[6]

Recent research on resilience training in the workplace has shown that it not only improves emotional wellbeing, it also leads to gains in performance too. In a review of relevant studies, a team of leading specialists in workplace wellbeing wrote:

> Findings indicated that resilience training can improve personal resilience and is a useful means of developing mental health and subjective wellbeing in employees. We also found that resilience training has a number of wider benefits that include enhanced psychosocial functioning and improved performance.[7]

We can teach ourselves skills that help us suffer less when times are hard and perform better under pressure too.

An insight about turning points

When I was working those hundred-hour weeks as a junior doctor, I gathered a group of colleagues together for a resilience workshop. We called the day 'Coping without Sleep', and our goal was to share strategies that might help us survive our difficult working conditions. We came to the conclusion that self-help strategies could play an essential role, but by themselves they weren't enough. We also needed to address the conditions we worked in and our ability to meet core needs like sleep.

Resilience is a bigger concept than endurance; it isn't just about putting up with awfulness. It is more to do with looking at what helps us when facing adversity – about how we find a better part two when the first part of the story starts off badly. While endurance is often useful and sometimes essential, there are also times when we are better served by self-compassion or the ability to bring about constructive change. Resilience requires different strengths at different times.

So how does this link to my crash? Well, there I was, sitting in the wreck of a car, at a time of crisis in my life, having nearly just died. Amazingly, I look back on that time and treasure it as a vital turning point.

One way that difficult situations can change for the better is when crisis acts as a wake-up call. The hitting rock bottom of addiction recovery is a good example – this is when someone is so shocked by how awful things have got that they make a deep-seated decision to change. Something like that happened with me. Crashing into that rock face woke me up to what was going on in my life.

When you drive yourself on and on and on, without taking enough time for recovery and renewal, you increase the risk of an accident. My crash was like a reflection of my life. I had a sense of dread that if I carried on the same way, going back to the same hazardous conditions of work after my holiday, it wouldn't be long before I crashed again. If not another car crash, there were plenty of other disasters I was heading towards, such as worsening depression or a serious medical error at work. There's a saying that, 'If you carry on the way you're going, you'll end up where you're headed.' I was heading for another crash. I got it. Resilience for me was about making life-preserving choices. I resigned.

My journey

With the two-part story of 'There's what happens, and then there's what happens next,' neither part happens all at once. There's a sequence of events that add together and develop over time. The big shift for me with my crash was really getting the point that my work stress was causing so much more than just unhappiness. It had become a matter of life and death. Missing that oncoming car had taken me within a few feet of a possible fatality – either my own or someone else's. I felt such deep and grateful relief for my near-miss.

When facing something horrible, a term I love is 'inspirational dissatisfaction'. I hated the way my life was going, and within me felt a powerful intention activated. It wasn't only my desire to escape the ghastliness of sleep deprivation and burnout. It also felt deeply wrong to be working as a doctor in a manner so harmful to health. I made a promise to myself to seek out a better way of practising medicine: one where I 'walked my talk', not only in countering illness, but also in actively moving towards wellbeing. So I started a journey, and the place where I needed to begin was with my own recovery, finding, step by step, the upslope of my dip.

I'd been interested in self-help approaches ever since my first degree, which combined medicine and psychology. For several years before my crash, I'd taught relaxation techniques to help my patients improve their sleep, reduce anxiety and cope with pain. Now my interest in self-help tools took on new meaning and deeper relevance. I wanted to learn everything I could about how people deal with stress, recover from depression and restore wellbeing after burnout.

Leaving medicine for a while gave me an opportunity to train in psychological therapies. When I came back to finish my GP training, I was struck by how often I'd see people in my surgeries who were struggling with stress. So I set up a stress management clinic and started running courses teaching core self-help skills.

I became so interested in this work that I left General Practice for Mental Health, working for nearly twenty years teaching recovery skills to people with serious alcohol problems. As crisis is a high-risk area for relapse of addiction, a big part of my work was training my clients in ways to build their resilience. I could see that the skills I was teaching were valuable in many other contexts too. So I began to pioneer the role of resilience training in the workplace and in adult education. More recently I've taken my trainings online, and my courses now reach people from more than fifty-five countries around the world.

So that's my two-part story. There was me facing this awful time as an exhausted, depressed junior doctor who for a moment dozed while driving. What happened next was that my car crash so shocked me I made a deep-seated decision to seek out recovery; in doing that I became so interested in resilience that I've ended up becoming one of the leading trainers in the field. It has become my life's work.

Post-traumatic growth

Resilience is often thought of as being able to reach a better than expected outcome *despite* difficult conditions. But in my two-part story there's something different going on. My leading role as a resilience trainer today is not *despite* my past breakdown from burnout, but largely *because* of it. If I hadn't gone through those ghastly years, I wouldn't be as passionate about the work I do or as effective in it. This is an example of 'post-traumatic growth'.[8]

Post-traumatic stress disorder is where traumatic experience leaves us with continuing negative effects. But difficult times don't always end badly, and even when they do, that's often not the whole story. Our experience of adversity can leave us with positive effects too, deepening us, teaching us important lessons and helping us find new strengths. By understanding more about how post-traumatic growth occurs, we can make it more likely. That's one of the goals of this book. And it starts with a simple thought experiment.

Try this – a thought experiment

Every time you face a difficult situation, experiment with the idea that resilience is something you *do* rather than *have*. Ask yourself: 'What would a story of resilience look like here?' and see where your answer takes you.

Life has no shortage of occasions that might frustrate, annoy or disappoint you. If you see each one as an opportunity to practise your resilience tools, you change the meaning of these events and, with that, the way the narrative develops. Instead of feeling so tormented, I invite you to view the awfulness as part one of a story, and then to be curious about what part two brings. Each of the Seven Ways we look at focuses on a different skill that might help you here.

The journey of this book

We start with the skill of storyboarding, as a storyboard is a way of mapping out different elements involved in the story of responding in a resilient way. We've already used a simple story-board framework with the two-part structure of 'There's what happens, and then there's what happens next.' In its simplest form, a storyboard invites you to reflect on both the situation you face and responses that might help. By filling in the gaps, you nudge yourself to consider steps you can take.

HERE'S ME, FACING THIS... (DESCRIBE THE CHALLENGE YOU FACE)	WHAT HELPS HERE IS... (DESCRIBE WHAT HELPS YOU)

Fig. 3: A simple two-part resilience storyboard

The First Way of the book looks more closely at how stories of resilience go, drawing out lessons from inspiring examples and mapping out a framework you can use to design constructive responses to any challenge you face. We'll also look at how to deal with common obstacles to resilience, so that you can better understand roadblocks in the way as well as how to move through (or around) them.

Advances in neuroscience in the last fifteen years have reshaped our understanding of what happens to our nervous system when we're feeling under threat. The Second Way focuses on the skill of emotional first aid, and begins by looking at how our brain works differently when we're agitated. This helps us understand why we might struggle to cope when highly distressed. Emotional first-aid practices are introduced that help us steady ourselves and step into a more resourced state.

While many self-development books encourage positive thinking, the Third Way focuses instead on the skill of thinking flexibly. Based on cognitive therapy, which research identifies as an effective treatment for anxiety and depression, flexible thinking tools are easy to learn, and help retrain our brains to think in a more resilient fashion.

Many people most need their resilience when facing pressures at work. Our Fourth Way takes a close look at the skill of overload management. You'll become more familiar with the 'coping under pressure' curve and learn to recognise stress symptoms at an earlier stage. We'll also look at how to step into a more focused high-performance state, while recognising and keeping within limits to your load-bearing capacity.

As well as introducing new tools and new thinking, resilience training is helpful when it reminds you of what you're already doing that might be working well. For example, many places of work have fire drills set up, so that we're prepared for the worst should it happen. When looking at what helps us deal with the overload of crisis situations, we'll extend the familiar 'worst-case preparedness' approach of fire drills to introduce the idea of a 'crisis drill', where we think in advance about how to respond to adversities we might face.

To open up new ways of moving forward in areas we feel stuck, we need to draw upon our creativity. What's recently become clear is that inventiveness is learnable – we can teach ourselves techniques that improve our creative problem-solving abilities. Research shows problem-solving training can be as effective as antidepressants in treating depression, though we don't need to be depressed in order to benefit.[9] With the Fifth Way, we look at insights and practices that help us develop this skill of problem solving.

In my coaching and training work, I've often seen people have breakthroughs when they stop struggling all by themselves in an area where they feel stuck, and instead reach out by asking for help. The Sixth Way – on the skill of strengthening support – explores how to draw in the help we need. We identify common obstacles to asking for and receiving support, as well as ways to help ourselves move through these. Moving from personal to interpersonal resilience, we also look at what helps us deal with bumpy patches in relationships, so that we can get better at repairing them when they go wrong.

Just as you can have resilience in relationships, so you can also have it in teams, groups, communities and organisations. Having a resilient team or group around you acts as a buffer supporting your personal resilience. A way of building support around you is to look at how you can strengthen the resilience of whatever larger groups or communities you belong to. In the Sixth Way, we'll look at how to do that, applying resilience tools to the purpose of improving conditions and cultivating a favourable environment around us.

The real key to making the resilience training offered here work is finding a way to make the practices part of your life. As with fitness, or playing a musical instrument, regular practice makes such a difference. But what helps us keep to our good intentions and make positive changes stick? Fortunately, the science of behaviour change is another area where significant advances have been made in the last twenty years. Focusing on the skill of stick-ability, the Seventh Way introduces research-informed strategies that help embed resilience-supporting choices and actions so they're still bringing you benefits in years to come.

To make these seven ways easier to remember, I use the acronym SETOPSS. Each letter points to a pathway to helping resilience grow.

The SETOPSS Programme
_____

S - Storyboarding
E - Emotional First-Aid
T - Thinking Flexibly
O - Overload Management
P - Problem Solving
S - Strengthening Support
S - Stickability

Fig. 4: The Seven Ways of SETOPSS

Who this book is for

Firstly, this book is for you, if you are facing something tough right now and want tools you can use. It might be you're under pressure at work, or you're feeling challenged in your personal life. Whether you've had a setback recently or have been struggling for a while, we're going to be looking at practical strategies and insights that can help.

Secondly, this book is for you if you'd like to get better at helping other people deal with difficult situations. If you want to pass resilience strategies on to people you work with, as a way of helping resilience grow within your team, organisation, clients, patients or students, then you'll find much here that is both easy to teach and effective to use.

Thirdly, this book is for you if you recognise resilience as a life-enhancing quality that helps you take on challenges and not be put off by setbacks along the way. If you have hopes or ambitions with inevitable hurdles in the way, resilience can help you survive the bumps and keep to your path.

Do you recognise yourself here?

If so, let's begin.

The First Way – Storyboarding

Storyboarding is a way of viewing the present moment as part of a larger sequence of events, as part of an unfolding story. When you use a storyboard to support resilience, you map out elements of the story you'd like to see develop, focusing on both the challenges you face and factors that help you address them.

The First Way includes:

1

Identifying Inspiring Examples

On a cold February morning in Afghanistan, Giles Duley was out on patrol. He was doing the work he'd been at for a decade – following the lives of people facing adversity. As a photographer, he told their stories through his pictures.[1] He captured images both of challenges faced and strengths expressed. The people he was with this time were US soldiers. Giles was doing a story about the impact of war, revealing through his camera an inside view of life on the front line. But then he took a step that turned his own life upside down. He trod on a landmine.

At first, it seemed his life might be over. Then, after a series of operations and two months in intensive care, Giles regained consciousness to find both his legs amputated and one arm too. He was told he'd never walk, and certainly never work, again.[2]

In a two-part story of resilience, this is part one. There's what happens, and sometimes this is completely awful. Yet even with extreme adversities, like for Giles here, the spider diagram we looked at in the introduction still holds true (see Fig. 1 below). Whatever situation we face, there will be different ways it can work out. The second part of a story of resilience involves finding and following one of the better possible timelines. That can be hard going. So we need to draw on helping factors that support the climb out of a dip.

Part 1: A turn for the worse

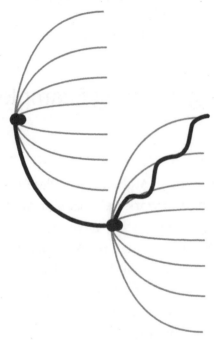

Part 2: Following a better timeline

Fig. 1: The spider diagram revisited

Something that helped Giles was remembering stories of people he'd photographed. In 2009, he'd spent time with Rohingya refugees in Bangladesh, a people described as the most persecuted on the planet.[3] Driven from their homes in Myanmar (formerly Burma), yet not at that time recognised as refugees by the international community, they were denied access to support from aid agencies and had raw sewage running through their camp. While their situation appeared hopeless, they didn't give up.

In 2010, Giles had lived alongside street children in Ukraine, looking through his camera lens to bring their stories to the world. Their squatted house in Odessa was in a state of partial collapse; materially they had nothing. Remembering their resilience helped Giles access his. Their stories were a source of strength.

What is resilience?

The word resilience comes from the Latin 'resilire', which means 'to leap back'.[4] An object or material is resilient when it springs back into shape after being stretched or squashed. Economies, communities, ecosystems and organisations are resilient when they cope with shocks or find their way back to wellbeing after periods of disruption. Our focus is on personal resilience, looking at what helps you cope with adversities and recover from setbacks, so that you can make the best of whatever situation you face. The definition I use when training is this:

> Resilience is the ability to deal with,
> find strengths in,
> and/or recover from,
> difficult times.

A principle I find helpful is, 'First what, then how'. When you want to learn something, first get clear *what* it is, then look at *how* you do it. In getting to know what resilience is, examples are often more revealing than definitions. Resilience shows itself in different ways; the same definition can be expressed in a variety of styles. Examples also have a power to teach and inspire us; they give us a pattern to follow. Our goal in this chapter is to become more familiar with the story of what resilience looks like. When you get to know this story well, and some of the different ways it can happen, it becomes easier to consider how a story of resilience might go in the situation you face.

A starting point here is to think about the difference between a tennis ball and a tomato. Imagine holding each in turn and squeezing. What happens? You don't have to exert much pressure before the tomato collapses in a mess. A tennis ball, by contrast, gives a little when squashed, but springs back into shape afterwards. When thrown at the ground, the ball bounces back. That image of a ball rebounding is often associated with resilience. But 'bouncing back' is just one version of how the story can go.

If you buried a tomato and tennis ball in soil, then came back after many years, what might you find? A partially decomposed tennis ball would most likely look a mess. But if you're at the right time of year, you might see plants bearing juicy fresh tomatoes ready to be picked. Each tomato contains seeds that carry life forward, plants dying down in difficult conditions like droughts or cold winters yet sprouting back year after year. When adversity is followed by new growth, where we rise again but in a different form, we can think of this as 'bouncing forward'.

For a third type of bounce, I think of a cork floating in a rough sea. It bobs up and down with the waves, having a buoyancy to bounce with the storm rather than be sunk by it. We can be like this too when we're holding it together in tricky situations, being with our own rises and falls without letting them get to us too much. This 'bouncing with' is about coping with challenging situations. We don't dip down so deeply because we've found ways to sustain, steady or protect ourselves.

When you're facing a difficult situation, it is easy to think the worst. The story running through your mind might follow the shape of 'Because of this . . . therefore that . . . ', where because the first part is awful, it is easy to assume the second part will be too. Each type of bounce described here gives the story somewhere different to go. They suggest a part two that either rises after the fall or resists continued descent. The tennis ball, tomato and cork bobbing with the waves remind you that a storyline of resilience has a range of routes it can follow.

What is storyboarding?

Years ago, I worked with a sleep specialist who taught me how to help people who experienced recurrent nightmares. If someone dreads going to sleep because they fear their bad dream will return, you invite them to think of ways it could have a better ending (see Fig. 2 below). Each nightmare has a story involving scary scenes. But even the most terrifying encounter is more manageable when you have a direction to move in that heads the way you want. When someone with nightmares has found a more encouraging storyline to follow, you invite them to close their eyes, imagine themselves back in the dream and then make their way to the good ending.

There's what happens

The nightmare

And then there's
what happens next

Finding a better ending

Fig. 2: A treatment for recurrent nightmares

What you're doing with storyboarding is thinking about how you'd like the story to go in the situation you face. You're mapping out a sequence that moves from one thing to another. If the starting point of 'Here's me facing this' has nightmarish qualities, think of ways the story of what's happening could have a good or better ending. While you don't know for sure what will happen, thinking about how you'd like the storyline to go can help you trace a possible pathway that heads the way you want.

The first of our Seven Ways to build resilience is to develop and apply this skill of storyboarding. It is a skill because it is something you can get better at. You can practise, improve your technique, and pick up tips that help you. A simple storyboarding technique we've already looked at is just to ask yourself, 'What would a story of resilience look like here?' and then consider some ways it might go.

We're going to be looking at tools that help you map out resilience narratives more clearly and in more detail, using proven strategies in a framework you can customise to fit the situation you face. So far, our storyboard has four key elements:

a) *The main character.* If you're storyboarding a situation you face, then this is you. If you're using this tool to help someone else, then they would be the main character here. You can also apply the storyboarding process to building resilience in a team, community or organisation. Ask yourself, 'Whose resilience do I want to build or cultivate?' The answer to that question becomes the main character in your story.

b) *The adversity faced.* A key part of what makes it a story of resilience is that there is something difficult or challenging. There's a hazard, risk or obstacle.

c) *Helping factors.* The other essential element in a story of resilience is something that helps the main character cope with, recover from or be strengthened by the adversity. That doesn't mean the story always has a happy ending – just that the main character is able to draw on factors (such as strengths, insights, actions, relationships etc.) that support them in facing the adversity. These helping factors make a better outcome more likely.

d) *Hoped-for outcome.* What we added with the treatment for recurrent nightmares is a better ending. The helping factors lead somewhere different than might have happened without them.

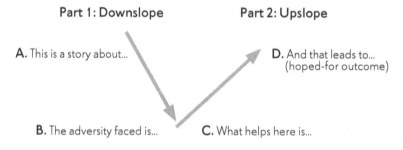

Part 1: Downslope   **Part 2: Upslope**

A. This is a story about...   **D.** And that leads to...
                                                        (hoped-for outcome)

B. The adversity faced is...   **C.** What helps here is...

Fig. 3: A two-part story with four elements

The three forms of bounce represent variations of this storyline, each expressing a different aspect of resilience (see Fig. 4 below).

Bouncing back is about recovery, where, after a period of disruption, the main character returns to a familiar starting point. Examples include getting well after illness or injury and regaining confidence after having lost it.

Bouncing forward is about transformation and growth; it is sometimes known as 'transformative resilience'. Here the story goes through a dip, but then rises again in a way that moves somewhere new. In this version of events, the main character emerges from adversity with added strengths, resources or wisdom. Difficult times might also be the trigger that provokes people to tackle issues and improve things.

In *Bouncing with*, there is a protective element that stops the character dipping so low during difficult times. Known as 'adaptive resilience', this is about coping in the face of hardship, adjusting to changing circumstances and maintaining an inner balance that resists being sunk by difficult conditions.

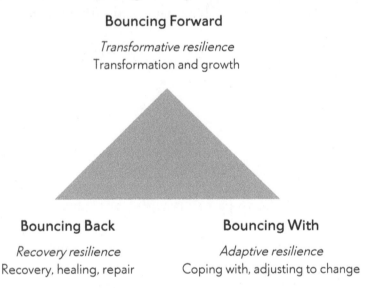

Bouncing Forward

Transformative resilience
Transformation and growth

Bouncing Back

Recovery resilience
Recovery, healing, repair

Bouncing With

Adaptive resilience
Coping with, adjusting to change

Fig. 4: Three types of bounce

Some examples demonstrate one style of bounce more strongly than others; more often they work together. When you're facing a challenge or find yourself dipping in some way, storyboarding resilience involves considering how things might go if you were to express one or more of these different forms of bounce. What would you do? And what might that lead to?

The journey of learning a skill starts from the place of not having it as much as you'd like. Don't be put off if at the moment you're not sure how best to do resilience in the situation you're in. To become skilful in anything, it helps to have models to follow. That's why a first step in resilience training is to become interested in examples, to collect and study them, to give them your attention. The more familiar you are with stories of resilience in general, the easier it is likely to be to bring them into your life.

The photographer returns

It might seem a small thing, but at the time it meant so much. When, after three months, Giles managed to sit up in bed by himself for the first time, he saw that as a great victory. 'From that point I knew I could make it', he said, describing his recovery. From there, he set himself goals so that he'd have achievable next steps to aim for. He wanted to walk (using artificial limbs) by Christmas, go for a drink in his local pub and get back to his home within a year.[5] Beyond that, he wanted to return to his work as a photographer who tells stories we can learn from and be moved by.

Andrew Zolli and Ann Marie Healey, two leading thinkers in the field, define resilience as:

> *the capacity of a system, enterprise, or a person*
> *to maintain its core purpose and integrity*
> *in the face of dramatically changed circumstances.*[6]

For Giles Duley, photography was central to his sense of purpose in life. In February 2011, he'd travelled to Afghanistan with a mission to take pictures, to show us the impact of a war.

Less than two years later, he returned to Kabul to complete the job. This is bouncing back.

Giles didn't stop there. Commissioned by the United Nations to document the refugee crisis across Europe and the Middle East, he travelled to Lebanon, a country where 25 per cent of the population are refugees. His book *One Second of Light* shares his pictures taken both before and after losing three of his limbs. His TED talk has been watched hundreds of thousands of times. 'The way I see it', he wrote, telling his story in the *Observer* newspaper, 'what I'm doing hasn't changed, but my voice has got louder.' In an inspiring example of post-traumatic growth, this is bouncing forward.

When I'm struggling and find myself thinking, 'It's never going to work out,' I say to myself, 'Maybe'. I also remember the spider diagram and think of, among others, Giles Duley. His example is a reference point reminding me we can never know for sure what can and can't happen. One of the most powerful influences on human behaviour is what we see other people do. When we give our attention to those who've got back up after the hardest of falls, it encourages us to do that too.

Recasting a story of defeat

Inspiring stories of recovery expand our sense of possibility. They remind us that even when all seems lost, we can still be surprised by the incredible capacity of life, including the life within us, to regenerate, bouncing back or forward. Yet there are also times when we don't recover, we don't get well, and the downslope is followed by further descent. For times like these we need stories that demonstrate the third kind of bounce. One of my great teachers here is a teenager called Stephen Sutton.[7]

Stephen did well at school, getting good grades in exams, enjoying music and excelling at athletics. He was just fifteen when diagnosed with cancer in his gut. Initially he seemed to have a good response to chemotherapy and radiation treatment. He was declared cancer-free. Then another tumour was found behind his knee.

Spending time in and out of hospital over the next two years, Stephen decided he wanted to study medicine. With top grades in his exams, he was selected for interview at Cambridge University and two other medical schools. However, before hearing whether he'd been offered a place, he withdrew his application. Cancer was in the way. It had spread to his liver and his lungs. His doctors told him his condition was terminal.

About a month later, Stephen did something that was to change the rest of his life. He posted a page on Facebook. Calling it 'StephensStory', this is what he wrote:

Hello everyone! I'm eighteen years old and in the last three years I have been fighting cancerous tumours in my bowel, knee, groin and pelvis. I have had to undergo surgery, radiotherapy and chemotherapy – all resulting in me spending a lot of time in hospital! Medical opinion has ranged from me requiring an amputation to now instead being incurable. This means that realistically I'm facing a very uncertain, and probably very limited, future.

Originally all I ever wanted to do was study hard and make a difference to the world by becoming a doctor, however in light of my current circumstances I have decided to be more pragmatic with my time. This will involve utilising as many short-term opportunities as possible to enrich my own life experience, and most importantly to try and improve the lives of others by fundraising and raising awareness of cancer in teenagers and young adults.

Under this he put details of how people could donate to the Teenage Cancer Trust, and a 'bucket list' of forty-six things he'd like to do in the limited time he had left.

His first goal was to raise £10,000 for charity. Other goals included skydiving for charity, writing a book, organising a charity gig, organising a charity football match, going busking, being part of a flash mob, to drum in front of a huge crowd, hug an animal bigger than him, crowd-surf in a rubber dinghy at a gig, star as an extra in a film or music video, inspire someone else to become a doctor or fundraiser and do some public speaking in front of a huge crowd.

While he didn't reach all the goals on his list, he did succeed in all those listed here. His first goal of raising £10,000 was reached fairly quickly, so he aimed for a million instead. He reached that too, raising more than £3 million for charity in just over a year.

Three zones of challenge

The examples we've looked at so far involve resilience in extreme conditions. The more everyday bumps and knocks of work pressures, tension in relationships or setbacks in our personal lives might seem a long way from these. A useful framework here is to consider three zones of challenge.

The green zone refers to challenges we can deal with easily. The orange zone is where we feel stretched beyond what's comfortable but we're just about able to cope. The red zone is where we're out of our depth, in ways that feel overwhelming or that push us over an edge into panic. What's interesting here is that the zone we're in doesn't only depend on how difficult the challenge is. It is also related to our coping capacity, as the graph in Fig. 5 below illustrates.

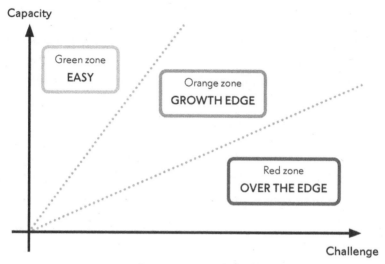

Fig 5: Three zones of challenge

When you're in the green zone, there might not seem much need for resilience – though it can be a good time to prepare yourself for challenges ahead. Nick, a successful businessman, told me, 'Things are fine for me now, but I'm interested in resilience because I want to future-proof myself.' He knew it was reasonably foreseeable that red zone times would happen for him too.

The orange zone is often referred to as our growth edge. In yoga, this is where you stretch just beyond what's comfortable, but in a way that helps flexibility grow. At work, orange days may bring you out in a sweat, but they can also be highly absorbing. You need to give your full attention if you're to step up to a higher level of challenge; the experience and practice you gain from this help your skill level rise. Eventually you reach a point where challenges that used to be stretching feel less daunting. Moving up the vertical axis takes you out of orange and into green.

Resilience training is a way to prepare for the orange and red zones in life. By learning skills that help you steady your nerves, mobilise energy, feel more motivated, think clearly and access support, you can build your bounce-ability. Rather than feel completely defeated when you're over the edge, you might see that what starts as a nightmare can go somewhere very different.

Try this - three zones of challenge

What zones of challenge do you recognise in your life? What zone are you in now? And how has the recent past been? What do you see coming up in the near future? If you're in the green zone, see this as a time to prepare. If you're in the orange or red zones, see this as a time to develop and practise the skills that support your resilience.

While the challenges someone else faces in their orange or red zone may be different to yours, the skills they use that help them cope are likely to be ones you can use too. There is a sequence of steps people take to find the upslope out of their dip. Becoming interested in stories of resilience is a good way of learning what these steps are.

Resilience practice – identify inspiring examples

For this practice exercise, think about examples of resilience you find inspiring. These start in the red zone of challenge, with a turning for the worse. But the main character then expresses one or more of the forms of bounce we've looked at, and this leads to things working out better than you might have expected. You can use the four-element story framework of:

a) This is a story about . . .

b) The adversity faced is . . .

c) What helps here is . . .

d) And that leads to . . .

Here's Stephen's story told using this four-part structure.

a) This is a story about Stephen, a teenager living in the UK.

b) The adversity faced is a diagnosis of cancer when he was fifteen years old. He wanted to become a doctor, but his cancer spread, and when he was seventeen years old, he was told his cancer was terminal, that he was going to die.

c) What helped here is Stephen recognising that although he had much less time left to live than he had hoped, he still had choices about how he spent that time, and he wanted to make the best of it. He wanted to use that time well. He said he saw cancer as 'a kick up the arse'. What also helped Stephen was an ability to make contact with people through Facebook, to get support and collaborators in his project to raise money for charity. Other helping factors included the support of his family and friends, his sense of humour, his creative thinking and his constructive outlook on life.

d) Tragically, Stephen died at the age of nineteen. He didn't bounce back. But the helping factors described here led him to find a much better leg of the spider than might have other-wise occurred. In his book, Stephen writes, 'My story isn't about a teenager with cancer. It's about using my time, however long or short that may be, to have the maximum positive impact. I might not be here forever, none of us will. Life's about making every second count.'

Try this - identifying inspiring examples

What examples of resilience can you think of? Start collecting them, guided by the four prompts of:

a) This is a story about . . .

b) The adversity faced is . . .

c) What helps here is . . .

d) And that leads to . . .

In the next chapter, we'll be looking at how we can apply what we learn from these examples.

2

The Journey Approach to Change

At one of my resilience workshops, there is a buzz in the air. I ask people to raise a hand if they feel inspired or energised by what they've just heard. Nearly everyone does. Acknowledging that her experience had been different, a young woman called Amy looks down, her hands held together in her lap. She shakes her head.

We've just done the 'identifying inspiring examples' process. The arms in the air demonstrate an important feature of resilience: *it is transmissible.* One of the ways we catch it is through stories – through hearing examples in narrative form. But that not everyone is boosted by this process demonstrates another important truth: there are blocks to resilience too. We need to understand what gets in the way. So I was curious about how it was for Amy.

'Doing that made me feel worse,' she told us. 'Here's these people able to cope with the most dire situations, yet I find myself crumbling at the smallest thing. I'll never be like them. I just don't have it in me.'

We live in a society that labels people. From an early age we get classified as 'good' or 'bad' on a whole range of scales. Once we have these labels attached to us, they often become internalised, shaping our sense of who we are and what we're capable of. So how can you build resilience, or help others grow theirs, if the title 'non-coper' gets in the way? It is here that we need to turn to the work of psychologist Carol Dweck.[1]

When Carol was at school, her teacher, Mrs Wilson, arranged the seating in her class to reflect how clever she thought the children were. Those with the highest IQ sat at one end of the room, and the lower their IQ the further away they sat towards the other end. The assumption Carol grew up with was that some people were naturally gifted, our aptitudes and intelligence being set at a particular point early in life. Back then, she thought this was just the way things were and there was little we could do to change it. Later in life, her research showed something quite different.

Carol's great discovery was that the way we think about intelligence influences our ability to learn. One approach, called 'the fixed mindset', sees intelligence levels as something we can't change. Like the colour of our eyes or our adult height, this view regards intellect as mostly the product of our genes. Another perspective, the 'growth mindset', views our brain as like a muscle that grows stronger with training. When we hit a problem, these mindsets take us different ways. If you're struggling, a fixed mindset takes this as evidence that you're not clever enough to succeed with this type of challenge, increasing the chances that you'll give up. The growth mindset sees struggle as an expected part of the journey of learning. Rather than thinking, 'I can't do this,' you're more likely to think, 'I can't do this *yet*.' The simple addition of 'yet' changes the story: it builds in the idea that you might find a way, encouraging you to persist. Research shows that having a growth mindset strengthens people's ability to stick with tasks they find difficult, this persistence helping their abilities grow.[2]

We can apply this same thinking to resilience. As an example, look at the following four statements and rate each one for how much you agree with it.

1) Your resilience is something very basic about you that you can't change very much.

2) You can learn new things, but you can't really change how resilient you are.

3) No matter how much resilience you have, you can always change it quite a bit.

4) You can always substantially change how resilient you are.

The first two are fixed-mindset statements; the last two are growth-mindset statements.[3] The danger of viewing resilience in fixed-mindset terms is that it creates a block. I think of this as a 'going nowhere story' that follows the pattern of 'Here's me, I want to . . . but I can't because . . . ' Amy, the woman shaking her head in my resilience class, had this. 'Here's me, I want to be more like the people in those inspiring stories, but I can't see that happening, I just don't have it in me.' If you ever find yourself thinking like this, where there's a strength you'd like to develop but doubt you have it in you, try adding the word 'yet'. Two recent scientific discoveries might give you some encouragement.

Our brains can change and grow

It used to be widely accepted that once we reach adulthood, our brains stop producing new cells. It was also commonly thought that our personality isn't likely to change much once we've reached our twenties. Over the last few decades, advances in neuroscience have turned both these views on their heads.

A key breakthrough came with the invention of brain-imaging technology. With the use of advanced scanners, we can literally look inside our heads. This kind of research has shown that, for example, an area of the brain concerned with spatial memory and the ability to navigate is better developed in London taxi drivers than London bus drivers.[4] While the bus drivers follow a limited number of routes, the taxi drivers exercise their navigational memory to much greater degrees, causing their hippocampus to grow.

This process of brain cell growth and development is called *neurogenesis*, and it has been shown to continue even in later life. Teaching elderly people to juggle, for example, led to brain growth in areas linked with hand-eye coordination, with results measurable after just three months of practice.[5] 'The reality is,' concludes Harvard Medical School neuroscientist Dr Amar Sahay, 'that everyone has the capacity to generate new brain cells that can help enhance cognitive functions.'[6]

As well as being able to produce new cells, our brains can also rewire and reorganise themselves in response to learning and experience – a process called *neuroplasticity*.[7] This has particular significance for resilience, because it means we can train our brains to become better at dealing with stress. If someone is naturally nervous, with an anxious personality, they can work on skills and practices that help reset their brain to a steadier, and less easily triggered, state. Even relatively small shifts, like being able to approach challenges with more of a growth mindset, can make a difference, as the psychologist David Yeager demonstrated in an experiment with high-school students from New York.[8]

One group of students was given a brief growth-mindset training intervention involving three elements. First, they read a short article summarising recent research that showed our brains and personalities can change. Then they read personal reflections written by older students looking back at how they'd struggled with social challenges, like feeling excluded, but then found ways to deal with this. These narratives normalised the experience of struggle, while also placing the difficult period in the context of a larger story where the students later found a way through. The third part of the growth-mindset training was getting the students to write encouraging advice they'd give to other students facing challenging situations.

The intervention group, together with a control group, were then asked to do something known to be stressful – to give a five-minute talk in front of others. Compared with the control group, those doing the growth-mindset training showed a more settled response to stress, as measured by heart-rate reactions and stress hormone levels. Further studies have shown that students receiving this type of growth-mindset training did better in their exams nine months later than those in a control group, and suffered less from depression too.[9]

From picture to filmstrip

The shift from a fixed to growth mindset is similar to the difference between a picture and a movie. With a fixed mindset, we paint a picture of ourselves a particular way: 'I am like this; I'm not like that' (see Fig. 1 below). Hanging a mental self-portrait on the wall of our mind, we might say things like, 'The idea of me doing that – it's not even in the picture. It's just not going to happen.'

Fig. 1: A fixed mindset

With a growth mindset, imagine instead a roll of movie film (see Fig. 2 below). Just because something isn't in the picture at the start doesn't mean it won't happen later on. Even when a limiting belief seems set in stone, it is possible to chip away at that thought, taking it apart little by little. It is the many small changes from one frame to the next that lead to larger movements and shifts.

Fig. 2: A growth mindset

Have you ever had the experience of succeeding in something that previously you thought you would never be able to do? Or seen someone else move through this process? If you have, it is worth remembering these moments, because they remind us that we can, at times, surprise ourselves. It is also useful to trace the sequence of events where someone moves from not believing they can do something to actually doing it. Here's an example.

Jane used to be terrified of public speaking. She saw herself as timid, and not the kind of person to be the centre of attention. But then a problem happened at work that she might have been able to prevent if only she'd had the confidence to speak out at a meeting. Her fear was undermining her effectiveness, so she decided to take on the project of training herself to find her voice.

Something that made this difficult for Jane was that she blushed easily. When starting to speak she would feel her heart pounding and know she'd be going red in the face. The feeling of embarrassment just made her heart pound even more, and she struggled to find her words. It was easier just to keep her mouth shut.

Then a friend told her about Toastmasters, a club giving people the opportunity to become more confident as speakers. In the group sessions, people took it in turns to talk for just one minute on a topic given to them. With the support of her friend, Jane decided to give it a go. The first time she spoke it was scary – but she also burst out laughing, felt encouraged and had a good evening. She began to see the speaking challenge as a kind of game. Joining the club and coming back regularly, she soon became more confident. Her heart still raced, but not as much. Some years later, she found herself teaching courses to help other people learn to speak in public.

The power of choice points

I think back to Amy, the woman shaking her head at the start of this chapter. Hearing inspiring examples hadn't worked for her. Yet she made an important shift that day. In the morning she'd seen the story of resilience as something that applied to other people, not her. By lunchtime that had changed. What made the difference was learning to use two specific practical tools that, when applied together, helped her face an area she was struggling with and move forward.

While Amy had found the growth mindset attractive as a theory, she wasn't sure how to put it into practice. The idea of choice points made this clearer. A choice point is a moment where we could turn this way or that. We have options facing us, and the path we choose steers us a particular way.

Jane, the woman who'd feared public speaking, came to a significant choice point after feeling regret that she hadn't spoken out at a meeting. She could have just accepted that she was shy. Instead, she decided to tackle her terror of talking in groups. What made her decision a powerful one was the way she followed through and supported her commitment again and again through her other choices (see Fig. 3 below). She opted to tell her friend about her resolve to find her voice. She said yes when invited to the Toastmasters meeting. When her turn came to speak she rose to the challenge rather than pass.

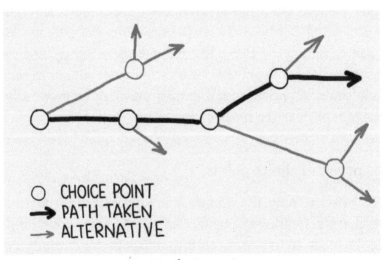

Fig. 3: Choice points

Amy recognised that she'd faced similar choice points. After not coping well with recent knocks at work, she'd made a decision to tackle her sensitivity to stress. That's what led to her coming to the resilience workshop with me. When everyone else raised their hand in enthusiasm for inspiring examples, Amy could have gone along with the crowd and pretended everything was fine, but she didn't. At that moment of awkwardness, there was part of her that felt like giving up and walking out. But she didn't. She stuck with it and told us how she felt.

For both Jane and Amy, many of these choices might not seem that big a deal when looked at in isolation. But taken together, each choice contributed to a larger journey that helped them both make significant shifts. I think of this as *the journey approach to change*, where we recognise the power of these smaller choices and steps, give them our attention and take them.[10] The growth mindset acts through our choices and our steps, not just the big ones, but also the many smaller moment-by-moment preferences we act on each day. By learning to recognise key places where we could turn this way rather than that, we steer ourselves in a direction that strengthens our resilience.

The skill of storyboarding

While the first tool Amy found useful was the idea of choice points, what helped her apply this insight in a more systematic way was the strategy of storyboarding. This involves mapping out a sequence that starts from where you are, and then adds steps in the direction you'd like to go. These steps take you on a journey, the storyboard focusing your attention on the route you'll take and the issues you'll face. Like looking at a map, the storyboard helps you plan, prepare and navigate. It is a practical way of applying the growth mindset.

The two-part storyboard we've looked at so far is useful for reminding you that the challenge you face is just the starting point, rather than the way things will always be. What Amy found helpful was a more developed, six-part storyboard process involving the following steps.

1) *Starting point.* Each story of resilience begins with a sense of 'Here's me facing this . . .' The challenge encountered will be different for each person. It might be a difficulty, a setback, an argument or disappointment. It might also be the challenge of a purpose calling them, a goal they find stretching. With this storyboarding process you start by describing the challenge you face.

2) *Hoped-for outcome.* If you think of the spider diagram, and the many different ways the situation could go, what are your preferred options? What's the best that could happen? And why would you like that? By thinking about better ways the situation could go, you give yourself a direction to head in and perhaps also a goal to head for.

3) *In the way of this, obstacles or difficulties include . . .* Great stories tend to involve a tension between a desire for something to happen and obstacles or difficulties that stand in the way. Our lives are often like that too. Seeing the challenging situation as an episode in a larger story makes it easier for us to consider the possibility that we might find a way to improve the situation. However, to address a difficulty we need to acknowledge it, which this part of the storyboard helps us do.

4) *Facing all that, what helps me is . . .* Developing helping factors is a central part of resilience training. We'll be looking at this much more.

5) *Turning point.* It is common for adventures to begin by presenting a challenge that seems overwhelming. But throughout the story turnings can happen. Real-life stories have this too.

6) *Specific achievable steps in the next seven days.* The storyboard presented here is a planning tool that takes in a larger view of the problem, including your hopes, the challenge and the helping factors, but which then focuses your attention on practical steps you can take. That's the goal of the process.

The letters S H I F T S can help you remember these six sections. Here's a template you can use for this process (see Fig. 4 below).

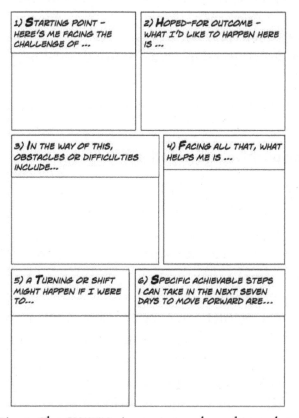

Fig. 4: The SHIFTS six-part storyboard template

In my resilience training work, I ask people to do this in pairs, with one partner as the storyteller, describing a story of resilience prompted by a 'sentence starter' – where there is an opening of a sentence for each section. The storyteller uses this as a prompt, and then follows the sentence starter in a way that is specific to the challenge they face. This way the storyboarding offers a general template that can be customised to a wide range of situations.

The listener's role is just to be interested. When we're speaking to someone else and we have their full attention, it is much easier to continue the story. Telling it as a story might take ten minutes – and people are often surprised by how easy they find it to talk non-stop for this amount of time, just periodically prompted by the sentence starter to begin the next section. If you don't have a partner to practise this with, you can, as an alternative, write or speak through the storyboarding process by yourself. Many people find this an invaluable planning tool.

Balancing positive and negative

What Amy most appreciated about this process was that it gave her space to describe what she found difficult, and to feel heard in this, without just getting stuck in the problem. The structured process has a balance of positive and negative focus, talking about hopes and helping factors as well what you're facing and what you find difficult.

Research by psychologist Gabrielle Oettingen has shown that to have only positive thinking, where you're focusing on your dreams and ideal outcome but avoiding thinking about the problems in the way, is often counterproductive.[11] In a wide range of settings, she has shown, giving attention both to what you hope will happen, and also the realistic hurdles and difficulties in the way, is more effective. Reviewing research on goal setting, the psychologist Heidi Grant Halvorson concludes, 'The optimal strategy to use when setting a goal seems to be to think positively about how it will be when you achieve your goal, while thinking realistically about what it will take to get there.'[12] That's what the storyboarding process does. Why not give it a try?

Try this – six-part storyboarding

Using the sentence starters below, or the template in Fig. 4, work through the six-part storyboard process to map out a response to a challenge you face.

1) Starting point – here's me facing the challenge of . . .

2) Hoped-for outcome – what I'd like to happen here is . . .

3) In the way of this, obstacles or difficulties include . . .

4) Facing all that, what helps me is . . .

5) A Turning or shift might happen if I were to . . .

6) Specific achievable steps I can take in the next seven days to move forward are . . .

What if I don't know what will help?

While this process often generates ideas for how to move forward, sometimes our minds go blank and we can't think of anything. When this happens for me, I remind myself that adventure stories can have foggy moments, when the path ahead is hidden from view. If that happens for you, you can storyboard the story-board. Here's an example (see Fig. 5 on next page).

1) **STARTING POINT –** HERE'S ME FACING THE CHALLENGE OF ...	2) **HOPED-FOR OUTCOME –** WHAT I'D LIKE TO HAPPEN HERE IS ...
filling in this storyboard when I don't know what to put here.	I'd love to find a way to make it work for me, but that isn't happening yet.
3) **IN THE WAY OF THIS,** OBSTACLES OR DIFFICULTIES INCLUDE...	4) **FACING ALL THAT, WHAT** HELPS ME IS ...
I feel defeated and don't know where to start.	Remembering the growth mindset, trusting the process, it may become clearer.
5) A **TURNING OR SHIFT** MIGHT HAPPEN IF I WERE TO...	6) **SPECIFIC ACHIEVABLE STEPS** I CAN TAKE IN THE NEXT SEVEN DAYS TO MOVE FORWARD ARE...
Read the next two chapters. Try this process with a friend.	Carry on reading. Try this process again later.

Fig. 5: Doing a storyboard

3

The Boat and Water Level

Have you had the experience of coping well with a problem one day, then a week or two later facing the same situation but struggling with it? Our resilience fluctuates – we have good days and not-so-good days. This chapter explores what makes the difference and how we can make good days more likely.

A picture of resilience

Over thirty years ago, when I was a medical student in London, I came upon a metaphor that has become one of my most valued resilience tools. It was described in a talk by the holistic medicine pioneer, and local GP, Professor Patrick Pietroni. Being well and healthy, he said, is a bit like rowing a boat. Illness, or other kinds of problems, can be thought of as crashing into a rock (see Fig. 1 below).

Fig. 1: The boat-and-water-level metaphor

Most approaches to tackling difficulties tend to focus on the rock. Healthcare professionals are like geologists who know lots about rocks you might hit. But the problem, or rock, is only half the story. The water level, said Patrick, represents our background level of resilience. When we're feeling good in ourselves, with our emotional reserves at a high level, we may float over rocks that on a bad day we'd hit. When we're feeling depleted, our water levels low, we're more likely to crash.

When I teach resilience, I use this boat-and-water-level metaphor as a mapping tool. I ask people to draw a horizontal line to represent their water level of resilience, then put in downward arrows for factors that lower this, and upward arrows for those that strengthen it.

To help people identify downward arrows, I ask them to complete a sentence starter such as: 'When I face a difficult situation, I'm more likely to struggle when ... ' For example, I'm more likely to struggle when I haven't been sleeping well, when my diet is poor and when I'm already overloaded or stressed. These are risk factors that increase our chances of a crash. The other side of this is the upward arrow sentence that starts with, 'I tend to cope better when ... ' This invites us to identify protective factors that feed our resilience, such as support from friends, feeling determined and having a well-developed toolkit of strategies (see Fig. 2 below).

When I'm feeling challenged or overwhelmed, I say to myself, 'Chris, how's my water level doing?' This reminds me to pay attention to the little steps I can take to nourish my capacity to face whatever's there. That includes things like self-compassion, taking renewal pauses or addressing any draining factors that leave me at a low ebb.

Fig. 2: Mapping resilience factors

Why now?

When I worked as a GP, I'd often ask my patients, 'Why do you think this problem is happening now?' Whether they had a head-ache, depression or a bad dose of the flu, the 'Why now?' question prompted them to tell me about background factors that increased their risk of becoming unwell. It might have been tension in their family life, stress at work, or perhaps they weren't sleeping well. When I drew the boat-and-water-level diagram, it made sense to them. They could see the link between feeling depleted and crash-ing into the rock of their health complaint.

If I ask a question like, 'What is the cause of the common cold?', the answer I most commonly hear is, 'A virus'. Until 2017, the NHS website went even further: 'The only thing that can cause a cold or flu is a cold or flu virus.'[1] The boat-and-water-level metaphor suggests this isn't the whole story, and the research backs this up.

In the mid-1990s, a team of researchers in Pittsburgh, Pennsylvania, arranged for 276 healthy volunteers to have measured amounts of cold virus squirted up their nostrils. The participants were kept in quarantine and had a battery of investigations both before and after virus exposure. They were also interviewed about their stress levels and social networks. Those who'd been experiencing higher levels of stress before the study were more than twice as likely to get a cold. People who were relatively socially isolated were more than four times more likely to get a cold than those with diverse social networks.[2]

Further studies by Sheldon Cohen, the lead researcher, have shown that people experiencing higher levels of positive emotion are less likely to get a cold.[3] Positive mood states have an impact on our immune system that strengthens our resistance to infection. Other research has shown that regular exercise and good sleep also have a protective effect.[4,5] The upward arrows – of positive emotions, a well-developed social network, good sleep and physical exercise – act as a buffer reducing our risk of colds (see Fig. 3 below).

Fig 3: Upward arrows have a buffering effect

Different types of causes

The way you think about the cause of a cold can influence your chances of catching one. If you believed the only cause is a virus, you might dismiss the impact of stress, sleep and exercise, and instead seek to prevent colds by avoiding contact with other people. Yet the research we've looked at shows that those with fewer friends were at higher risk. What can lead to confusion here is the way we think about cause and effect. It is helpful to think about three types of cause: a necessary cause, a sufficient cause and a contributory cause.

The cold virus is a good example of a necessary cause – the virus is necessary for the infection to take place. However, not everyone exposed gets infected; the bug by itself isn't a *sufficient cause*. The third type of influence is more relevant here – as high stress levels, social isolation and poor sleep make colds more likely, they are *contributory causes*.

There's a shift in thinking when we move away from the idea of *the cause* and look instead for *contributing causes*. For example, which square in the diagram below is the cause of the circle (see Fig. 4 below)?

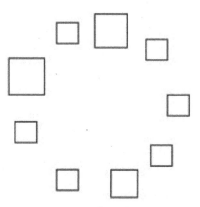

Fig. 4: A circle of squares

What causes resilience?

When people ask me, 'What is the cause of resilience?', I draw this circle of squares. While some causes may be more significant than others, even the small squares can play a role in creating the circle. In a similar way, many factors work together to generate resilience. Psychologist Martin Seligman, when looking at how different influences work together to shape our long-term happiness, identified three groups of causes.[6] The first of these is our genetic make-up; the second is the circumstances of our life; the third involves factors under our voluntary control. Our resilience is shaped by the balance of downward arrows (risk factors) and upward arrows (helping or protective factors) in each of these three areas (see Fig. 5 below).

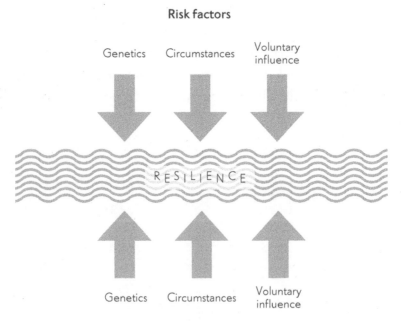

Fig. 5: Three groups of factors causing resilience

Genetic factors

The fixed-mindset view that some people are naturally more resilient than others has some basis, even though it isn't the whole story. Hundreds of studies have shown that genetic factors play a role in shaping our personality. 'Roughly 50 per cent of almost every personality trait,' states Martin Seligman, summarising the research, 'turns out to be attributable to genetic inheritance.'[7] If your parents tend to become anxious or depressed when things go wrong, you're more likely to be like this too. So if you suspect that genetic factors make you less resilient, this downward arrow is part of your larger picture.

On the other side, though, is a reassuring statistic. Over 99 per cent of our genetic make-up is identical for all humans, so you have almost exactly the same genes as any person you're inspired by.[8] Through evolution our species has developed a natural resilience that is hard-wired into us. It is part of the way we're built. I'm reminded of this every time I see a toddler learning to walk. They fall down, then get up, fall again and rise another time. This is an example of a natural bounce-backability that isn't put off by the repeated experience of failure. We can count this natural resilience as a strong upward arrow. It is something we all have: it is part of the way we're built.

Circumstances

Do we need to have had favourable conditions in early life in order to develop our strengths and live well in adulthood? To answer this question, Emmy Werner and Ruth Smith followed the progress of nearly 700 children in Hawaii over a period of more than four decades.[9] Thirty per cent of these had been born and raised in difficult circumstances that included poverty, trauma at birth, and families troubled by discord, divorce or mental illness. By the age of ten, children with difficult early years were more likely to have developed learning or behaviour problems. By age eighteen they were more likely to have mental health problems or be labelled as delinquent. Unsurprisingly, adversity in infancy was seen here to act as a downward arrow increasing the chances of hitting rocks in later life.

But there were some significant exceptions. A third of those with very difficult early life circumstances succeeded at school, didn't get into trouble with the law, and managed their home lives well. By the age of forty, they had grown into competent, confident and caring adults with accomplishments in work and education equal to or better than those who'd grown up in economically secure and stable home environments.

A striking finding of the study was that most of those who'd experienced serious coping problems in their teenage years had turned a corner by midlife. By the age of forty, most were in stable marriages and employment. There had been some casualties along the way, this group having a slightly higher mortality, particularly from accidents and AIDS. The majority, however, seemed to have found their way to recovery and wellbeing. In looking at what helped them do this, Werner and Smith identified key 'protective factors' that made good outcomes more likely.

Some of the protective factors were related to personality and personal strengths. Even as toddlers, the children who later did well were rated by independent observers to be more friendly, agreeable, cheerful and sociable. At age ten, they scored higher on practical problem-solving and reading skills. At age eighteen they were more likely to help others, and to have developed confidence in their ability to make progress with problems they faced.

A second group of protective factors were found in family relationships – the children who did better were likely to have at least one close relationship with someone they trusted who was sensitive to their needs. If this wasn't one of their parents, it might be an older brother or sister, aunt or uncle or grandparent.

A third important protective element was a trusting relationship with a friend or mentor in their community, particularly someone they could seek out for advice and support in times of crisis.

Voluntary influence

What if your family history sets your genetics against you, you've had a difficult start in life, and then you don't find the protective factors identified by Werner and Smith's research? For many years, I worked with clients who might recognise themselves here. The source of support they'd come to trust and rely on was alcohol. Tom, a young man in his twenties, told me how it began:

> When I was twelve I discovered that drinking made me feel normal. Before that I'd spent most of my childhood with my stomach in knots from anxiety. Drinking took that away. It was wonderful.

For Tom, alcohol felt like an upward arrow. Without it, he feared crashing into the rocks of panic attacks, depression and social anxiety. His story of resilience went along the lines of, 'Here's me facing this, feeling on edge and miserable, and what helps me here is drinking.'

If you find a way of dealing with problems that seems to work incredibly well, you might think, Why bother with other ways?

While most of us spend our teenage years learning, through trial and error, a range of ways to deal with the challenges of adolescence, Tom relied on alcohol. As his brain got used to it, he needed to drink more to get the same effect. Eventually his nerve cells became so adapted to the presence of alcohol that he experienced withdrawal symptoms when his blood level fell. He had become physically dependent.

While drinking gave temporary relief from anxiety and depression, when the effects wore off, his symptoms would return in amplified form. He felt trapped: the more he drank the worse he got, and the worse he got, not knowing how else to deal with problems, the more he drank.

There are many ways we can undermine our own resilience. Often this starts with behaviours that offer short-term relief, yet which make problems worse in the longer term. Comfort eating, reckless spending and habitual lying are other examples. Each might seem like an upward arrow in the moment, but can lead to hangover effects later. Choice points are like votes that can support our resilience or weaken it – learning to recognise and use our voluntary influence well is the key to building resilience.

Tom came to see me after he'd had an epileptic fit caused by alcohol withdrawal. He was shocked. While scared of facing life without alcohol, he'd come to accept that continuing to drink was making his life much worse. A big part of our work together involved exploring ways he could build his resilience – so that he'd be able to face life without returning to his old prop.

The boat-and-water-level mapping tool is a great starting point here. And the place to begin is with the basics, with four key areas of voluntary influence that support our capacity to cope. The first is to choose to nourish ourselves. The second is the choice to exercise. The third is the choice to support our sleep. The fourth is to strengthen support. Let's look at each of these essential upward arrows in turn.

The choice to nourish ourselves

According to research at the University of Connecticut's Human Performance Laboratory, even mild dehydration can interfere with our ability to think clearly. It can also influence our mood and energy levels.[10] The problem is that we're not likely to feel thirsty until the problem is more severe, as physiologist Lawrence Armstrong explains. 'Our thirst sensation doesn't really appear until we are 1 or 2 per cent dehydrated. By then dehydration is already setting in and starting to impact how our mind and body perform.'[10] If we're looking at simple things we can do that might strengthen our ability to cope with challenges in the day, ensuring we drink at least six cups of water a day is a good starting point.

Does it matter what we drink when seeking to rehydrate ourselves? We've already mentioned the problems Tom had with alcohol. While an upward arrow of comfort in the short term, in the longer term it had toxic impact on both his mood and health. In addition, alcohol affects our hormones in ways that lead us to urinate more, adding to dehydration.

Fizzy soft drinks might seem like refreshing upward arrows, but they too can have harmful effects on our mood, energy levels and health. A study of fizzy drinks on sale in UK supermarkets found more than half of them had over seven teaspoons of sugar per can.[11] Sugary drinks give us a short-term lift, but this can then be followed by a 'sugar crash', as Dr Oz, a leading wellbeing author, explains. 'Simple sugars, such as those in candy bars, soft drinks and white bread, are a recipe for an energy crash. . . . You'll get an initial energy boost, but then crash as soon as the effects wear off.'[12]

We get energy from carbohydrates in our diets in two main forms: the 'quick carbs' from simple sugars that taste sweet, and the 'slow carbs' from complex carbohydrate in vegetables, brown rice, cereals etc. Because the 'slow carbs' take a while for our body to digest and break down into sugars, they lead to a gradual release of energy and blood-sugar levels remain more stable in a healthy way. But when we have the 'quick carbs' in sugary drinks or food, our blood sugar shoots up, triggering the release of insulin, a hormone that lowers blood sugar. That causes the sugar level to crash down again, leaving us feeling on edge, tired, tense and irritable.

An erratic blood-sugar level, where it shoots up and down, is a cause of mood swings. The impact is so powerful that a young offender unit was able to reduce significantly the level of violent episodes just by moving to a sugar-free diet.[13] Other studies in prisons have shown that dietary supplements of key vitamins, minerals and essential fatty acids can also help stabilise people's emotional states, in ways that make violent episodes less likely to occur.[14] More recent research has also shown that reducing sugary and highly processed foods, while having more fruit, vegetables, olive oil and nuts, can help reduce our risk of depression.[15]

One useful approach to dealing with difficult behaviour is to focus on the rock of the problem. The dietary research shows how the water-level approach can also be effective. By raising the water level of people's wellbeing and resilience through the upward arrow of healthy nutrition, crashing into rocks becomes less common.

We can take the same approach with our own difficult behaviour. Do you ever behave in ways you regret afterwards? Is this more likely when you're under pressure? By nourishing yourself well, ensuring you have a diet and fluid intake that supports your wellbeing, you raise your water level. When you look at the food you have in a day, what is the balance between the upward and downward arrows (see Fig. 6)?

Fig. 6: Does your diet support your resilience or weaken it?

The choice to exercise

If there was a treatment you could take every day that would make your brain work better, improve your mood and give you a sense of having more energy, while at the same time reducing your chances of getting ill or dying from a long list of medical conditions, would you be interested? In a popular YouTube video, preventative medicine specialist Dr Mike Evans presents evidence that taking half an hour of exercise a day can be one of the most powerful things we can do to improve our wellbeing.[16] His question to us all is, 'Can you limit your sitting and sleeping to just twenty-three and a half hours a day?'

While you might know this already, and it seems like common sense, common sense is not always common practice. If you'd like to benefit from the energising and mood-improving influence from regular exercise, you can adapt the boat-and-water-level mapping tool, using it in a slightly different way to support your intention. Here's how.

The boat-and-water-level mapping tool is an example of a 'force-field analysis'. It is a way of visually representing forces or factors that influence something. The something we've been looking at so far is our resilience, but the water level could instead represent anything else you'd like to change, where low levels of this increase the chances of a problem, represented by hitting a rock. If you want to use this tool to support increasing exercise, then we make the water level represent your level of exercise. If our exercise levels fall too low, we're more likely to run into any of the rocks that sitting too much can lead to.

So what helps you exercise more? Draw these in as upward arrows. And what gets in the way – what makes it less likely that you will exercise? Draw these in as downward arrows. Here's an example.

Three important upward arrows for me are:

a) Being convinced that exercising will help me feel more energised and happy.

b) Finding ways of exercising that I enjoy.

c) Having nudges that prompt me to exercise more.

The long-term health benefits are another upward arrow, but aren't as compelling for me as the attraction of feeling better in myself in the short term.

Downward arrows for me are:

a) I don't see myself as very sporty.

b) When I've tried exercise programmes, I haven't got on very well with them and they haven't lasted, mostly because it feels more like a 'should' than a 'want'.

c) I'm too busy to have time for this.

d) I've got lots of other things I'd prefer to do with my time.

When I map this out, it looks like this.

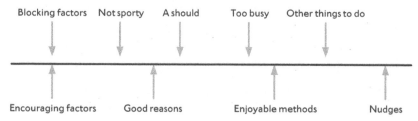

Fig. 7: Mapping factors influencing exercise

Try this – force-field analysis of factors influencing exercise

If you'd like to exercise more, try this mapping process to identify factors encouraging you and also those blocking you:

Identify factors that make it more likely you'll exercise (upward arrows). E.g. I'm more likely to exercise when . . .

Identify factors reducing the chances that you'll exercise (downward arrows). E.g. I'm less likely to exercise when . . .

See if you can reduce, remove or counter any of the downward arrows. See if you can strengthen, add to or enhance any of the upward arrows.

A nudge is anything that prompts me, that makes me more likely to do something in that moment. When I walk into the kitchen and our dogs, Millie and Zac, look at me in a pleading way, wagging their tails, that is a nudge to go for a walk. A few years ago, I bought a wearable step meter, which counts how many steps I take each day. I have a goal to reach 10,000 steps a day. I notice it when I miss my target. Just having a way to give myself feedback like this, with a clear goal that I know whether I'm reaching or not, is another nudge to walk more. Something else I've done is get a step board; when it is raining I put on music and do steps to dance music. It is fun. It energises me, and I feel better afterwards.

Something that makes it more likely that you'll achieve any goal is to make it near and clear. Near means it is doable in the short term. Clear means you know exactly what you'll be doing, and when. Research shows that simply making goals more imme-diate and specific dramatically increases the chances that you'll do them. In a study on students exercising, students were asked if they intended to exercise more. A second group was also asked a second question: if they did want to exercise, when were they going to do that and how? Just adding the second question about when and where increased the proportion of students who actu-ally exercised from 37 per cent to 91 per cent.[17]

The choice to support your sleep

Good-quality sleep is an important upward arrow, yet sleep disturbance is so common that most people have experienced it, and one person in ten suffers so badly it significantly interferes with their daytime coping, energy and mood.

If sleep is a problem for you, you can apply this same mapping tool, but with the water level representing sleep quality rather than resilience or exercise. When the water level of sleep quality gets lower, you're more likely to hit the rock of a sleep problem. You can use this tool to map out the factors that interfere with your sleep (downward arrows) and also those that help it (upward arrows).

Here are four important upward arrows that help promote sleep quality:

a) *Physical exercise during the day.* Sleep is part of your body's natural rhythm of activity and rest. Increasing activity in the day, especially physical exercise, can help you sleep better at night. 'The evidence is out there', says sleep specialist Michael Grandner, 'that people who are even getting mild exercise are sleeping better than those who aren't.'[18]

b) *Winding down before sleeping.* Sleep is often helped by a 'winddown' time of reduced activity before you go to bed. Try things you find relaxing, such as having a hot bath (especially with added essential oils), reading or listening to calming music.

c) *Relaxation exercises.* It is easier to move into sleep from a relaxed state than it is from full alertness. Learning ways to move towards sleep, by lowering your level of tension and arousal, can help you get closer. This is where you can be helped by learning relaxation practices or listening to recorded relaxation exercises that talk you into a state of greater calm. Even if you can't sleep, it is worth trying relaxation and resting, as this may help you get halfway there. If you are already relaxed, you may find yourself more easily drifting off.

d) *Reinforcing your biological clock.* Your body has a natural 'body clock' that tells it when it should be awake and asleep. Having a regular time to go to bed and wake up helps reinforce this biological rhythm. You can also strengthen this rhythm by avoiding daytime naps of more than thirty minutes, increasing exposure to sun and light in the day, and looking at the sky first thing in the morning when you wake up (this tells your body-clock the day has begun).

The idea of 'sleep hygiene' involves clearing away anything that might be interfering with sleep, as well as adding factors that improve it. So it can be helpful to identify downward arrows of sleep-disrupters. Here are some common ones.

a) *Drugs that interfere with sleep.* Tea and coffee contain caffeine, which is a stimulant, so high levels, especially in the evening, may disturb sleep. Nicotine is also a stimulant: if you smoke when you wake up in the night, this may interfere with sleep (nicotine withdrawal can also interfere with sleep, which is why heavy smokers may notice improved sleep when they've given up for a while). Even fairly small amounts of alcohol interfere with the deep 'stage 4' sleep needed to feel refreshed. Someone may think they've been asleep but wake up feeling underslept.

b) *Stress or worries.* These activate the 'fight-or-flight' response that increases our level of arousal. Busy thoughts spinning in our minds can be toxic to sleep. Finding a way of putting them down, whether by writing or drawing before we go to bed, or learning relaxation exercises or mindfulness practices, can all help settle ourselves in a way that helps sleep.

c) *Anything else that interferes with sleep.* Noise, an uncomfortable bed, too much light, too much heat – all these are downward arrows that you can take steps to address.

The choice to strengthen support

When following the two-part story of 'Here's me facing this . . .' and 'What helps here is . . .', a common helping factor identified is support from other people. As this can be such a pivotal upward arrow, giving attention to this is one of our Seven Ways, and the focus of the Sixth Way that we look at later.

For now, I encourage you just to get used to using the boat-and-water-level process. When you're struggling, ask yourself, 'How's my water level doing?' And then carry out the following practice.

Try this: the Boat-and-Water-Level Process

1) The first stage is to draw a horizontal line to represent the 'water level' of your resilience.

2) The second stage is to identify any background factors that have a negative effect on your resilience (even if small effects). Represent these by drawing arrows pushing the line downward.

3) The third stage is to identify any background factors having a positive influence on your resilience. Represent these by drawing arrows pushing the water level line upward (see Fig. 8 below). Anything that lifts the line strengthens or supports resilience.

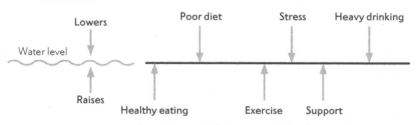

Fig. 8: Identifying background factors
influencing our resilience

4) The fourth stage is to identify specific practical steps you can take to raise your water level – are there any downward arrows you can remove or reduce or find ways to counter? Are there any upward arrows you can give more attention to so that they grow stronger?

   Once you've recognised steps you can take, focus on a few of these and take them. Then identify areas you can give attention to that might help your resilience grow.

Things that reduce or undermine my resilience include:

Things that support or strengthen my resilience include:

4

Develop Your SSRI Toolkit

'Would you like to make your treatment more effective?'

I'd always ask this question when prescribing antidepressant medication. Everyone said yes. So, here's the tip I'd give: *don't let your tablets do all the work*. If you can work with them, they'll be more likely to work for you. If you can catch depression at an earlier stage, and engage in proven self-help practices, you might not even need the medication. The key here is to understand how our choices and actions can also have an antidepressant effect. This is where the SSRI Toolkit comes in.

Mind tools

There's a debate happening about whether we live in the midst of an epidemic of depression, or whether sadness has become over-medicalised. Both views have evidence to support them.[1,2] Either way, what is clear is that the prescribing of antidepressant medication has risen dramatically in recent decades. More than one in ten adults in the USA now takes them, and use in the UK has more than doubled since 2005.[3] The commonest variety is a group of drugs called Selective Serotonin Reuptake Inhibitors, or SSRIs for short. Prozac is a well-known example. However, a different way of thinking about these letters links them to proven pathways to mood improvement that don't involve tablets. In addition, you don't have to be depressed to benefit.

The starting point here is the concept of 'mind tools'. If a tool is something we use to help us achieve a purpose, a mind tool is where our purpose is to change our state of mind. When I worked in mental health, I'd often ask people to think about a time they had felt low in mood and then recovered. We'd explore what helped them find the upslope of their dip. Sometimes it seemed it was just the passage of time that made the difference. More often, there were triggers to mood improvement that included things like a good conversation, becoming involved in an activity or going for a walk in a park. In the boat-and-water-level mapping tool, these are upward arrows. We can also think of these activities as tools.

When looking at how our choices and actions can have an antidepressant effect, I use the letters SSRI to point towards four types of tool: **S**trategies, **S**trengths, **R**esources and **I**nsights. This is our Self-Help SSRI Toolkit (see Fig. 1 below). The goal of resilience training is to add to this, as well as strengthen our skilfulness in using the tools already available to us.

Fig. 1: Our Self-Help SSRI Toolkit

Strategies involve practical steps that take us in a desired direction – for example, taking regular exercise, using relaxation techniques, spending time with friends or paying attention to our diet.

Strengths are the inner qualities we draw upon that help us get through challenging times. Included here, for example, are patience, determination, courage, sense of humour and the ability to communicate.

Resources refer to whatever we turn to for nourishment, guidance, inspiration and support. Included here are people who help us, services we use, special places where we feel safe, informative websites and self-help books.

Insights are the guiding ideas, wisdom or perspectives we find useful. The idea of the growth mindset is a good example: this way of thinking helps people become more determined and stick with challenges rather than giving up. The idea of choice points is an insight that helps us recognise how even our smallest decisions can play a role in strengthening our resilience and protecting our mood. Using the water-level mapping tool is a strategy based on applying this insight.

When you're doing the storyboarding process and you come to the sentence starter 'What helps me is . . . ', the self-help SSRI framework encourages you to look in four specific directions:

1) With strategies you're looking at yourself and practical actions you can take. Each strategy involves a larger plan that can be broken down into smaller steps. 'Exercise more' is a larger plan, but for that to be effective, I need to bring it into my life, using a sentence starter like, 'If I applied this strategy today, what I'd do is . . .' You can use that opening phrase as a springboard for any strategy. If I applied the strategy of paying more attention to nutrition today, one

thing I might do is drink more water; another is avoid snacking on sugary cakes and have some fruit instead.

2) With strengths, you're looking inside yourself at the qualities or capacities you can draw upon. While the strategy is about what you do, the strength is about how you do it – and what helps you do it. You need the strengths to follow through with the strategy.

3) Some strategies, even with your strengths, you can't implement all by yourself. You need to look beyond yourself for reinforcements, sources of nourishment and help. I think of the roots of a tree – resources are what we draw upon outside of ourselves (see Fig. 2 below). My direction of gaze turns outwards, considering places I might go to or materials I might use, people I feel supported by, pets I might stroke, books, pictures or websites I might look at.

Fig. 2: Resources are like roots from which we draw nourishment

4) When looking at the kind of thoughts you have, an insight is a guiding thread you follow. For example, when you think like this ... (describe the insight) then you're more likely to ... (describe where following this insight takes you in terms of how you feel and act). Each insight encourages you to follow some courses of action more than others; each leads a particular way.

Insights about dips, turnings and adventure

In his book *Reasons to Stay Alive*, Matt Haig describes his deep dips into, and out of, depression. A line from the opening pages grabbed my attention: 'The bottom of the valley never provides the clearest view.'[4] When I'm at a low ebb, I look at things more bleakly. That phrase about the valley carries an insight: it reminds me that my view of things is influenced by the state I'm in. With the valley image in mind, I'm more likely to be patient with myself, accepting that a pessimistic perspective from the bottom of a dip is not the final word on how things are.

Another insight I link with the valley theme is that turnings can, and do, happen. If I'm in a situation that is going horribly wrong, I know that it won't always be this way, that periods of decline often level out and find their upslopes too. However, improvement isn't guaranteed – the challenge of resilience is to find ways to make upward turnings more likely and effective. That's why the sentence starter of, 'A turning or shift might happen if I were to ...' is built into the six-part storyboard. There is a more challenging side to turnings, though, as my friend Sheri reminded me.

Sheri used to work with technology giants like Microsoft, helping them design workplace improvements to support innovation and wellbeing. In the summer of 2011 she had an awful headache that wouldn't go away. A brain scan showed three tumours, and she was told she'd need surgery. Her doctor added that an operation might not be successful, and that it could lead to brain damage or even kill her. 'I went into free-fall,' Sheri told me, describing how she felt when hearing her diagnosis. Deciding against a risky surgical intervention, she opted for radiotherapy instead. With brain swelling as a side effect of this, there was a concern she'd lose her eyesight. It looked bleak.

An idea Sheri found helpful was that of a 'call to adventure'. There is a particular point in adventure stories, often after something awful has happened, when the main character makes a choice to rise to the challenge and seek out whatever is needed to find a better way forward. That motivational impulse becomes a guiding purpose that moves the story forward.

For Sheri, her desire to find the best way forward was the call to adventure that pulled her on. Helped by a cancer coach, she considered what she could do if unable to travel or even to see. She decided to train as a coach – work she could do from home over the phone or internet, using her strengths and experience in supporting people design better futures or make the best of difficult ones.

Sheri has become one of my teachers of resilience; we've run online courses together and spent many hours talking through the storyline of 'Here's me facing this; what helps here is . . .' Looking at the down-and-up shape of my two-part story picture, she said, 'It is more of a zigzag for me.' After plunging downward when her scan revealed the tumours, she was buoyed up by finding a medical team she had confidence in. Then when epilepsy emerged as a side effect of the radio-therapy and brain swelling it produced, she dipped again.

Following her call to adventure once more, she studied approaches to wellbeing, engaged in practices that supported her recovery and started to feel better again. Just when she thought she was through the worst of it, she had another setback when feeling unwell again. An important insight about turnings is they happen both ways – from worse to better, and also from better to worse. 'It feels like a circular process,' Sheri said, 'a rollercoaster ride that keeps repeating.' There was an important difference though, each time she went around the loop.

Fig. 3: The rollercoaster loop of resilience

'When I fall down now,' Sheri said, 'I'm better at picking myself back up. I don't tend to fall so deep, and I get up more quickly.' What helps her do this is applying the resilience tools she was learning about, which each journey round the loop gave her more experience of using. Sheri found the SSRI-Toolkit framework particularly useful, as it pointed her attention to what was already available to her: to strategies, strengths, resources and insights she found made a difference. Recognising what helped her, she had something to build on that she could develop and take further.

Starting from where you are

Before learning new tools, it is useful to review what you're already doing and finding helpful. Try this process to review your resilience toolkit.

Try this – reviewing your Self-Help SSRI Toolkit

For this exercise, think back to a past situation you found difficult but which you got through in a way you now feel happy about. What helped you do this? Focus particularly on **Strategies** you used, **Strengths** you drew upon, **Resources** you turned to and **Insights** you found useful. These helping factors are your 'Self-Help SSRIs'. Our resilience grows when we develop them. You can use the table below to write in Self-Help SSRIs you recognise.

Strategies Practical things we do, e.g. asking for help, using problem-solving approaches, meditation, attention to diet and exercise etc.	
Strengths We draw upon these within ourselves, e.g. courage, determination, sense of humour, flexibility, ability to communicate etc.	

Resources We turn to these for nourishment, inspiration, guidance or support, e.g. friends, mentors, self-help books, places we feel safe, support groups, telephone helplines etc.	
Insights Ideas, perspectives or sayings we find useful, e.g. 'I can't; we can', the idea of timelines, the journey approach to change etc.	

Beyond tablets or talking, there's a third choice

When I was a medical student, I was taught that the treatment of depression involved a choice between tablets and talking, where talking involved referring people for counselling or psychotherapy. A third choice that wasn't so well known or used is *psychoeducation* – where people learn skills that help them deal with dips and difficult times. With over 300 million people around the world suffering from depression, the World Health Organization is now coming behind this third path. It has developed a treatment package called PM+, or Problem Management Plus, that brings together self-help tools proven to help people manage stress, depression and anxiety.[5]

My discovery of these self-help tools came largely out of my personal journey of recovery from burnout and depression after my harrowing years as a junior doctor. In the months that followed my departure from medicine, I searched out self-help books and courses to find out how I could get well again. When, in the early 1990s, I went back to work as a GP, I saw patients every week who had stress-related symptoms similar to those I'd suffered, such as anxiety, low mood and emotional exhaustion. The tools I'd learned about include some of those now taught in the World Health Organization PM+ intervention and in many resilience programmes. I found myself teaching them in my GP surgeries, sometimes having the same conversation with different patients several times in a day.

Seeing so many people who'd benefit, I wondered what it would be like to teach these self-help skills in a group setting. So I proposed to the other doctors I worked with that I set up and run a stress-management group. They were delighted to have a resource to refer their own patients to as well.

As stress causes or aggravates such a wide range of conditions, the experiences of people in the group varied greatly. For some it was a triggering of depression or worsening of anxiety; for others it was a skin condition flaring up, or a problem in a relationship. In spite of facing different triggers and consequences of stress, everyone identified with the shared storyline of, 'Here's me facing this and I'm struggling.' They also all described feeling a social pressure to put on a brave face and not reveal to those around them how much they were struggling. If everyone puts on a brave face, all we see is everyone else's apparent lack of struggle, which can give us the idea that we're deficient if we're not coping. So it came as a great relief to many present to find they weren't alone, that similar struggles were experienced by so many others.

The writer C. S. Lewis, who wrote the Narnia novels, once remarked, 'Friendship is born at that moment when one person says to another: "What! You too? I thought I was the only one".'[6] It felt like that in the groups – the transformative impact was not just in what people were learning, but also in the feeling of community and support they experienced. In terms of the SSRI-Toolkit model, the group was a resource, while what they were learning were insights and strategies that helped them find their strengths.

The buffet-meal model of training

When you eat a meal served as a buffet, you're invited to make your own choices from a selection of offerings. You're not expected to like every dish, though you're more than likely to find something that nourishes you. I present resilience training in a similar manner – as a range of offerings where each item might not suit every person, but within the range of options it is most likely they will find something useful. To find out which offerings might help them, people need to have an open mind, and a willingness to experiment, to try things out.

As the focus of resilience training is more on the water level than the individual rocks, people facing quite different rocky patches can find the same upward arrows useful. The resilience strategies we've looked at, such as giving attention to improving nourishment, hydration, exercise, sleep and support, can bring benefit whether the problem faced is depression, anxiety or a physical condition made worse by stress.

Pulling it together and applying the storyboarding process

The storyboarding process works best when accompanied by the boat-and-water-level and SSRI-Toolkit review. The structure of the storyboard sets out the challenge you face, your hoped-for outcome if you deal with this well, and also the obstacles or difficulties that stand in the way of this. The boat-and-water-level process is a way of mapping the difficulties (downward arrows) as well as the helping factors, and the SSRI-Toolkit review nudges you to describe in more detail what you find helpful. To develop the skill of storyboarding, what helps most is practice. It is for you to fill in the gaps in customising the storyboard to fit the situation you face.

Try this – the practice of storyboarding

Each time you encounter a difficult situation, use this as an opportunity to practise the storyboard process. Use the boat-and-water-level and SSRI-Toolkit processes when considering what might go in box 4.

Our journey now is to add to and strengthen the toolkit you have available to you, so that when you do the sentence starter of, 'Facing all that, what helps me is . . .', you have a wider range of tools you're familiar with to draw upon and use.

Storyboarding –

The First Way at a glance

What does it look like when you do this skilfully?

When confronted by adversity, you ask yourself, 'What would a story of resilience look like here?' When you're familiar with how this type of story goes, it is easier to recognise steps you can take to support your own resilience or help other people develop theirs.

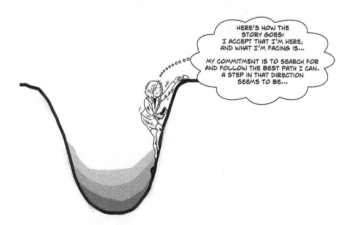

What helps you do this?

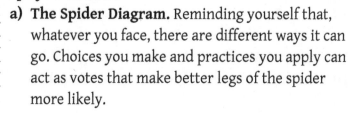

a) **The Spider Diagram.** Reminding yourself that, whatever you face, there are different ways it can go. Choices you make and practices you apply can act as votes that make better legs of the spider more likely.

b) **The Water-level Mapping Tool.** Asking yourself, 'How is my water level doing? What is pushing it down, and what can I do that will help nudge it up?'

c) **Remembering your Self-Help SSRI Toolkit.** Reminding yourself of times you've faced challenges well and what has helped you do that, particularly reflecting on Strategies you've applied, Strengths you've used, Resources you've turned to and Insights that have guided you. Then consider what new tools you can add, and try these in the situation you face.

d) **Telling it as a story.** Prompted by a storyboard template, such as the two-part sequence of 'Here's me facing the challenge of . . .' and 'What helps me here is . . .', or the six-part SHIFTS framework

(**S**tarting point, **H**opes, **I**n the way is, **F**acing that what helps is, a **T**urning might happen if I were to, **S**pecific Achievable Steps are . . .)

80

e) **Applying the Growth Mindset**. Life isn't a fixed picture. You can instead view each moment as one frame in a larger unfolding sequence or process. If you're struggling and can't do something, consider adding the word 'yet', and then continue the journey of looking for a way.

The Second Way – Emotional First Aid

Whatever challenges you face, your capacity to respond will be influenced by your emotional state. Emotional First Aid involves simple practical steps you can take to support your resilience when you're feeling distressed. It includes a combination of:

Emotional self-awareness – where you notice what you're feeling.

Emotional engagement – where you are able to benefit from the energy, aliveness and guiding signals emotions can offer.

Emotional self-regulation – where you're able to steady your state during turbulent periods.

Emotional recovery – where, if you're feeling hurt, bruised or wounded, you take steps that help restore wellbeing.

The Second Way includes:

5

The Emotional Capsize Drill

Can you think of a time when you've been grateful for your anxiety or appreciative of your anger? While these feelings are often unwelcome and can be problematic, they also play essential roles in a threat-detection and -response system that supports our natural resilience. In his classic book *Emotional Intelligence*, psychologist Daniel Goleman describes what might happen if we didn't have this.[1]

Goleman tells the story of Elliot, a successful corporate lawyer found to have a tumour the size of a tangerine at the front of his brain. Surgical removal seemed a success, and before long he was back at work. Only he wasn't his old self. He appeared disorganised, squandering both time and money while neglecting important tasks. He lost a series of jobs and his marriage broke down. Even though a battery of tests showed his sharp intellect was still intact, he was struggling to make decisions.

Further investigation revealed the cause of Elliot's difficulties: he had lost his ability to feel emotions. The operation to remove the tumour had severed the connections between parts of his brain involved with emotional experience and logical reasoning. Describing the impact this had, Goleman writes, 'Elliot's thinking had become computer-like, able to make every step in the calculus of a decision, but unable to assign values to differing possibilities. Every option was neutral ... Lacking that awareness of his own feelings, he had no preferences at all.'[1]

How can you make a decision if you don't know which option feels better? How would you ever know you'd taken a wrong turning, unless you had that uncomfortable gut feeling that you were heading off course? Our emotions, both the pleasant and the challenging ones, are essential for navigating our way through life. More than just guiding us, though, they also energise and motivate our responses. You might know you're drifting off course, but if that doesn't generate any alarm, what is there to rouse you to do something about it?

Before Goleman's ground-breaking book, it was rare to see the words Emotional and Intelligence placed side by side. Indeed, the phrase, 'You're being emotional,' was more likely to be used as a put-down. Part of the reason for this is that our emotions, while sometimes guiding us well, can at other times take us places we don't want to go. When they are intense they can be experienced as overwhelming, or lead us to do things we later regret. That's why a common request at resilience workshops is for tools that help us deal with feelings better.

In this chapter, we will look at how we can respond to, as well as recover from, feelings of distress in an emotionally intelligent way. We'll explore how we can benefit from the gifts our feelings offer us, while at the same time being able to steady our nerves and nurse our wounds when we need to.

How to begin

The first step in growing emotional intelligence is to recognise its value. When we see the importance of something, we're more likely to give it our attention and be open to skills that improve our technique. If our emotions are seen as too hot or difficult to handle, and we don't see their value, the danger is we may look for ways to shut them down. David, a surgeon I used to work with, gave me an example: 'I remember the day I stopped caring,' he told me, 'I was in an impossible situation. However hard I tried, it still wasn't enough.'

With a heavy workload and disturbed sleep from working long hours, there were days David knew he wasn't at his best. When a patient died after he had operated on them, he felt awful, and wondered whether he was to blame. He was a conscientious and caring man, so it hurt when those he'd treated died. In the three zones of challenge described in Chapter One, the emotional burden of David's work took him far into the red zone. Closing down his caring seemed like a necessary strategy to survive.

If we're bruised or physically injured, a first-aid approach involves taking early or immediate steps to protect wellbeing and promote recovery. When we're emotionally bruised or wounded, we need something like this too. Failing to care for psychological injuries can make their effects worse. David's 'compassion fatigue' is an example, his deadening of empathy and emotional experience being a symptom commonly seen in helping professionals who are burning out.

The biology of fear

Another time we need emotional first aid is when our fear of our feelings stops us doing things we want to do. For Jane, the woman mentioned in Chapter Two who was afraid of speaking in public, her biggest fear was not the speaking itself, but feeling exposed and experiencing embarrassment. We can apply the two-part storyboard here: there's what happens, and then there's what happens next. The emotion that takes us into the orange or red zone is part one.

Part two is what follows. And that's where choices Jane made influenced the way things went. Telling me what she'd gained from my resilience course, Jane said, 'I remember the spider diagram. It helped me recognise that when I felt fear, there were different ways it could go. The old route was to step back and keep my mouth shut. But I realised that response was blocking me. The question, 'What's the best that can happen here?' got me thinking I could change this – that I might, one day, become someone who used to be blocked by her fear, but isn't any more.'

An important shift for Jane came with learning about the biology of her nervous system. When she used to go red in the face and feel her heart pounding, she thought there was something wrong with her. The more her heart raced, the more worried she became, and the more worried she became, the more her heart pounded. Recognising her body reactions as a normal response to threat changed the meaning she gave to her experience. 'Instead of telling myself I'm going to have a heart attack, I found a more reassuring voice inside myself. I knew that my body alarm system had been switched on and that this was preparing me for physical action. I also knew it was temporary, and that if I slowed down my breathing and practised my emotional first-aid skills it would pass.'

The more Jane learned ways to settle her body reactions to anxiety, the less fearful she felt of speaking in public. As her confidence grew, her body response didn't charge up as much. She had a self-amplifying loop going the other way: the more settled she felt, the less she reacted; the less she reacted, the more settled she felt.

Fig. 1: Two self-amplifying loops

Learning about the Resilience Zone

In April 2015, a massive earthquake hit Nepal, killing over 9,000 people and injuring over 20,000. In the months that followed, Dr Laurie Leitch, one of the world's leading resilience trainers, went out with her team to join the relief efforts. Laurie has worked with survivors of tsunamis, hurricanes, genocide and a range of other disasters around the world. Her work focuses on teaching people skills that target their autonomic nervous system.[2] She starts her trainings by describing the biology of our response to stress.

Laurie shares a picture of a gentle wave (see Fig. 2 – the wave image here is adapted from a graphic used in Laurie's work).[3] 'Inside the body, just like in nature,' she tells people, 'there are all kinds of cycles and rhythms: day follows night, some places in the world have seasons, the phases of the moon. We have the same kinds of cycles in our body, and when they're in balance with each other, then this rhythm is a smooth wave. Thoughts, feelings and inner sensations fit together, in balance. Do you remember a time when you felt like this? We call it the resilience zone.'[4]

Fig. 2: The Resilience Zone[3]

Laurie is describing the action of two complementary nerve pathways: the sympathetic nervous system that charges us up ready for action, and the parasympathetic nervous system that settles us down. When we feel anxiety, stress or anger, our sympathetic nervous system activates our 'fight-or-flight' response that prepares our body for combat or escape. The racing heart, tensed muscles, faster breathing and increased sweating this leads to gave our ancestors an edge that helped them survive attack by predators. Our sympathetic charge-up system can also be activated by excitement, helping us become physically poised to make the best of opportunities.

While this 'stress response' increases arousal, our 'relaxation response' goes the other way and calms us down. 'Think of a parachute coming into landing,' Laurie says, describing how our parasympathetic nervous system can gently bring us back into equilibrium after a challenging time. Like an automatic gear system running in the background of our lives, these parallel nerve systems are called 'autonomic' because they happen automatically, without us needing to think about them. When they're in balance, we live our lives in this resilience zone, with a natural rhythm of engagement and renewal in our readiness to act.

Laurie teaches neuroscience to survivors of disasters because it helps explain the symptoms many experience after the traumatic times they've been through. Problems arise when either our charging-up or winding-down systems go too far. 'After a shock, our system can be bounced out of kilter,' Laurie explains. 'When you're in hyper-arousal and stuck on high, you may be irritable or even rageful. You may have pain syndromes, you may feel anxiety and grief. When you're bumped below the zone, you're in hypo-arousal: you can feel depressed and disconnected. Learning about your mind–body system helps you understand what's going on.' (See Fig. 3 below, adapted from a graphic used in Laurie's work.)[3]

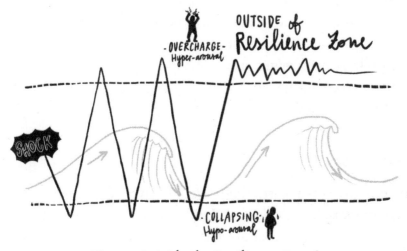

Fig. 3 – Outside the Resilience Zone[3]

Hyper-arousal

When we're over the top line, in hyper-arousal, we not only get the body symptoms of stress, such as a pounding heart, but our brain works in a different way too. Daniel Goleman uses the term 'Amygdala Hijack' to describe this. Part of our brain linked with our emotions, the amygdala, can take over when we're in states of extreme distress. This rapid-response survival mechanism can cause us to jump out of harm's way even before we've consciously acknowledged there might be a problem. As Goleman explains, 'The amygdala can have us spring to action while the slightly slower – but more fully informed – neocortex unfolds its more refined plan for reaction.'[5] When we lose our temper, or freak out in a panic, our amygdala has taken over.

Another important change that happens in these Amygdala-Hijack moments is that our neocortex, the thinking brain, becomes less active.[6] This explains why we may find it more difficult to think clearly when we're very distressed. When you're facing a difficult situation, it often helps to have your sympathetic nervous system charge you up for action. If you're crossing a road and see a car speeding towards you, your amygdala taking over might save your life. Emotional intelligence involves recognising when these survival reactions are helping us and when they are not.

Hypo-arousal

In our primitive past, there would have been times when running wasn't possible, and fighting would have been suicide. For times like these, nature has installed in us another emergency survival response – to freeze. We can see this in rabbits that go completely still when they see a car headlight. If you freeze, the predator might not notice you. An invading tribe might think you're dead and leave you alone. In extreme fear, it can feel like we're turned to stone, which is what the term 'petrified' means. We can freeze in milder forms too. Our mind might go blank, we can be speechless, unable to find anything to say or feeling at a loss for what to do.

There are a range of ways we can fall below the resilience zone into hypo-arousal. The physiological freeze response, in its varying intensities, is one. We also dip down below the line when we're feeling defeated or depressed. The sadness of loss can take us here too. There is a collapse of energy, a withdrawal from engagement.

Dissociation, where part of our mind splits away and takes us somewhere else, can also be part of the picture. A study of survivors of the *Herald of Free Enterprise*, the ferry that capsized in 1987 killing 193 people, found more than ten per cent reported a sense of leaving their body during the disaster. Some even felt they had entered a tunnel leading to a bright light. 'Such experiences as these,' writes the psychologist Stephen Joseph, who carried out this research, 'are a protective mechanism intended for use in dire situations where no options remain. It kicks in when the circumstances are such that struggling might only make things more dangerous.'[7]

Tracking

The first skill Laurie teaches is 'tracking', where you identify and track symptoms that tell you which branch of your autonomic nervous system is most active. As you pay attention to what's happening in your body, are there signs of sympathetic nervous system arousal, such as sweatiness, heart pounding, muscle tension and shakiness of your hands? Or does your body show your parasympathetic nervous system is activated, with a slowing of heart rate, feeling light-headed or faint, and floppiness rather than tension in your muscles? When we're above the line in hyper-arousal, we're more likely to feel tense, irritable, on edge. When we're below the line in hypo-arousal, our energy levels are lower, it can be a struggle to motivate ourselves, we might seem to have blanked out or be daydreaming.

When I worked in mental health, I'd sometimes see clients who had explosive responses to anger. When I met Don, he told me he got into fights when losing his temper, yet afterwards felt awful about this. He nodded his head when I explained about the Amygdala-Hijack process. 'That's exactly what happens to me,' he said, adding that he felt reassured by understanding why he flipped out. I taught him the skill of tracking, so he could notice the early warning signs that he was getting angry. Once his amygdala had taken over, it was difficult for him to control his behaviour. But at an earlier stage, more choice points were available. One thing he learned was to take his own pulse.

Try this - take your pulse

Hold out one hand, palm upwards. With the other hand, place two fingers below the base of the thumb, in the upper part of the wrist. Rest them between the bone above and ligaments below.

Fig. 4: How to take your pulse

Have a timer or second hand of a clock visible. Count the heart-beats for 15 seconds and then multiply by four. Do this from time to time, so you get a sense of what your normal resting pulse rate is. Do this also when you're angry, stressed or anxious. If your resting heart rate is more than 30 beats a minute faster than usual, it isn't a good time for a conversation or argument. Find a way to step back and give yourself some cooling-down time.

Two different directions for dealing with distress

I was running a workshop with my friend Margo when a wasp entered the room. I noticed my heart rate rising. I've been stung before, so I get a bit nervous when I see a potential threat flying by. Then all of a sudden, the wasp hovered right in front of me. I froze.

I thought of the spider diagram and, related to this, a perspective-check process taught in the Penn Resilience Program.[8] It involves asking three questions: 'What's the best that can happen here? What's the worst? And what's most likely?' The best was that the wasp would fly away very soon. If the worst happened and someone, perhaps me, got stung, we'd survive. It would be a bit uncomfortable, but not too bad. And the most likely thing was that the wasp would fly away before too long. So, I reassured myself that everything would be fine, took a deep breath to settle myself and carried on with the workshop.

Meanwhile, Margo had got up and opened all available windows. She looked uneasy. She told us why. She was allergic to wasp stings. The worst possibility for her was that if she got stung, she could die. The wasp moved on, buzzed against one of the windows and flew out. Everyone breathed a sigh of relief.

Strategies to address distress fall into two broad categories. I'd followed one and Margo had taken the other. I'd opted for an 'emotionally focused coping' approach. After recognising arousal of my sympathetic nervous system and then my freeze response, I did the three-question perspective check. On reflection, I thought the wasp was not too big a threat, so I reassured myself. I breathed deeply and slowly as a way of settling my stress response.

Margo had instead taken a problem-focused approach, where her attention was more on the source of the distress, the wasp, than her emotional reaction to it. Because of the risk to her safety, her priority was to remove the threat. She considered different ways to do this: chasing after the wasp and trying to swat it would likely make it more aggressive and increase the chances that someone would be stung. Opening the windows seemed the best bet. Her approach worked.

Margo faced a potentially deadly peril. What if she had panicked or freaked out? She knew that rapid movement near a wasp is something they react to, so panicking could be dangerous. If instead her reaction had been to freeze, she might not be stung, but being stuck in a state of terror would block her ability to run the workshop with me. Wanting to find out how she kept her cool, I interviewed her afterwards.

'I know if there's a wasp in the room, I need to keep my focus on it,' she said. What helped her rise to the occasion in this scary moment was preparation. Margo had a daily practice of mindfulness meditation. Just as someone who exercises regularly will be physically fitter and better able to cope with exertion, Margo's regular meditation strengthened her ability to be more steadily alongside whatever was happening in that moment, and to maintain her focus.

We can use emotionally focused strategies in two different ways. One is in the moment, when we notice we're out of balance, to bring ourselves back. The other is more preventative, helping maintain our balance and keep us in better shape. Because Margo supported her emotional wellbeing on a daily basis, not just through mindfulness but also by paying attention to diet and exercising regularly, she was able to have the presence of mind needed to focus on a problem more effectively. As Margo demonstrated here, problem solving and emotionally focused coping can help each other: they are complementary.

In SETOPSS, E comes before T

Several years ago, I changed the way I taught resilience. I used to have the practical problem-solving and thinking strategies much earlier on. But my friend David Peters, a professor at the Centre for Resilience at Westminster University pointed out that 'when people are drowning, they don't need tips on how to improve their swimming style. They need something much more immediate and easier to grasp.' When your amygdala has taken over, and you're either stuck on the high arousal of 'fight or flight', or below the line in freeze, you need tools that are simple enough to use even when your mind goes blank. This is where emotional first aid comes in.

In later chapters we'll map out a range of problem-solving strategies that help us address different types of challenge out there, whether overload and stress, conflict in relationships, or worries about the future. In this chapter and the next, we'll look more at emotionally focused strategies, because if we can get ourselves in a good state, we're in a better position to apply a problem-solving approach. Getting ourselves in a more settled state allows us to consider a wider range of possibilities, our thinking can be more flexible, and our reasoning capacities are more available to us. A core purpose of emotional first aid is therefore to get us into a better state, so that we can then identify and take the steps that follow.

Capsize drill

As a younger man, I loved canoeing. But every now and then, perhaps when a big wave took me by surprise, I'd capsize. An important skill I learned was how to do the kayak roll. When I found myself upside down and under water, I continued the movement round, lifting my upper body, flicking my hips and pushing down with the paddle so that I came back up again. I needed to practise this again and again so that it came more easily when needed. This was my capsize drill.

In a similar way, there will be times when we get tipped over by situations. We find ourselves emotionally under and need to find ways to pull ourselves the right way up again.

In the next chapter, we'll look at a range of strategies for steadying yourself when you're feeling on edge or outside the resilience zone. By learning ways to settle yourself, you're learning the skill of emotional self-regulation. But what about those times when you have lost it, when your conscious thinking brain isn't working so clearly? What simple first-aid tools can you use then?

When looking at our reactions to shock and distressing events, self-awareness is the starting point for emotional first aid. Just asking ourselves the question, 'Am I in the resilience zone?' can prompt us to notice which state we're in and the impact this has.

Here are five first-aid approaches for bringing yourself back to the resilience zone. The first four are designed as self-help strategies. The fifth was developed to use when helping other people in distress, although it can also be adapted for self-help use.

a) The traffic-light system. This is what I taught Don for when he noticed his fist clenching or his voice sounding angry. These were warning signs that he might lose his temper.

First, think of a red traffic light. Imagine seeing one in your mind, and as you do this, say to yourself, 'STOP'.

Then think of the amber traffic light. While that is showing, identify one simple step you can take that moves you towards a safer, less aggravating situation. You might say something like, 'Hang on a minute: I'm just going to the loo.' Or, 'I'm going to put the kettle on to make some tea.'

When you have an action in mind, imagine the traffic light turning to green. Then go and do it: take the step. This technique is useful when we spot ourselves heading in a direction we don't want to go, and we want rapidly to change course.

A traffic-light system is not about blocking or suppressing emotions. It is more about being better able to give ourselves a pause and a choice point, where we have an opportunity to redirect our flow if previously we've felt swept away or out of control.

b) The Mindful STOP. I learned a similar strategy from Dr Clay Cook, a psychologist at the University of Washington.[9] In his online resilience course, he taught a mindfulness practice that uses the four letters of S T O P to encourage us to:

Stop – imagine a stop sign: this gives you cause for a pause
Take a deep breath
Observe with an open and gentle attitude
Proceed positively

If we're ever caught up with worry or distress, the O here offers a helpful vantage point. The observer position of just noticing involves a stepping back from being entangled. The open and gentle attitude invites a curiosity about our experience, together with a tone of compassion towards ourselves and others. Strategies that encourage us to pause like this help us acknowledge what's happening, while also inviting ourselves to consider choices that support our resilience.

c) The ABRAH Approach. When I was a child, we'd sometimes see magicians who'd use the magic word 'Abracadabra'. An emotional first-aid tool I teach, and also use, is to say to myself the word 'ABRAH', then following these letters to remind myself to:

Acknowledge
Breathe
Respond with
Active
Hope.

Acknowledging is the starting point, where I'm noticing both inner and outer events. I might say to myself, 'What I'm facing is . . .' or, 'OK, I'm acknowledging that . . .' If I'm feeling upset or angry, I reinforce my recognition of that by naming the emotion I'm experiencing. Research shows that the simple act of naming a strong emotion can help us take a step back from it.[10]

Then I Breathe, with a three-breath pause where I breathe in to a count of five and breathe out to a count of six, doing this three times. Slowing down our breathing stimulates our parasympathetic nervous system, and the three-breath pause is short enough that I can do it even while on the phone, or in the middle of a meeting.

I think of Active Hope as a three-step process that involves starting from where you are, identifying what you hope for in this situation, and then taking active steps to make your hopes more likely to happen.[11] When I respond with active hope, I think of the spider diagram, where each leg represents a different version of how things could work out. Where do the better legs lead? They are my hopes. And if I'm not sure what step to take, a simple next step might be just to continue the emotional first-aid process of bringing myself into a better state. This next process might help here.

d) ACT – Acceptance and Commitment Therapy. There is a well-developed psychological treatment approach called Acceptance and Commitment Therapy that I'm much influenced by.[12] I use the term here in a slightly different way. Like a great book title that delivers the main message of the pages inside, I find the phrase 'Acceptance and Commitment Therapy' therapeutic in itself. When troubled or struggling, I say to myself, 'Chris, A–C–T: Acceptance and Commitment Therapy.' It is a verbal touchstone, something I reach for and hold on to.

By repeating those letters and words, I'm reinforcing the two-part story with the twin qualities of acceptance for Part One and commitment for Part Two. Acceptance is about acknowledging what's there, being alongside reality without shutting any of it out. Then my commitment is to expressing a story of resilience in Part Two, searching out the best leg of the spider and responding with active hope.

e) The RAPID model for psychological first aid. I remember feeling shocked as a medical student when a doctor stood at the end of a patient's bed, told them they were going to die, then busily strode off to their next task. The patient was left stunned and alone. A short while later, I saw a nurse come and give support. While the doctor gave a great lesson in how not to be alongside people in distress, the nurse provided a model to follow. She sat down next to the dying man, she told him she'd seen what had happened, and wondered how that had left him. She listened. She built rapport.

A robust finding of research into survivors of tragedy is that social support is a protective factor, while isolation increases the risk of post-traumatic stress.[13] Yet when dealing with those in distress, it is common for people to feel awkward and not know what to do. A 'flight response' to stress may be, like the doctor here, to speedily retreat into a task more familiar. While physical first aid is widely taught, psychological first aid hasn't been, at least until recently.

We've been using the term emotional first aid when looking at how we deal with our own distress. The term Psychological First Aid refers to supporting others, particularly after traumatic events. It has been defined as 'a supportive and compassionate presence designed to stabilise and mitigate acute distress, as well as facilitate access to continued care'.[14]

To give people a clearer framework to follow, Dr George Everly and colleagues at the Johns Hopkins School of Public Health developed the RAPID model for Psychological First Aid.[15] Designed to be easily learned, it guides potential responders to crisis situations through five steps. The letters R A P I D help us to remember these, as they stand for **Rapport**, **Assessment**, **Prioritisation**, **Intervention** and **Disposition**. We can follow this sequence when supporting others. We can also apply this guiding framework to supporting ourselves.

The starting point for building **Rapport** is caring attention. That's what the nurse showed. Her body language, direction of gaze and tone of voice added together to let the man know someone cared how things were for him and wanted to help. But it is difficult to know how to help someone without an understanding of what they want or need. So, the next step in building rapport is listening.

Think how you might approach someone if you wanted them to know you cared, that you genuinely wanted to help, and that a first step in that was finding out how things were for them. Can you approach yourself in the same way? I've sometimes looked at myself in a mirror and imagined I'm speaking to a dear friend. 'Hey Chris, what's up?' Then I've listened to myself.

Assessment is guided by three questions:

1) Is there any evidence this person needs assistance?

2) Is there any evidence this person's ability to function is, or may be, compromised?

3) Is further exploration of this person's capacity to cope warranted?

After a traumatic event, an assessment needs to address the risk of injury – you might ask someone how they are and whether they've been hurt, while also looking for any evidence of injury. If we've just had a traumatic experience, we can ask these three questions of ourselves. Do we need help? Are we finding it difficult to function or cope? Do we need to be checked out in any way? If the answer to any of these questions is yes, then the next step of assessment is considering how much so, particularly looking at whether the distress is leading to any impairment or collapse in their (or our) ability to function.

Prioritisation involves considering the degree of urgency for any further action. Any of us might experience a collapse of our ability to cope when in extreme distress. Falling apart with grief can be a normal part of our coming to terms with loss, and it can be unhelpful to over-medicalise or therapise healthy emotionality. But where do we draw the line and seek further help, either for ourselves or others? A useful reference point is to look at what's happened in the past, and how this has been dealt with. If someone has felt like this before, and usually feels better a short while afterwards, that's reassuring. If there's been a past history of harmful stress reactions, particularly involving a threat to personal safety, that needs taking more seriously.

A question I'd explore is: 'Are you worried about yourself?' We can ask this of others and ourselves. If we're worried, what are our worries? And what additional support might address these? That leads to the next stage of intervention.

While we've looked mostly at how to help ourselves in difficult times, what Interventions can we offer to others? The Johns Hopkins guide identifies interpersonal support as the single most powerful factor to foster resilience: 'Enlisting the support of friends and family of those affected by adversity can be not only effective but also highly efficient as well.' A simple intervention might just be to explore with someone where they can get support from.

The Disposition phase of psychological first aid considers the question of 'Where do we go from here?' If you're helping someone else, a key issue is what your role is. If you're just someone who happens to be in the right place at the right time to offer support, do you need to have a continuing role? You're looking at their needs – and also at yours, reflecting on both what might be needed and also what you can realistically offer. If in the intervention phase you've helped them identify other sources of support, then this may be the time to say goodbye and move on. If you've agreed to be part of their continuing support, then the next stage is to work out when and how.

Whatever your next step, there are practices you can use every day that help build your inner reserves, so that you are better resourced to face whatever challenges lie in front of you. It is to these that we turn next.

6

Self-Steadying Practices

Nick's hand was in a bucket full of ice cubes. I asked him to keep it there for as long as he could. It didn't take long before his hand was so cold it hurt. Yet focusing on his breathing, and breathing more slowly, helped Nick remain calm. He glanced every now and then at the computer screen nearby, which showed what his heart rate was doing. At first it was steady and slow, then, as the pain increased, it began to rise. Eventually it was too much. 'That's it,' he said, as he pulled his hand out.

That was in 1983, and Nick was a volunteer in a research project I was doing for my first degree, which combined medicine and psychology. I was using heart-rate biofeedback to help people learn to relax. Each subject could see how their heart rate responded when they tried different settling strategies. If they found something that worked, they could see their heart rate slowing down. Then I asked them to dip their hand in the ice bucket, to see whether being in a more relaxed state would strengthen their ability to withstand pain. It did.

It was this piece of research that started me on my journey of learning about resilience. From it I gained two important lessons.

The first was that our physical reaction to distress, like our heart pounding, is not completely outside our influence. We don't consciously control our heart rate, but with some practice we can learn to slow it down. Speeding it up is easier – we just need to be physically active or remember a time we felt frightened. These both activate our sympathetic nervous system. Stimulating the parasympathetic nervous system, and the relaxation response that goes with it, takes a bit more skill. But it is such a useful skill to learn.

My second lesson was that our perception of pain is influenced by the state we're in. When we're deeply relaxed we may still notice pain but be less bothered by it. I began studying different ways of calming myself down. I found self-hypnosis was so effective that I was able to have fillings done at the dentist without any local anaesthetic. I also learned that using strategies like this helped me deal with psychological pain too. When I felt miserable or upset, spending time in a relaxed state settled me.

Later, when I finished my training as a medical doctor, I found that teaching simple relaxation skills was an invaluable aid to my work. When I took blood samples, I'd ask patients to focus their attention on a spot on the wall, then count backwards from ten, and when they reached one to imagine themselves somewhere they felt safe and relaxed. When people had been feeling nervous about needles, this practice helped reduce their anxiety and the discomfort they felt. What I was teaching was a self-steadying practice.

There are many different ways we can bring ourselves back into the resilience zone when we're either too charged up or have dipped down into hypo-arousal. We have looked at awareness and understanding as the first important steps. We have also introduced quick-to-use strategies that open up a pause, so that we're better able to choose our next step rather than react in an impulsive way that we might later regret. But what next?

The four quadrants of emotion

Is the goal to become more relaxed? Not always. It is more about making choices that move us towards a state that serves us well in that moment. It is here that an emotional mapping process can help us address the questions of 'Where am I now? And where would I like to get to?'

One way our feelings change is in their energy level. Some feelings charge us up, while other feelings have the effect of draining energy away, even leaving us feeling as though our batteries are flat. There's also another axis of variation, which is linked to how safe and satisfied, or unsafe and dissatisfied, we feel. We can plot these two axes to map out four quadrants of emotion.[1]

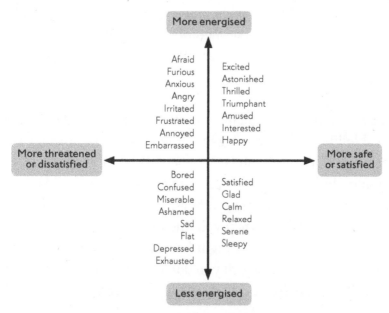

Fig. 1: Four quadrants of emotion

Each of the four corners of this graph is linked to a different state of activation in our brain and nervous system. The upper two quadrants engage our sympathetic nervous system; the lower two engage our parasympathetic nervous system. The active satisfied state of the top right-hand corner is highly desirable, but if we spend all our time there it can be exhausting. We also need recharge moments, which tend to happen when we're in the bottom right-hand corner. Many of the strategies to recharge and settle ourselves take us to this quadrant. But not all of them. If we're feeling too calm, perhaps even a bit sleepy, and we need to charge ourselves up before an event, emotional first aid here might be a wake-up and charge-up strategy like a burst of physical activity.

Try this – four-quadrant check-in

Which corner of the graph represents how you feel right now? What are you feeling, and where would you put yourself? What quadrants have you been in recently? And where would you like to get to?

Learning ways to regulate your mood state is one of the most valuable life skills you can gain. When you find a strategy that works well for you, it can become a friend for life and an ally to call upon in times of need. Yet, like friends, there will be some we get on with better than others, so it is worth trying out a range of approaches. When you find one that fits for you, practise it regularly, so that using it becomes second nature. When you know a practice so well you don't even have to think about it, it will be there for you more easily when you need it.

Developing a playlist

How many times each week do you find yourself feeling on edge or even pushed over an edge and outside the resilience zone? (See Fig. 2 below.)

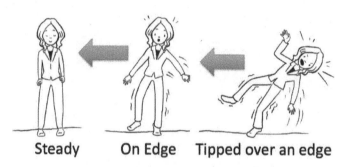

Steady   On Edge   Tipped over an edge

Fig. 2: Self-steadying strategies
help bring us back into a steadier state

Each of these times is an opportunity to practise one of your self-steadying strategies. Rather than use the same technique every time, it can be helpful to have a 'playlist' of a few you're working on, or already have confidence in. Each has different benefits and will suit some situations better than others. You might also use them in combination.

Try this

When you notice yourself feeling on edge, and you'd like to settle your state, use this sentence starter as a prompt to practise a self-steadying strategy:

'What I do to settle myself is . . .' – and then use the strategy you describe.

To encourage you to experiment with different approaches, here are ten options.

1) Mindfulness

2) Expressing the feeling

3) Expressive writing

4) Processing the feeling

5) A water-level check

6) Distraction

7) Gratitude practices

8) Support from people and places

9) Body-focused practices

10) Cognitive reappraisal

1) Mindfulness

Have you had the experience of sitting down for a meal, then a short while later find yourself looking at an empty plate and wondering where the meal went? If you're busy, with things on your mind, you might not give much attention to an everyday action like eating. Mindfulness is the opposite of being on automatic pilot like this. It is about being present in the moment, so if you're eating, you give this your full attention, noticing the textures and flavours of food, as well as the movements of your mouth.

John Kabat-Zinn, a pioneer of mindfulness research, described it as 'a way of connecting with your life . . . cultivating attention in a particular way – paying attention on purpose in the present moment non-judgementally'.[2] Integral to this approach are the qualities of gentleness and curiosity. If your mind wanders, you notice that, then gently and kindly bring your attention back to what's in front of you in the present moment.

When I teach mindfulness as a practice to support resilience, I use the phrase 'subtle yet powerful' to describe it. On the surface, this form of paying attention might not sound like a big deal. But research shows the benefits of regular mindfulness practice include stress reduction, improved mood, strengthened memory, improved ability to focus, enhanced immune function and reduction in psychological distress.[3] Mindfulness has also been shown to counter anxiety and depression, as well as reduce the risk of relapse of depression.[4]

The term mindfulness is used in different ways. Sometimes it refers to an experience or a state of being, at other times to a meditation practice or to a programme of training. The experience of mindfulness is where you are paying attention, in a non-judgemental way, to whatever you notice in the present moment. This includes the thoughts you're thinking, the emotions you're experiencing, the sensations in your body, as well as what you're seeing, hearing, smelling or tasting.

Our attention is like a spotlight that moves from one thing to another. We control where we point it – we can consciously choose to focus on a sound, or on what we see, or on the feeling at the tips of our toes.

Try this – the five-sense check-in

A simple mindfulness practice is to move your attentional focus through your five senses, one at a time, prompted by the questions below. Spend a short while on each sense and then move on to the next. You can do this while sitting – you can also do it while out for a walk.

What am I seeing? (Look around you.)
What am I hearing? (How many sounds can you hear?)
What can I smell? (Take in a big sniff.)
What can I taste? (Allow your tongue to wander round your mouth.)
What can I feel in my body? (What sensations can you feel? Do a body scan where you move through the different parts of your body, giving your attention to any sensations related to that part, and then move on to the next.)

While directing our attention is easy to do, what's more difficult is to keep our focus where we've chosen to aim it. After a few minutes, our mind tends to wander, to remember something, or go off on a train of thought that moves from one thing to another. Like a monkey swinging from branch to branch, our minds are active and can range widely in their thought journeys. That can be useful. Where it becomes a problem is when we ruminate – where we dwell on events, real or imagined, in a way that pulls us down or winds us up.

A research study involving over 32,000 people in 172 countries identified rumination as a key predictor of someone's risk of depression or anxiety after a stressful event.[5] Mindfulness helps us take a step back from troubling thoughts or feelings, so that we observe them rather than getting caught up in them.

There is a difference between looking *from* your stress and looking *at* your stress. When you're looking from your stress, or your anger or anxiety, it is as though there is a storm cloud above you casting a shadow on all you see. When you step back, and look *at* your stress, or anger, or anxiety, you see the storm cloud too. When you notice the stressed, angry or anxious thoughts or feelings, you can name these, together with any associated body sensations. For example, I might say to myself, 'I am experiencing some anger, I am feeling tension in my neck, I feel a tightness in my belly.' Each moment is a bit different, and if we sit with our experience, it changes. Mindfulness is about being with whatever is there, just noticing it.

What we do with a mindfulness practice is exercise the muscle of our attention by having a chosen focus that we come back to again and again. For example, with mindfulness of breathing, our chosen focus is our breathing. We pay attention to the sensation of air coming in and going out, and to any movement or sound associated with our breathing.

A mindfulness practice usually involves setting aside a period of time on a regular basis to focus your attention in a particular direction. It might be that when brushing your teeth, you do this in a mindful way, where you notice each movement of your brush. You can eat a meal in a mindful way, giving your full attention to the taste and texture of your food and the experience of taking it to your mouth, smelling it, and eating it. Eating can become more satisfying this way.

The way you respond to distractions is a key part of the mindfulness process. As Mark Williams and Danny Penman write in their bestselling book *Mindfulness*, 'After a while, your mind may wander. When you notice this, gently bring your attention back to your breath, without giving yourself a hard time. The act of realising that your mind has wandered and bringing your attention back without criticising yourself is central to the practice of mindfulness meditation.'[6]

I've seen people who previously felt on edge for much of the time learn to settle their nervous system through regular mindfulness practice. For some people, this is a breakthrough discovery. But not everyone. Yet even if you've tried mindfulness and found it hard to maintain a regular practice, just to move in a mindful direction can bring many benefits. Shawn Achor developed a workplace wellbeing training programme in which he invited people to engage in a three-week challenge, where each day they did at least one short wellbeing activity, one of these being to give mindful attention to their breathing for just two minutes. Four months later a survey of those who'd taken part showed they had a significant increase in their life satisfaction.[7]

Try this - two minutes of mindfulness of breathing

If you're short of time, set a timer for just two minutes. In that period, pay attention to your breathing, to the sensation of air coming in and going out.

How do you know you are breathing? What do you notice? Is there a sound you hear, or a sensation of air moving, or can you feel your chest or belly moving with each breath?

If you notice your attention drift, finding yourself thinking about something else, acknowledge that, and gently bring your focus back to your breath. Each time your mind wanders, the act of noticing that is part of the practice, as is gently returning to your chosen focus of attention.

As you practise this, you'll find it easier to stretch for longer than two minutes. If a regular mindfulness practice takes root in your life, it has a powerful restorative influence. You'll also become more aware of a range of emotions. Some of these you can just sit with: they will come and they will go. And also, there will be some feelings you'd like to give more attention to. That's where this next practice helps.

2) Expressing the feeling

Joan had been feeling uncomfortable all morning. Her partner had said something that upset her, and she wasn't sure whether to mention it or not. She'd done her mindfulness practice, noticing tension in her shoulders plus some hurt and angry feelings, too. Over lunch, crying as she spoke, she told her partner what had been bothering her. He listened, heard her and apologised. The storm cloud that had been with Joan all morning disappeared.

Have you had an experience like this, where a feeling bubbles under the surface for a while and is then expressed in a way that clears the air? Joan told me she felt physically different afterwards. 'I felt lighter, energised and clearer in my mind,' she said. Yet even though emotional expression is linked with health benefits, we're not always encouraged to open up. Fears of burdening others, appearing too negative or provoking an argument can lead people to keep quiet and stifle their unease.

Research suggests that habitually suppressing feelings or dwelling on them carries a cost that can include increasing depression and anxiety. Reviewing over thirty studies, the psychologist Johanna Schäfer and colleagues reported that 'habitual use of maladaptive emotion-regulation strategies such as rumination and avoidance may result in prolonged and intensified experiences of negative emotions.'[8] Being able to give form to a feeling, whether in words or other expression, can allow you to release it and move on. That is a lot easier if you have a context of safety and support, and where you've grown up with healthy models of emotional expression. In more hostile or less supportive contexts, showing how you feel might risk exposing vulnerabilities that others can use against you. Fortunately, there are many ways to express how we feel, and not all of them need to be public. Expressive writing is an example.

3) Expressive writing

In the early 1980s, the psychologist James Pennebaker found that recently bereaved widows and widowers had fewer health problems in the first year of their loss if they were able to talk about the death of their partner.[9] But what if someone didn't have anyone to talk to? Would expressing your thoughts and feelings to yourself also have benefit?

Pennebaker and his team tested the impact of expressive writing by asking students to write about personally upsetting experiences and the feelings they had about these.[10] A control group were asked to write instead about matter-of-fact topics like the shoes they wore or the rooms where they lived. While writing about upsetting events left people feeling sad around the time of writing, it was followed by better health in the next six months compared with the control group. Later studies have shown that expressive writing has a positive impact on the immune system, improves mood and can reduce symptoms in a range of medical conditions, including asthma and rheumatoid arthritis.[11] 'Writing about upsetting experiences,' concludes Pennebaker, 'although painful in the days of writing, produces long-term improvements in mood and indicators of wellbeing.'[12]

Expressive writing is a way of moving through troubled feelings, either from recent events or from traumas in the past. In some of the research studies, people wrote about events from their past that they'd never spoken about to anyone. The writing doesn't need to be seen or commented on by anyone else, and if you're trying this yourself it can be a relief to know that this is for your eyes only, so it doesn't have to make sense or be grammatically correct. You just identify an upsetting issue or event and pour out any words that come. It can help to set a time – many of the research studies suggested fifteen minutes once a day for four days in a row, but shorter periods were also used. Once you start, don't stop to think too much: just let the words flow.

While the earlier studies looked at writing about past events, more recent research has shown that writing about troubling events in the future can also be useful. Several studies have demonstrated that writing about exam nerves not only helps settles people's mood, it can also lead to improved results.[13] In one study, people with high levels of maths anxiety found writing for just seven minutes before the exam steadied their nerves and improved their performance.[14]

Try this – expressive writing

When something has upset you, or when you're worried about an event coming up, try writing about it. Get a notebook or blank sheet of paper, set a timer for a time that feels comfortable for you – perhaps ten or fifteen minutes – and start writing. A good place to begin is with a sentence starter like, 'So here I am; what I'm facing is . . .'

Don't worry about spelling, grammar, punctuation or sentence structure; just continue until the time is up. If you find this a useful process, consider adopting it as a habit, as a form of 'emotional maintenance' for dealing with thoughts and feelings on a regular basis.

If you've written about something disturbing, don't be surprised if you feel upset afterwards. That's a normal reaction. Working through a feeling is a journey that tends to include feeling it. Writing can be an important step in this, and is sometimes enough to move you through to the other side of the emotion.

However, if you're feeling too much distress is coming up, you can shift the focus of your writing to exploring what helps you deal with disturbance. Rather than looking back at past events or forward at things that might happen, you can develop a sentence that begins like this: 'When I'm feeling like this, what helps me is . . .' This might take you to trying some of the other self-steadying strategies here.

4) Processing the feeling

Every emotional experience can be thought of as the start of a story that wants to go somewhere or do something. The feeling is a 'call to action' – that's part of its purpose: to call your attention and motivate a response. In the last chapter, we saw what happened to Elliot when he had lost this valuable capacity. If you think of a feeling as a messenger, one of the best ways to settle that feeling is to take the message seriously. Processing a feeling is where we take it on a journey that moves the emotion along. Sometimes, as with Margo and the wasp, there is a simple action that resolves the situation the feeling alerted you to. But other times it can be less easy to work out what the message is or whether it is something you want to act on. That's why it can be so useful to have a process, or a sequence of steps, that helps you clarify what the emotion is and how best to respond.

In this sequence there are three main parts:

awareness – identifying what the feeling is (or feelings are)

understanding – recognising what the feeling is (or feelings are) about

response – considering a range of options and choosing your next step

To be aware of what you're feeling, you need a moment of your attention. If you're busy and moving at high speed you may miss this – which is why people can be surprised at how much sometimes bubbles up when they do stop. If you're not sure what you're feeling, developing a 'listening practice' can strengthen emotional self-awareness. This could be mindfulness, but could also be through creative expression, writing or drawing, or conversation.

To become clearer why you're feeling something, a useful question to ask yourself is: 'If this feeling were trying to tell me something, what would it say?'

Try this – listening to your feeling (or feelings)

If you're aware of a feeling, but you're not sure what it is about, try using these two sentence starters as prompts, completing them by writing or speaking:

   'What I'm feeling is . . .' (consider the four quadrants if you're not sure)

   'If this feeling had a voice, it might say . . .'

When we looked earlier at how resilience develops, we moved away from the idea of a single 'root' cause, and instead considered a range of contributing causes. We can do the same with our feelings, helped by the framework of the three P's. In this, the question 'Why am I feeling this?' is answered in three ways, considering the Predisposing or background factors, the Precipitating or trigger factors, and the Perpetuating or maintaining factors.

Predisposing factors

Every emotional experience has a history of past events that sensitise us to feeling a certain way. These are the predisposing or background factors. For example, past scary events can increase someone's tendency to feel anxiety, and a recognised symptom of post-traumatic stress disorder is an increased startle response, where someone might jump if they hear a loud noise. If we haven't eaten for a while, low blood sugar leads to adrenaline release, and this will put us on edge, making us more likely to feel angry, tense or irritable.

Precipitating factors

These are the trigger events that are often seen as *the* cause of the feeling. For example, John said something that upset Penny. However, if we think of the boat and water level, John's comment might trigger a crash, but whether Penny became upset would also have been influenced by predisposing factors like whether she'd had breakfast, what mood she was in that day and her history with John. On a different day, with Penny in a different mood, and with the relationship with John in better shape, the same comment might have been floated over without causing any bumps.

Perpetuating factors

What keeps a feeling going once it has started? A common perpetuating factor we've looked at already is rumination, where someone dwells on an event, replaying it in their mind in a way that re-triggers distress – for example, if each time Penny thought about what John had said, she had another burst of adrenaline and renewal of her annoyance. While thinking about past events can be a way of working through them, if the thinking is stuck in a repetitive loop it can keep a feeling going.

Another perpetuating factor that can amplify stress is where someone is too busy to eat or drink, so remains dehydrated and low in blood sugar, in a way that reduces their capacity to deal with stressful events.

Wherever there is a vicious cycle of a cause that rebounds back to make itself happen more, there is a perpetuating factor at work. Another example is in the relationship between depression and heavy drinking. Each makes the other more likely, in a feedback loop where each is a contributing cause for the other.

Heavy drinking   Depression

Fig. 3: A vicious cycle

Processing a feeling involves unpacking it, looking at the different factors involved. Sometimes just getting clearer on what the feeling is about helps move it on. But at other times the call to action needs to be answered; a response is needed.

5) A water-level check-in

The question 'How's my water level doing?' reminds me to pay attention to simple steps I can take to nourish myself in times of need. When we're depleted, our water level low, that question draws attention to any unattended appetites or needs. A check-in sentence I often use is, 'I feel . . . (report in how I'm feeling), I need . . . (identify any unmet needs requiring attention).' As we have touched on previously, mild dehydration, low blood sugar and loneliness have an impact on our water level, leaving us feeling at a low ebb. Sometimes it might be a glass of water, a meal or some good company we need rather than a relaxation session. If we're not clear what we need, asking ourselves what we'd like or prefer can draw attention to simple steps of self-care that help us steady ourselves. For example, it might be, 'I'm feeling a bit cold, I'd like to put on a jersey,' or, 'I'm feeling bored, I'd like to go for a walk.'

Try this - attending to needs and preferences

At periodic intervals in a day, pause and do these three check-ins:

How's my water level doing?

'I feel . . . I need . . . (or, if no needs are apparent, I'd like . . .)'

'If I took my needs seriously, what I'd do now is . . .'

In my work with clients in recovery from addiction, these check-ins were important for dealing with cravings. If someone relies on a particular substance or behaviour to comfort themselves, they're likely to experience cravings for that whenever they're feeling something is missing. This applies more broadly than just with addictions: there might be other habits of choice we turn towards when feeling uneasy, whether social media, checking our emails or watching TV.

If our self-comforting habits work well for us, that's fine, but if we're relying too much on something, or it has unwanted after-effects, then we may want to steer ourselves in a different direction. Each time we feel drawn to our familiar crutch, we can ask ourselves, 'How is my water level doing? Could my desire for my habit be like a warning light telling me I'm depleted in another area?' It might be I'm lonely, hungry, thirsty, tired or need to replenish in another way. What we're doing here is using the experience of uneasiness as a prompt to pay attention to our needs.

6) Distraction

When I used to take blood from people in my work as a doctor, I found distraction an invaluable technique to help them deal with pain. I'd ask my patient to focus their attention on a spot on the wall and count backwards from ten. I'd do something similar myself when at the dentist. There's a simple principle at work here: how we feel depends at least in part on what we focus our attention on. If we're watching closely as someone sticks a needle in our arm, we'll likely feel the *ouch* more than if we're looking out the window enjoying the view of trees blowing in the wind. It is similar with emotional pain too: if we dwell on our distress, we'll experience it more.

There's another side to distraction, though. Habitual avoidance of uncomfortable thoughts and feelings has been shown to be unhelpful.[9] Hiding from problems doesn't remove them, and when they remain unaddressed, they tend to get worse. So, when is it OK to distract and when is it not? To find out, researchers in Sweden recruited people to take part in a survey asking about how much they accepted their feelings, how they dealt with them, and also how they were in a range of measures of wellbeing.[15] They found that if people first accepted their feeling but then chose to 'constructively refocus', they tended to score more highly on measures of wellbeing. If people tended to avoid feelings (scoring low on acceptance) and used distraction as a coping strategy, their wellbeing levels were lower. They concluded that 'distraction may be either adaptive or maladaptive, depending on whether it is combined with an attitude of acceptance or avoidance'.

With the storyboarding starting point of 'Here's me facing the challenge of . . .', you're beginning by accepting where you are and what you feel. You're then looking at where you go from there, and distraction can sometimes be a useful option. With any of the strategies we're looking at here, it is important to review the impact of what you do. Any tool can be used well or over-relied on in a way that is limiting.

In addictions recovery, there is a saying, 'Look, don't stare.' If you find your attention stuck on a source of distress in a way that undermines your coping capacity, distraction can help break the spell. When I teach intentional refocusing, I invite people to ask themselves a question that directs their attention a different way. For example, if you ask yourself, 'What ten things can I see that are yellow?' you start looking around the room for them. I invite you to try this.

Try this - intentional refocusing

If you're finding an emotion too intense and you'd like to settle yourself, ask yourself a question that gets you looking in another direction. For example, 'What ten things can I see that are purple?' When you've reached ten, clap your hands. If you can't find ten, then aim for as many as you can, and when you've had enough of looking, clap your hands. The goal is to shift your focus, give yourself a pause and then come back to what you were doing.

7) Gratitude practices

When people look for ten things that are yellow or purple, they're often surprised by how much they see that they hadn't noticed before. Some things we only spot when we actively look for them. This insight is the starting point for intentionally cultivating gratitude, as there are valuable benefits we receive from others that we might take for granted or not be consciously aware of until we look more closely and think about them.

Take, for example, your favourite meal. What do you like about it? The first step in appreciating something is to notice what you like, and just as you can look for ten things that are yellow, so you can also look for ten things you like about a meal. Positive psychologist Karen Reivich uses the phrase 'hunt the good stuff' to describe this active searching-out of positive aspects of something.[16]

There are two sides to gratitude. One is appreciation, where you're noticing what you value, like or love. The other is thankfulness, where you identify those you've received from and experience gratitude. You can take both these sides further. You can stretch your noticing by savouring, where you let your attention linger on the aspects you appreciate most. You can stretch thankfulness by actively considering those who've played a part in benefits you value and expressing your gratitude rather than keeping it to yourself. For example, you might thank whoever cooked your favourite meal, even if it was you. And then extending further, trace the chain of those involved in supplying or creating the food. That might include not just shops and farmers, but also the bees that pollinated plants and the earthworms that improved the soil. Gratitude is a social emotion that points our attention outwards beyond ourselves, strengthening our awareness of the networks we receive from. This strengthens resilience by reminding us we're not alone.

When you give your attention to appreciation and thankfulness, notice how you feel. Often people report feeling lighter, happier, more open and warmer inside. Research by Barbara Friedrikson, one of the pioneers of positive psychology, shows how positive feelings like these play a role in settling our emotional state after disturbance. 'Mild joy and contentment,' she writes 'share the ability to undo the lingering cardiovascular after-effects of negative emotions.'[17] She refers to this as the 'undoing effect'.

Is the glass half full or half empty? It depends which side we give our attention to, and while that's influenced by our habits of perception, it can also be a matter of choice. When we hunt the good stuff, we notice the value of what's here already and the fullness of the glass. That creates a feeling of safety and contentment that buffers us against emotional knocks, as well as helping us recover more quickly from them. Gratitude practices are a form of mind training that have been shown to powerfully influence our mood. While the storyboarding of resilience starts with 'Here's me facing the challenge of . . .', how might the story be different if we started it with the phrase, 'Here's me, and what I'm appreciating is . . .' A two-part story of gratitude might have a second sentence starter of, 'I'd like to express my appreciation by thanking . . .'

Try this – a two-part story of gratitude

Look around you, allowing your attention to be guided by the questions 'What do I appreciate here? What do I value, like or love?' In this 'hunting the good stuff', each time you find something, let your attention stay there a while, savouring it and taking it in. Then consider who or what has played a role in creating or supporting that which you appreciate. How could you thank them?

Then write, or speak, a two-part story with the following sentence starters:

'Here's me, and what I'm appreciating is . . .'

'I'd like to express my appreciation by thanking . . .'

Let these sentence starters invite you to describe in detail what you appreciate, what it is about it that you like or love, who has played a role in creating it, and how might you thank them.

I use the term 'appreciative gaze' to describe the process of noticing and valuing what we like or love. This type of seeing is a learnable skill. Just like some people are birdwatchers – they notice birds, they look out for them and spot them from afar or even when they're hidden – we can learn to look out for what we appreciate. Research has shown that keeping a diary of things we notice each day that we're thankful for helps improve our mood.[18] It is a powerful self-steadying strategy.

8) Support from people or places

Where do you turn for support when you're upset? Support from others is such an important pathway to resilience that we'll be looking at it more closely in the Sixth Way. But as well as support from people, we can also benefit from the restorative and settling impact of places that are special to us.

Just five minutes in a beautiful garden has been shown to have a profound impact on mood[19] – even more so if we give our full attention with mindfulness or appreciative gaze. Research has shown that people recover from operations more quickly if their hospital bed gives them a view of trees and nature, rather than concrete and buildings.[20] There might also be special places you go when you need to recharge. We can develop relationships with such places, and a practice of sitting in nature. We have touched already on the antidepressant impact of exercise – if you combine exercise and nature, you strengthen the effect.

9) Body-focused practices

We've looked already at how the activation of our autonomic nervous system leads to changes in our physiology, such as heart rate speeding or muscles tightening when we're anxious. The body is also a powerful route into settling ourselves. Perhaps the simplest way of doing this is through touch, through physically holding ourselves. It is natural to pick up and hold a baby as a way of settling them, but we too respond to be being held, and a hug from the right people, or even stroking a pet, has been shown to trigger release of the mood-lifting hormone oxytocin.[21]

10) Cognitive reappraisal

When we meet someone, our brains decide from a brief glance at their face whether they are trustworthy or not.[22] We might find ourselves warming to a stranger or feeling suspicious before we know anything about them. Our initial appraisal of 'friend or foe' isn't always right. Bringing our judgements into view and reconsidering them is called 'cognitive reappraisal', and it is one of the most research-evidenced pathways to settling our mood. If we're upset, angry, frightened or hurt, we look at the thoughts that lead us to feel this way and review them. Finding a different story about what's going on involves the ability to change our mind. It is such a powerful route to resilience that it is the focus of our next way: Thinking Flexibly.

Emotional First Aid –

The Second Way at a glance

What does it look like when you do this skilfully?

Imagine you've just experienced a difficult situation that in the past might have tipped you over an edge. Perhaps it left you feeling furious, frightened, or hurt. Yet you're pleased with how you deal with this. First of all, you notice: you acknowledge both the challenge you've faced and the feelings it has left you with. Secondly, you're able to take a pause and reflect on your state, noticing if you're unsettled in a way that might need some attention. Thirdly, you're able to respond to how you feel and to the situation you face, reflecting on choices and tools available to you, applying ones that move you in a direction you'd like to go.

What helps you do this?

 a) **Listening to your heart.** Valuing the role your feelings play as guiding signals, as reminders of your values and sources of energy, you pay attention to your emotional experience. Practices like journaling, mindfulness and personal check-ins enable you to be more in tune with yourself.

b) **Insights from neuroscience.** You recognise that your brain and nervous system may respond differently when you're in a state of distress. The idea of the resilience zone can make you more alert to times when you're in an over-charged state of 'fight or flight', or when you're blocked by a freeze response.

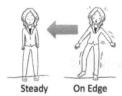

Steady   On Edge

c) **Self-Steadying Strategies.** When you feel on edge or outside the resilience zone, a range of practices are available to you that move you in a more settled direction. Whether through slowing your breathing, mindfulness, thinking differently or seeking support, you recognise choice points and actions for emotional self-regulation.

ACT d) **Acceptance and Commitment Therapy (ACT).** You feel how you feel. Acceptance isn't the same as approval: it is about acknowledging where you are and what you experience. Commitment is about reminding yourself what matters to you, what directions you want to move in, which legs of the spider you want to follow. Then you do that, you ACT. While Acceptance and Commitment Therapy is an approach in its own right, the letters ACT remind you that combining acceptance and commitment can itself be therapeutic.

The Third Way – Thinking Flexibly

We have flexible necks that allow us to view the world from different angles. We can look up and see opportunities in the distance, look down and see hazards we might otherwise trip over, look around us and take in an overview of our situation. Flexible thinking is the ability to have similar manoeuvrability in our thinking perspective. We start by recognising that, whatever we face, there are different ways we can think about it, and some thinking pathways will be more useful to us than others. With practice, and with the tools we'll look at, we can get better at noticing the impact of how we think and trying out a different perspective if that might improve our resilience.

This way includes:

Chapter 7 – The Skill of Failing Better
Chapter 8 – Psychological Self-Defence

7

The Skill of Failing Better

There is an old Chinese tale about a farmer who depended on his horse to plough his fields. One day the horse ran away.

'What terrible luck,' his neighbours exclaimed.

'Maybe so, maybe not, we'll see,' the farmer replied.

A few days later the horse returned home, bringing with it three beautiful wild horses too.

'What great luck,' the neighbours said, feeling envious that the farmer now had three more horses.

'Maybe so, maybe not, we'll see,' replied the farmer.

The farmer's son began work training the wild horses. A few days later he was thrown off one of them and broke his leg.

'What terrible luck you've had,' the neighbours said.

'Maybe so, maybe not, we'll see,' said the farmer.

The next week soldiers marched through the town conscripting all able-bodied young men. The farmer's son, still recovering from his injury, was judged unfit and left behind.

'How lucky is that!' said the neighbours, fearing for the safety of their sons.

This story follows a pattern: events initially judged as bad luck bring unexpected benefits, while an event that seemed at first to be good news turns out later to be a source of suffering. Have you had this experience too - where your initial judgements about an event were later turned on their head? Here's a time this happened for me.

When I trained in group work years ago, participants on the course took it in turns to run a workshop, so that we could give each other feedback about our facilitation. When it came to my turn, I was excited by the day I had planned. Only it didn't work at all well. I felt such a failure afterwards that when I got home I collapsed in a heap and burst into tears.

Looking back, I now see that day as one of my most important learning experiences. I recognise where I went wrong, and my determination not to repeat that mistake has shaped the way I work with groups, making me much more effective as a facilitator. This is an example of post-traumatic growth. The long-term benefits of that event go further than just improving my group skills, though. I also learned something that has helped me develop the skill of failing better.

Different flavours of failing

I grew up with the view that success is good and failure bad. So, no surprise that I found my workshop disappointment upsetting. I'd been building the event up in my mind, I was looking forward to it – but then my positivity popped like an overblown balloon, leaving me deflated and empty. What made this setback worse was the thinking track I got stuck in after the event. I had a harsh, self-critical voice that took my poor performance as evidence of incompetence. A sequence of pessimism played out in my mind: because I'd failed, I was no good at this and my plans to develop a career in training weren't going to work. A dismal tale rolled on from there, and with it an excruciating experience of sadness and shame. I felt like giving up on my plans and hiding myself away.

I wish I'd known about the Chinese farmer and his horse. When he says, 'Maybe so, maybe not, we'll see,' he's expressing the spider diagram in words. Whatever we face, there are different ways it can go. When his horse ran away, maybe it was bad luck, but the story was still in play, so the farmer was keeping an open mind. When we fail, or things go wrong, our story is still in play. We don't know how it will turn out in the long run. But choices we make influence what happens; a pivotal choice point available to us is the meaning we give to events. The meaning we give to what happens shapes our emotional experience and our behaviour.

The meaning I gave to my flop of a workshop was that it implied I wasn't good enough at running groups to make a career as a trainer. In my mind was a sequence that went, 'because of this . . . therefore that . . . which will lead to . . . and then also . . .' This train of thought left me feeling so awful that I was on the verge of giving up.

Reflecting on the perspective-check questions of: 'What's the best that can happen here? What's the worst? And what's most likely?' I had got stuck on seeing the worst. So, what's the best that can happen when you mess up? Have you ever made a mistake that worked out well in the end? Sir Alexander Fleming did. It was only when a sample of bacteria in his untidy laboratory went mouldy that he discovered penicillin. He saw that the bacteria had died back around the mould. He then went on to extract the antibiotic substance the mould was producing.

The invention of crisps is another example of a failure that worked out well. In a restaurant in New York in 1853, a customer complained that his potatoes were too soggy and thick. The chef, George Crum, cooked them again with thinner slices. The customer didn't like these either and complained. Mr Crum patiently chopped the spuds another time. These got sent back too. Eventually the chef was so fed up he sliced the potatoes as thin as he could, fried them and covered them with salt. The crisp was born.

Thomas Watson, the founder of IBM, once said: 'If you want to succeed, double your failure rate.'[1] The meaning he's giving to failure here is that it is useful preparation that helps us become more experienced and, from this, successful. Thomas Edison had a similar view. When a journalist asked how he felt after failing a thousand times in developing the electric light bulb, Edison replied, 'I didn't fail a thousand times. The light bulb was an invention with a thousand steps.'[2]

The skill of failing better involves using our setbacks as sources of experience and learning. That is helped by a thinking track that keeps us engaged in the process of looking for better ways forward, rather than one that leaves us feeling like giving up. Rigid thinking is where we get stuck in a particular view and find it hard to see things any other way. Just the shift to recognising that there are different flavours of failure is a step towards a more flexible view.

Flexible thinking is like having a flexible neck

Try this for a moment. Look down. See what's in front of your feet. That's useful for seeing hazards on your path that you might otherwise trip over. Look up, see the sky, and faraway places you might reach in the distance. Look around you, see what you're facing. Flexible thinking is similar to this, but we do the looking with our mind. Looking down is negative thinking, looking up is positive thinking, looking around and seeing what's likely is realistic thinking. Looking from a range of different, and perhaps even unusual, angles is creative thinking.

Our necks have evolved to be flexible because this gives us survival advantage. Being able to look from different angles

Fig. 1: Four types of thinking

strengthens our ability to recognise threats, be reality-orientated and spot opportunities. Flexible thinking is applying that same principle to the way we think.

So how do we know which is the best way to think? Are they all as good as each other? One way is to ask ourselves, 'What is

Fig. 2: If we always look up
we may not spot hazards in our way

the evidence for this?' Some thoughts are interesting but have no factual support. The self-help writer Tony Robbins compared any belief to a table: it needs to be held up by supporting legs.[3] Evidence is like a supporting leg. So if we have a deeply negative view that isn't helpful to us, one way of challenging that is to ask, 'What's the evidence for that?'

The creative thinker Edward de Bono, who coined the term 'lateral thinking', suggested another way of assessing our thoughts.[4] As well as 'judgement value', where we judge them as true or false depending on the evidence, there is also 'movement value', which is about where they take us. It is possible to have two or three views each with factual evidence behind them, but which take us to different places. For example, with my difficult day learning to run groups, the thoughts 'I've messed up' and 'I've gained valuable experience' are both true, but the second view is more encouraging in helping me develop a career as a trainer.

Learning to change our thinking track

Research shows that two factors making depression more likely after a setback are rumination and being overly self-critical.[5,6] With rumination, our thoughts are stuck on a track that drives our mood and our behaviour in a particular direction. Self-critical commentary after we've made a mistake is an example of this.

When I think like this   I tend to feel like this   And behave like that

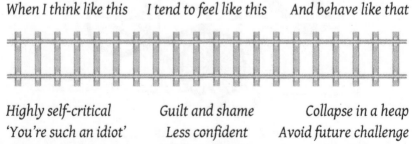

Highly self-critical   Guilt and shame   Collapse in a heap
'You're such an idiot'   Less confident   Avoid future challenge
Fig. 3: A thinking track of harsh self-criticism after failure

Cognitive therapy is a proven treatment for anxiety and depression. It helps us recognise the thinking tracks we habitually fall into and then learn to change these if they're leading us somewhere we don't want to go. The ability to switch tracks is a learnable skill that can take our mood and behaviour in a different direction. A tool that helps here is the ABC thinking check.

Doing the ABC thinking check

Taught as part of the Penn Resilience training, the ABC thinking check is a way of drawing attention to the way we're thinking about challenging events, and the impact this has.[7] **A** stands for **A**dversity – whatever it is we're facing. **B** is for **B**elief, the thoughts or beliefs we have about this. **C** is for **C**onsequences, in terms of where this leads in our emotional reaction and behaviour. First, we notice the thoughts we're having, and look where these lead. Then we ask ourselves, 'What other ways are there of thinking about this?' and do the ABC check on these too.

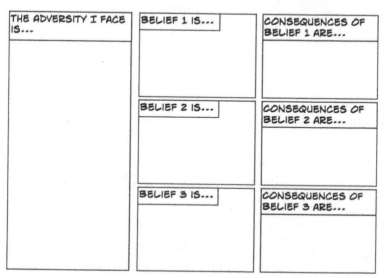

Fig. 4: The ABC thinking check

Applying this to my botched workshop, the adversity (A) is having failed to do as well as I'd hoped. For beliefs (B), my first thoughts come from the self-critical voice that says, 'Chris, you've messed up here. You're such an idiot.' I call this voice the 'crap channel'. It is like a radio station that provides a running commentary of everything I'm doing wrong, or that is wrong with the situation I'm in.

Fig. 5: The crap channel

When I think this way, I tend to feel defeated and disappointed with myself. I'm more likely to go quiet and step back from challenge. If I have this feeling too much, I'm less likely to carry on. But I've come to recognise this one. What helps me here is the question, 'What other ways are there that I can think about it?'

Creative thinking is where we generate a range of different perspectives. The key with flexible thinking is that we're able to recognise that any thinking track is just one of a number of possible views. So how else could I think about this? When I told a friend, she said, 'Don't worry – everyone messes up sometimes. It is part of life. *C'est la vie.*' This is a more accepting view. When I think this way I feel calmer, I brush aside the guilt and shame. I'm more likely to stick with my path. But perhaps I could also become complacent.

I like Thomas Watson's view that the way to succeed is to double your failure rate. This encourages me to look at what I can learn from this, and to see this as a step along the way. In research on creativity, one of the factors that distinguished more creative people was that they were less likely to give up after mistakes. They were more likely to see mistakes as just part of the learning journey.

A meaning that fits well with resilience training is to see each failure as an opportunity to practise applying my resilience tools. I ask myself: 'What would a story of resilience look like here?' – and challenge myself to find some tools that might help, then practise using them.

All four of these beliefs have some truth, in that they all have evidence to support them. But as thinking tracks they lead different ways, and some are more useful than others. Flexible thinking stops us getting stuck in one track. It opens up a choice, giving us the ability to move to a more constructive view.

Pre-traumatic growth

If you've got on the wrong bus and see yourself heading off course, having gloomy thoughts along the lines of, 'Because of this mistake, I'm going in the wrong direction, and if that continues, it could be awful,' might be not only true but also useful. It prompts you to abandon your bus journey and get off at the next stop. This is an example of defensive pessimism, where our fears for the worst motivate preventative action. This is the thinking behind the precautionary principle, where even when we don't know for sure that a path will lead to problems, if risks are considered likely, choosing a safer path is viewed as a wise precaution.

In my addictions recovery work, I saw this type of defensive pessimism as essential for recovery. It is when someone has negative thoughts and, linked with these, feelings of alarm – about where their addictive behaviour is taking them – that they become more motivated to change. As leading positive psychologist Martin Seligman writes, in the notes to his book *Authentic Happiness*, 'In spite of the many advantages of positive thinking, there are times when negative thinking is to be preferred.'[8] The danger of overly-positive thinking is that minimising risks makes it easier to ignore them.

What we're looking at here is a healthy side to worry. Positive anxiety is where our fears about things going wrong activate us to take steps to address risks and improve outcomes. I think of this as 'pre-traumatic growth' – where our concerns about potential traumatic events ahead of us rouse our preventative or preparatory response.

How do we know if fear is helpful or blocking?

Fear acts to alert us to threats; it has evolved to serve a life-preserving purpose. Yet, like an overprotective parent guided by good intentions, caution can exceed its optimum dose. Where do we draw the line in appropriately applying the precautionary principle? If we're never held back by fear, we might become reckless, but if we're held back too much we become blocked. This is particularly important after failure and things going wrong, because sometimes our failing is feedback that we're on the wrong track, while at other times, as with Edison and his light bulb, a disappointing result might be a vital step on a longer journey.

When I was working with clients struggling with relapse from addiction, the way they thought about failure made a crucial difference. If they had the 'crap channel' in full play, with highly critical self-commentary about what a mess they'd made of things, they'd be more likely to drink again as a way of shutting out the shame. To learn to see their failure as a step along the way paved the way to learning from it, allowing a crisis to become a turning point. This was failing better.

When I teach in my workshops about changing thinking tracks, people tend to accept the theory but sometimes struggle with the practice. What's hard here is that we can get stuck in deeply ingrained habits of mind. Is it possible to change our mental pathways when they seem just part of how we are? What helps here is the learnable skill of psychological self-defence. It is to this that we turn next.

8

Psychological Self-Defence

I sit on a hill, feeling nervous. I've just given up my job and don't know where I am going to live or how I am going to support myself. I just know I couldn't go on the way I'd been going. My legs feel like jelly; it is as though the ground under me is unstable and might give way at any moment. I'm feeling fear.

Then, in a fraction of a second, my outlook shifts in a most extraordinary way. I burst out laughing, because suddenly it seems so clear. Something I hadn't seen swings into view. I've discovered mystery.

This was me a few months after my car crash and those hundred-hour weeks as a junior doctor. I had given up my job and didn't know what was coming next. Feeling on edge and worried about how I was going to manage, I'd gone to sit on a hill to have some reflection time. That 'Ah-ha' realisation completely changed the way I felt, my heavy sense of dread lifting and being replaced by an enthusiastic openness to a new phase in my life.

Though it is now thirty years since my moment on the hill, I still remember it vividly as a vital turning point. The shift in my mind and heart involved a new and liberating perspective coming into view that revealed something about uncertainty I hadn't seen or appreciated before. Before the flip point, I'd been thinking, 'I don't know what I'm going to do, I don't know where I'm going to live, I don't know how I'm going to support myself.'

144

I was finding it difficult to tolerate the uncertainty of not knowing because the meaning I was giving to it was one of threat.

In my mind I had a 'because of this ... therefore that ...' sequence that went like this: because I didn't have a job, I wouldn't be able to afford somewhere to live, I'd end up on the street and my life would fall apart. I'd been focusing on the lower legs of the spider, which left me in a state of fear about the worst that could happen. The shift was not in what I was seeing, but in the way I was seeing it and the meaning I was giving to this.

Imagine how a novel or a movie would be if you knew exactly what was going to happen? If a story is too predictable, it becomes boring. It is the not knowing that keeps your attention: a good storyteller draws in interest by raising important questions, and then leaving you on tenterhooks wanting to find out which way the answer goes. That cultivated anticipation builds our desire to turn the page of a novel or continue watching a film.

Something similar happens in life, and that's what mystery is. If you can open to the mystery of life, to not knowing what's around the corner, then life becomes more of an adventure. In that moment on the hill, the meaning I gave to not knowing switched from adversity to adventure. I was still seeing the bottom legs of the spider, but my not knowing also included the upper legs too. In shutting one door by leaving my job I was inviting in the possibility of opening others. My life had become an open book, and I experienced a sense of liberation.

When asked about qualities that help in life, the psychologist, author and meditation teacher Jack Kornfield replied: 'One quality that enabled my success is a certain kind of trust and flexibility. The trust is not that things will work out, but that if things don't work out you can do something else. That's the real trust.'[1]

That's the kind of trust I opened to, and it plays a key role in resilience. In this chapter we'll explore how you can cultivate it. First, though, we need to understand more how the sort of mind shift I experienced happens, and what we can do to make helpful shifts more likely.

Mind shift, mood shift

Working closely with people with depression, and also experiencing my own past times of depression, I've seen rapid shifts both up and down. Someone might be feeling just fine, but then one small thing happens that tips their view into a bleak take on things that seems absolutely real. It might be a collapse of confidence – that earlier in the day they were happy to do something that by mid-afternoon seemed impossible. In the depth of a dip like this, 'positive thinking' can be experienced as unhelpful as it often doesn't fit with what seems real and true. Yet what I'd experienced on the hill was that I can move from one version of the truth to another in an instant. This didn't make the old view no longer true. It was just that one version felt more encouraging and supportive of a constructive response.

How can we flip from one version of reality to another in an instant – whether from a satisfied view to bleakness, or the other way? Learning about image reversals offers some clues. When our mind sees an image that is ambiguous, where more than one thing can be true, it tends to settle on one version. But if you keep looking, the other version may suddenly jump out at you. A way to demonstrate this is with the Necker cube (see Fig. 1 below).[2] You can see it with the front square slightly higher to the right, or slightly lower to the left (see Fig. 2 below). When it's seen one way, it seems that is the 'right way', yet if you switch, the other way seems right too.

146

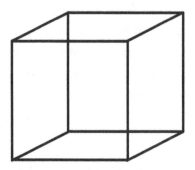

Fig. 1: A Necker cube – which side of the cube is in front?

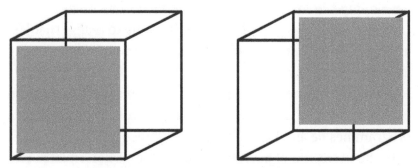

Fig. 2: A Necker cube – if grey marks
the front side, which view is correct?

Once you know it is possible to shift view, then even if one view seems absolutely true to you in that moment, you can hold in your mind the idea that it isn't necessarily the only way of looking that can be right. Why is this important? Because something similar goes on in our brain when we shift between seeing a glass as half full or half empty. We can flip between views.

It used to be thought that some people are just naturally 'glass-half-empty people' who tend to see what's missing and experience a lack. Other people are naturally 'glass-half-full people' who focus more on the half-full side, leaving them more satisfied with what's there. With flexible thinking it is possible to recognise the value in both views while also being able to choose and switch between them. We can learn to get better at doing this moving between views. Seeing the half-full side more easily helps improve mood, while seeing the empty side helps us identify where improvements can be made.

Learned helplessness to learned optimism

Martin Seligman first became well known as a psychologist for developing the leading theory for understanding depression – the learned-helplessness model. But he came to realise that just as people could learn to get stuck in the empty side of seeing lack of possibility, and then giving up hope, it was also possible to learn to lean the other way. This led to his work on learned optimism, which has played such a central role in the resilience programmes he and his colleagues developed.

In the literature of psychology, optimism is described in two main ways. The first is dispositional optimism, which is closer to the more everyday understanding. This is where, when looking forward in time, someone tends to look on the bright side and think things will go well. For example, if you're an optimist you're likely to agree with statements like 'In uncertain times, I usually expect the best' and 'Overall, I expect more good things to happen to me than bad.'[3] Research shows there are clear health benefits to thinking this way, and in particular it helps protect against depression and anxiety.[4]

But telling people to think more positively about the future can be experienced as not taking their concerns seriously. It can seem inauthentic or even in denial if those concerns are realistic. It can also seem difficult to change, as Alice, someone on one of my courses told me. 'I know worries build up in my mind and get a bit out of proportion,' she said, 'but that's just the way I am. I can't see how to change it.'

The second type of optimism is linked more to the way we think about the causes of events. When looking back in time at why a problem occurred, people tend to fall into habitual styles of explanation. Two important aspects of our 'explanatory style' are whether we see the cause as permanent and whether we see its impact as pervasive.[5] If we see a cause as permanent, then we're more likely to believe the problem will recur, leading to a more pessimistic view. In contrast, if we see the cause as temporary, then it is easier to see a problem as a one-off, leading to a more optimistic view. 'If you think about bad things in terms of "always" and "never" and abiding traits,' writes Seligman, 'you have a permanent, pessimistic style. If you think in terms of "sometimes" and "lately", using qualifiers and blaming bad events on ephemera, you have an optimistic style.'[5]

If we see a cause as having a wide-ranging impact, and the problem that occurred as just one symptom of a more pervasive issue, then we're more likely to believe there will be other problems occurring in the future. On the other hand, if the problem is ascribed to a very specific fault, which isn't likely to have other effects or spread to other areas, then that leads to a more optimistic view. While permanence is about a problem extending in time, pervasiveness involves extension geographically. Both follow a 'because of this, therefore that' sequence that brings out a bleaker view of how things will be.

Seligman and his team found that approaching optimism and pessimism this way, where the focus is on the way we think about events that have already happened, makes it easier to teach new thinking habits. If we find ourselves caught in an overly gloomy view of a situation, this 'explanatory-style' approach to learned optimism involves a simple check on how we view what's taken place. When a difficult event happens, there are three key questions:

1. Why do I think this happened?

2. Do I think the causes are permanent or temporary?

3. Do I think the causes have pervasive or specific effects?

Here's an example: Alice was going through a difficult time at work, finding it hard to cope when covering for an absent colleague who was unwell. Here's her reply to the three questions:

Why? I'm struggling because we're short-staffed. But I used to cope much better when things were tough. I don't think I've got it in me any more – I'm getting old.

Permanent or temporary? A colleague off sick is temporary, though they've been struggling for a while and might not come back. Getting old is progressive: I can't see that one improving.

Pervasive or specific in impact? Being short-staffed has an impact on everything we do at work, but there are some areas worse affected than others. The effects also spill over into my evenings and weekends, as I'm feeling exhausted most of the time.

Alice had been depressed in the past and felt herself sinking again. While some of this was linked to exhaustion, what made it worse was worry, with a sense of dread about how things would work out and whether she'd be able to cope. She didn't find it helpful when people told her to cheer up and be more positive. She felt the way she did, and the work pressures she faced were real: they couldn't just be wished away. She was fed up with worry, though, and interested in what she could do to tackle this. This is where psychological self-defence comes in.

How to dispute unhelpful thoughts

If someone you didn't like accused you of something you hadn't done, would you remain silent, or would you defend yourself by disputing their false claim against you? Most people are better at arguing back against others than they are at standing up to over-critical parts of themselves. This forms the basis of psychological self-defence, as Seligman explains: 'The key to disputing your own pessimistic thoughts is to first recognise them, and then treat them as if they were uttered by an external person, a rival whose mission in life was to make you miserable.'[6]

A technique used to argue back builds on the ABC thinking check we looked at earlier. It adds a **D** for **D**isputing and an **E** for the **E**nergisation that happens when you're able to shift to a different thinking track.[6] Here's how it might work for Alice.

A – the Adversity is being short-staffed at work with a colleague off sick. The increased pressure is leaving her exhausted and constant worry about this is getting her down.

B – Beliefs. The thoughts Alice finds most depressing are that she's struggling to cope because she's getting old, suggesting that problems will only get worse. She also thinks her colleague might not come back to work, so the work situation won't improve.

C – Consequences. The thought that the problems will get worse plays on her mind, keeping her awake at night, increasing her exhaustion, and also leaving her feeling low and bitter.
But then we add:

D – Disputing. Four important questions used in disputing thoughts are:

Evidence – what's the evidence here?
Alternatives – how else could I look at this?
Implications – what is the effect of thinking this way?
Usefulness – what perspectives might be useful here?

'It is essential to stand back and distance yourself from your pessimistic explanations,' advises Seligman, 'at least long enough to verify their accuracy.'[7] If our habitual explanatory style views the cause of the problem we face as permanent and with pervasive impact, that leads us to focus on the worst even when this isn't likely. Alice recognised that she didn't know how long her colleague was going to be off for. She had made a pessimistic assumption here that she could challenge. Also, there were other explanations for her tiredness than getting older. Her poor sleeping, which was linked to her worrying and was something she could tackle, was likely to be a bigger factor. Seeing her struggle as down to her age left her feeling hopeless. A more useful perspective was to focus on aspects of her situation she could change, like checking with her colleague how she was, addressing her worry rumination and exploring what she could do to improve her sleep.

E – Energisation. Alice felt relieved to see things weren't as hopeless as she'd been thinking. If her colleague was going to be off long-term, she could tell her manager she was feeling the strain and had concern about a recurrence of depression. If they didn't find a replacement within a reasonable timeframe, she could consider looking for another job. If her sleep improved, she might find ways to recover the satisfaction she used to feel in her job.

Real-time resilience

Karen Reivich, who has worked closely with Martin Seligman in developing the Penn Resilience training, offers a short form of disputing that can be used in the moment if you notice yourself on a thinking track that undermines your resilience. She suggests 'sentence-starters', similar to what we've used in the storyboarding, where you give yourself a start of a sentence as a launch point for talking yourself into shifting track.[8]

The first step is to notice the counterproductive thought pattern. Reivich identifies five common thinking traps, or unhelpful thinking tracks, that undermine resilience.

1) *Mind reading* – where we assume we know what other people are thinking. Alice had this, thinking other people were judging her as 'past it' because of her age. But the truth is she didn't really know what other people thought.

2) *It's all me.* The self-blame mind trap, where we're overly focusing on ourselves as the cause of the problem. Thinking this way leaves us feeling guilt and shame, and defensiveness can be used as a way of batting this one away.

3) *It's all them.* Where we see other people or circumstances as the cause of the problem. Thinking this way leaves us feeling more angry and resentful. It also reduces the chances that we'll see our role in events, and so reduces our capacity to identify choice points to change things.

4) *Catastrophising.* Sometimes known as 'awfulising', where we are on a thinking track of 'because of this, therefore that', and a sequence plays out that has an awful or catastrophic ending. That's what Alice was doing. Being able to do the

ABCDE was useful, but the thought was deeply ingrained, and it kept coming up. Having a name to call it was helpful. Alice found the term 'crap channel' (which we looked at earlier) helpful. She could say to herself, 'There goes my crap channel again.'

5) *Helplessness* – where we see ourselves as powerless to change anything. This is a recipe for depression.

If you catch yourself following one of these tracks, just to recognise that is a positive step. As you get better at spotting them, it becomes easier to say to yourself, 'Ah, there's that thinking trap – here I go again.' Then you can challenge the mind trap with one of these sentence starters.

1) *Evidence.* Consider whether the thought track is accurate by looking at the evidence. If you see it as inaccurate, challenge it in the moment with a sentence that begins, 'That's not true because . . .'

2) *Reframe.* Look at the situation from a different perspective, with a sentence starter that begins, 'A more helpful way to see this is . . .'

3) *Contingency plan.* If you're catastrophising, then think about what you could do if the worst did happen. See this as a two-part story of resilience, with the sentence, 'If . . . (name the fear) happens, then I will . . .' (map out your coping response).

Alice looked at some thoughts she often found herself having and planned how she might use these psychological self-defence techniques. There were times when she saw someone look at her and assumed they were having judgemental thoughts about

154

her being too old for her job. She could counter the 'I-know-what-they're-thinking' thought by replying, 'That's not true because I'm not a mind reader: I can't know for sure what someone else thinks unless I ask them.'

Reflecting on how she could counter the 'I'm too old to do this job' thought, Alice came up with the reply, 'A more helpful way to see this is that it is about energy rather than age, and my energy is influenced by factors I can change, like how well I'm looking after myself and how well I'm sleeping.' With this approach, each time she felt weary, she was reminded of her project of looking after her personal energy, recognising when she needed to step back and recharge, or take other steps that supported her wellbeing.

Alice's fear was that the stress at work would become too much for her, and that she might struggle to cope if her colleague remained off sick. She prepared a reply for when these thoughts came up. 'If I do reach the point where I'm finding it too much, then one option available to me is to discuss this with my manager. Another is to see my doctor. But in the meantime, I'd like to see dealing with stress as a challenge that I can story-board.' In the next section we look at the tools Alice found helpful here.

Thinking Flexibly –

The Third Way at a glance

What does it look like when you do this skilfully?

Periodically you pause and remind yourself that, however you're thinking about the situation you face, it is just one of a number of possible perspectives. You check with yourself: 'Is the thinking track I'm on serving me well? Are there other ways I could think about this?' You might consider how a range of people you admire might view this, and what thoughts they might have.

You're able to test both the validity and usefulness of alternative thinking tracks, choosing from these one that encourages constructive responses. You're able to draw on guiding thoughts that support resilience, while also recognising when the way you're thinking might be limiting you or your response. You also find yourself more curious and less threatened when your view meets another. You get into arguments less often and learn more from people who see things differently to you.

What helps you do this?

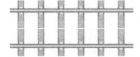 **a) Noticing your thinking track.** Each one leads you to particular consequences, in terms of how you feel and act. For example,

'When I think like this, I'm more likely to feel like that, and act like this.'

b) Recognising you have choice. Each way of looking is only one of many. Flexible thinking is similar to having a flexible neck – it allows you to look from a range of angles and switch between different views.

c) The ABC Thinking Check. When you have an Adversity (A), your Beliefs about this (B) have particular Consequences (C). Comparing the B-C pairings (e.g. B1 – C1, B2 – C2, etc.) lets you look at where each thinking track takes you, helping you choose between them.

d) Generating Alternatives. To consider a wider range of thought pathways, ask yourself, 'What other ways are there of thinking about this?' Imagine how different people you know might think about this.

e) Psychological Self-Defence. If a thinking track takes you somewhere you don't want to go, you can argue back against the unhelpful thoughts. Useful sentence starters are: 'That's not true because . . .' (drawing on evidence), 'If that happens, I can respond by . . .' (developing a contingency plan), or 'A more helpful way to see this is . . .' (reframing the situation).

The Fourth Way – Overload Management

Overload management involves both an active approach to regulating your level of loading or pressure, and taking steps that strengthen your capacity to cope with strain. The goal is improving your ability to function well under pressure, as well as to prevent, reduce and/or recover from harmful levels of overload.

This way includes:

9

Knowing Where You Are on the Hill

On 2 May 1845, a crowd gathered on the suspension bridge at Great Yarmouth to watch a circus clown floating on a barrel in the river below. As he went under the bridge, people rushed from one side to the other, so they could continue watching the spectacle beneath them. The strain of sudden movement was too much for the bridge, which then collapsed. Seventy-nine people, mostly children, drowned.

In 1891, a train travelling from Basel in Switzerland was so overcrowded that the Münchenstein Bridge couldn't take the strain. When it collapsed, over seventy people died. Five years later, a tram in British Columbia was so packed with people that Port Ellice Bridge gave way beneath them. Fifty-five people died.

This listing of nineteenth-century bridge disasters might seem morbid, but there's a story here of post-traumatic growth. Prior to 1900, overload was a relatively common cause of bridge collapse. After 1900, it wasn't.[1] We got the message that exceeding weight-bearing capacity was a dangerous thing to do and we became more serious, as well as more skilled, in preventing overload. We've learned this lesson with bridges. Could we apply the same insight with people?

Unfortunately, current trends are heading the wrong way. A recent report from the Chartered Institute of Personnel and

Development (CIPD) describes how people are increasingly being asked to meet tighter deadlines with fewer resources.[2] Do you recognise this in your workplace, or in services you use or communities you belong to? We are living in the midst of a stress epidemic where too many people struggle with having too much to do. This chapter explores how we can protect ourselves.

Understanding about overshoot and collapse

In the study of ecosystems, the term 'overshoot' is used when the population of a species exceeds the carrying capacity of its environment. If this happens too much for too long, environmental conditions decline, leading to a collapse in that population. This can happen with algae in ponds or with swarms of locusts when they strip a region's vegetation bare. Overshoot is too heavy a load; collapse is where it can lead.

Might a similar dynamic occur with electronic communications? In 1971, the very first email was sent. By 2003, 30 billion were going out each day. By 2015, that had grown to over 200 billion.[3] Just in the time it takes to read this sentence, more than 20 million emails are sent. That number goes up each year. So, what happens when our carrying capacity for electronic communication is exceeded? Reading and writing emails already consumes more than a quarter of many people's working week. If swarms of electronic messages gobble more and more of our attention, will we reach a point where our ability to function well collapses?

What bridges, ponds and our ability to deal with emails have in common are capacity limits. Beyond these lies a state of overload where more is less and less is more. After a critical threshold is reached, more traffic on the bridge makes it less safe, more emails in our inbox make it less likely we will read them. If we push further, a breakdown of some form may occur. This is overshoot and collapse.

The coping-under-pressure curve

To give graphic form to this insight that 'When in overload, more is less,' think of someone spinning plates. Before they reach overload, there may be a 'more is more' relationship between the number they spin and their coping ability. As with many challenges, when we're bored and under-stimulated we're less likely to be at our best. I think of this as the 'doze zone'. As pressure increases, we tend to perk up. Rising to a challenge helps bring out our best performance.

| Doze zone | Sustainable pace | Top of the hill |

Fig. 1: Before overload, more plates make us more engaged

We can plot this relationship between increasing pressure (in this case number of plates spinning) and coping or performance ability in a graph I call the 'coping-under-pressure curve' (see Fig. 2 overleaf).

At peak performance, seen on the graph as 'top of the hill', we are so engaged that time goes by quickly (see Fig. 3 below). Psychologists call this a 'flow experience'; it can be deeply

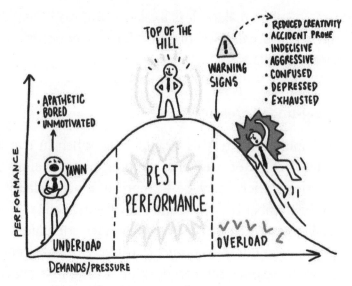

Fig. 2: The coping-under-pressure curve

satisfying. But if we then get pushed further, with more plates thrown our way, we tip into overload, where our coping capacity starts to decline. This is where we start experiencing stress, as we struggle to cope with a level of challenge that exceeds what we are able to deal with.

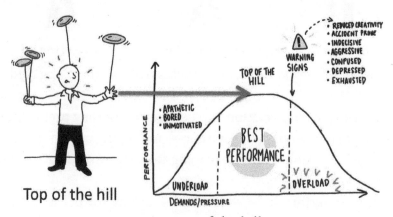

Fig. 3. Top of the hill

Why does performance decline when we're in overload? Think back to a time when you've struggled to cope with too much to do. When you're past the top of the hill, you might find your mind racing so quickly you lose track of things, find it difficult to concentrate or feel anxious about the risk of mistakes. As pressure increases you may also notice changes in your body: you sweat more, breathe differently and your heart races. In the early stages of being 'over the hill', our fight-or-flight response is activated. As we saw in Chapter Five, over-arousal of our threat-response system can push us out of the resilience zone. Our brain works differently when we're too charged up, with reduced activity in the parts of our brain involved with rational perspective and clear thinking. This is the 'more-is-less' part of the graph, as more pressure makes us less effective.

It is useful to recognise three phases of overload. First are the 'warning signs', the very first changes that alert us to being under stress. So long as it doesn't continue for too long, we can think of this phase as 'functional overload', where we're still able to function reasonably well. But if we're not able to step back, and the pressure increases, the risk is we get pushed into 'dysfunctional overload', where we experience harmful consequences of stress. The second phase of overload is where we experience symptoms. If the stress extends too far or for too long, and we don't have recovery time, we can be pushed into the third, and more damaging, phase of overload – breakdown. This is where some form of collapse occurs. It may be in our health, our mood, our confidence, our performance ability or our relationships. With chronic stress, this collapse stage is known as burnout.

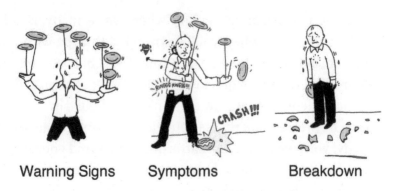

Warning Signs   Symptoms   Breakdown

Fig. 4: Three phases of overload

Your personal stress signature

How do you know when you're stressed? What are the first signs you notice? Each of us has a characteristic stress signature of signs and symptoms we experience when stressed. By learning to spot our personal warning signs earlier, we give ourselves an opportunity to take preventative action before stress reaches harmful levels.

You can identify your personal stress signature by looking at five distinct areas: your emotional state; what happens with your thinking; what happens in your body; the impact on your behaviour; and the impact on your relationships. For each of these five areas, what are the first things you notice when you start to become stressed? These are your warning signs. And what would happen in each of these areas if stress got worse or continued for longer?

Try this - your personal stress signature

Over the next few days, pay special attention to your degree of loading or overloading. Where are you on the hill? To recognise early warning signs or symptoms, reflect on your unique 'stress signature' in terms of what you notice when you're experiencing stress. What do you notice in terms of:

a) how you feel
b) how and what you are thinking
c) what happens in your body
d) how your behaviour is influenced (e.g. what are you more likely to do? What are you less likely to do?)
e) what happens in your relationships

For each of these five areas, what are the first things you notice (your warning signs)? What happens after this if stress continues or gets worse?

When I'm stressed, what I notice is . . .

Domain	Warning Signs	Symptoms
Feeling		
Thinking		
Body		
Behaviour		
Relationships		

Table 1: Stress signature

Example

John worked as a GP and was often highly stressed. For lunch, he'd sometimes eat a sandwich while stuck in traffic, out doing his calls. When asked about the difference between good days at work and more difficult days, he identified characteristic changes in each of the five areas. On quieter days, he'd feel relief at being able to get on with the work he loved at a pace that felt manageable. Just that little bit of extra time meant he could build rapport with his patients in a way that made his work more satisfying and more effective. But when over the hill, he felt tense and irritable, his mind raced, he came out in a sweat. He'd feel tense in his shoulders, he could sometimes notice himself clenching his fist. He'd be short and grumpy with people.

When he'd been through a particularly stressful time, he'd found it difficult to concentrate and made a mistake at work. He also crashed his car. He felt awful afterwards, becoming anxious and depressed, leading to a period of time off work.

A key learning for John was understanding the difference between 'functional overload', where he was coping, and 'dysfunctional overload', where he was so stressed he wasn't able to think clearly. This was a safety issue, both for himself and his patients. He wanted to get better at recognising the tipping point from the 'more-is-more' part of the curve, where a bit of pressure brought out his best performance, to the 'more-is-less' downslope of the hill, where feeling more stressed made him less effective. Spotting his warning signs told him he was at or just over the top of the hill.

When I'm stressed, what I notice is . . .

Domain	Warning Signs	Symptoms
Feeling	I'm tense, sulky.	Anxiety, depression.
Thinking	My mind is racing.	It is hard to concentrate.
Body	Sweatiness, tension.	Skin rash, headache.
Behaviour	I go quiet, withdraw.	Mistakes, accidents.
Relationships	Tension, irritability.	Rows, I become isolated.

Table 2: Example of stress signature

The difference between optimum and maximum

Years ago, I gave a talk about stress management and introduced the graph of spinning plates. Someone in the audience
raised their hand. 'That's interesting,' he said. 'I used to work in
a plate factory. Because of rising demand, they'd turn up the
speed of the factory conveyor belt in the months leading towards
Christmas. We could work faster and produce more plates – but
only for about six weeks. If the higher speed continued for
longer than that, we'd become exhausted and the breakage rate
rose to unacceptable levels.' What the plate man is describing
here is the difference between optimum and maximum speeds.

Under emergency conditions, most of us can push ourselves
and squeeze out that extra ounce of performance. But if we keep
at our top speed for too long, just as if we're sprinting in a mara-
thon, we don't complete the course. Our maximum speed is fine
for short dashes, but it isn't something we can maintain for
longer stretches. That's why the best place to be on the curve is
a bit before the top of the hill. Our optimum pace is more sustainable (see Fig. 5 below). It also gives us a hidden reserve so that
we're better able to respond to emergencies.

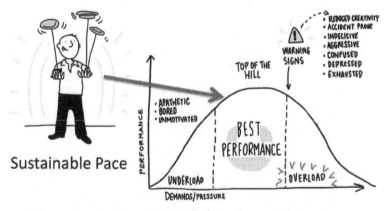

Fig. 5: Our optimum pace is less than our maximum

Symptoms can be wake-up calls

On the outside, Patricia's life in 2004 seemed a great success. Being at the top of her field, she had arrived at the position she had wanted for so long. But this had come at a high price. All she did was work. That left her with no time for people, no time for herself, no time to even think about what she really wanted. She just ploughed on. Until, that is, she crashed.

When I interviewed Patricia about her experience of this time, she told me that with hindsight she realised she had been deeply unhappy, severely overworked, chronically stressed and wasn't sleeping well. Her situation had imploded when a vice-president of the company said something at a meeting that so upset her she just got up, walked out and went home. 'I remember crying my eyes out when I got home,' she said, 'because something had broken.'

Deciding to resign, Patricia worked out her notice. Thinking she'd take a little time off before her next job, she was shocked to find that on one of her first mornings after leaving, she couldn't get out of bed. 'It got to the point where my body said, "If you're not going to stop, we're going to stop for you."'

A return to work was out of the question, as Patricia found her severe tiredness continued for months. Some days she experienced an almost complete lack of energy; other days she felt better and could get up and about. But if she pushed herself at all, she'd find herself back at the point where she struggled even to get out of bed.

Patricia's collapse of energy is an example of what can happen in the exhaustion phase of stress. While acute stress is linked to increased activity of the adrenal glands, which pump out adrenaline, with severe chronic stress the adrenal glands run dry. At this stage, the body is in a disturbed state, with abnormally low levels of essential hormones. For Patricia, this exhaustion phase of stress developed into Chronic Fatigue Syndrome that took her years to recover from.

The long journey of recovery forced her to become much more energy-aware. She studied the impact of stress, diet and exercise, learned the self-care practices of yoga, meditation and the skill of being kinder to yourself. Now running her own career resilience and wellbeing business, I asked her what her most important tools were for helping others deal with stress.[4] 'One of my favourites is the stress signature and the graph with spinning plates,' she said, having learned about these from studying with me some while ago. 'It demonstrates so clearly my lived experience of overstretch, and helps my clients to understand how easy it is to tip from being in peak performance into overwhelm and dysfunction.' Once you know about the hill, and how to find out where you are on it, you're then better placed to apply interventions that help you perform at a sustainable level.

A pivotal shift for Patricia was to change the way she lived with and experienced her symptoms – seeing them not as an enemy to fight, but as life-preserving signals alerting her to overstretch. If a warning indicator tells you you're low on fuel in a car, you don't just drive on and on regardless. You stop and refuel. We need to take a similar approach with our body symptoms and energy. Once we learn to listen to our body, we can then develop ways of working towards better performance.

The power of saying no

The other side of 'More is less' is recognising the times when 'Less is more'. If you want to be more effective, it helps to do fewer things. For that you need to develop the skill of saying no. Key here is recognising that 'Saying yes involves saying no.' In order to save your focus and energy and attention for the things you most want to move forward with, you need to strengthen the ability to clear the clutter in the way. In resilience training, I focus on two different ways of saying no. The first of these is the short-term no of renewal pauses. The second, which we'll look at more later, is the longer-term strategic no of commitment cropping.

The short-term no of renewal pauses

Research shows that our ability to cope with stress is enhanced if we can punctuate it.[5] Ongoing continuous stress is more harmful than shorter periods interrupted by renewal pauses. This principle has been applied for decades by professional athletes, who strengthen their endurance through using 'interval training'. In this they alternate periods of effort with time out or lower-intensity exercise. Something similar happens in sustainable agriculture, where crop rotations include a fallow period for the soil to renew its fertility.

More recent research at the University of Illinois suggests this interval-training principle can help us improve our brain function too. Taking a short break within a fifty-minute work period led to an improved ability to focus.[6] 'Our research suggests that, when faced with long tasks (such as studying before a final exam or doing your taxes),' suggests psychologist Alejandro Lleras, 'it is best to impose brief breaks on yourself. Brief mental breaks will actually help you stay focused on your task.'[7]

What we do in these breaks can add to their regenerative impact, and four factors in particular have been shown to boost renewal.

a) **Exercise.** Dr James Levine at the Mayo Clinic coined the phrase 'Sitting is the new smoking' after his research, and

172

others', showed that we're more likely to die and get sick from a range of conditions if we spend more than three hours each day sitting. 'Sitting is more dangerous than smoking,' he says. 'It kills more people than HIV and is more treacherous than parachuting.'[8] Exercising for twenty-five minutes has been shown to improve both mood and creativity, while even ten minutes of exercise can boost our ability to focus.[9,10]

b) Time in nature. A study compared the impact on memory function of walking through an arboretum with walking the same distance along city streets. Walking in nature improved scores in a memory test.[11] Other studies have shown significant improvements in mood.[12] Hearing about this research, a team I was working with decided to take walks together for their breaks rather than sitting drinking tea or coffee in their rest room. They found their breaks became more enjoyable and left them energised afterwards.

c) Social connection. The Gallup organisation surveyed more than 15 million people, asking about their wellbeing, work engagement and social networks. Those having a best friend at work were seven times as likely to be engaged in their jobs, had higher levels of wellbeing, produced better-quality results and were also less likely to have accidents at work. Reviewing this and other research looking at the impact of our social connectedness at work, Tom Rath and Jim Harter report that 'idle chitchat might actually be valuable to productivity ... Even small increases in social cohesiveness lead to large gains in production.'[13] If our social interactions at work improve both wellbeing and work performance, then breaks for renewal are likely to be more effective if they include company and support our friendships.

d) Micro-naps. While very short naps haven't been shown to improve performance, five to fifteen minutes of napping can give us a second wind and improve performance in the afternoon.[14] If a nap is more than thirty minutes, it is more likely to leave people feeling groggy afterwards, and if over forty minutes, the danger is it can upset that person's sleep cycle and interfere with night-time sleeping.

While taking breaks in the day can improve performance and mood, as well as protect us from stress, breaks outside of work have been shown to make a difference too. Holidays are known to leave people feeling energised and happier – but the effects often wear off within a few weeks. For more sustainable benefits, we need to build a culture that supports regeneration on a routine basis.

In a four-year study based at the Harvard Business School, Leslie Perlow and Jessica Porter tracked staff of a Boston consulting company.[15] They asked people to take a day off in the week, and to experiment with deliberate rest periods in evenings and at weekends. Although many of the staff resisted the instructions at first, after five months they were more satisfied with their jobs, more likely to see themselves working with the company in the longer term, and more content with both their work–life balance and work achievements.

There are many gains from stepping back – the problem is it can be hard to do when we've already got too much on our plate. That's where we need the commitment-cropping strategies we look at next.

10

Commitment Cropping

Elizabeth was struggling. Standing at the front of a room packed with people, her task was to squeeze several big rocks into a large glass jar that was already more than half full of gravel. There wasn't room. She tried shifting the gravel around, but she still couldn't do it. It felt impossible.

Fig. 1: The frustration of trying to squeeze in big rocks

The glass jar here represents the limited amount of time available to us. That easily gets filled up by the many lower-value calls on our attention, symbolised by the gravel. The big rocks are the more important things in our lives, which we often have trouble finding room for. Do you have this experience?

In a much-watched YouTube video, the bestselling author Stephen Covey reveals a solution to Elizabeth's dilemma.[1] 'You can take a fresh approach,' he says. 'You can start again.' Starting with an empty glass jar, he puts the big rocks in first. Then the gravel. The gravel often fits around the big things. But it is much harder the other way around.

Stephen Covey uses the big rocks story to teach an essential principle of time management: that of *putting first things first*. First make time for whatever matters most to you. Then see what else there is room for. However, this principle by itself is incomplete: it needs to be joined by a complementary insight about making choices. And I learned this from a plum tree.

Each year, we had a huge harvest of plums in our garden. But I didn't know what to do with them, because they didn't taste that nice. Then I discovered the secret to growing tasty plums. If earlier in the year I thin out the crop, removing at least half the fruit, the plums that remain become larger and tastier. Less is more.

When I look at my to-do list and feel overwhelmed, I remind myself of the plums and Stephen Covey's big rocks. The metaphor of pruning gives me the confidence to apply the second type of powerful no, the longer-term strategic no. This is about choosing what not to do, what to cut out altogether. I have three tools that help me do this. The first is an insight, the second is a strategy, the third is a skill.

Insight part one: the 80/20 Principle

Towards the end of the nineteenth century, the Italian economist Vilfredo Pareto noticed that 80 per cent of the peas in his garden came from about 20% of the pods. Recognising this ratio of 80/20 in other areas too, such as land ownership and income distribution, he wrote an article about it. Years later, modern-day management consultants talk of this 80/20 ratio as 'the Pareto Principle', where 80 per cent of an effect comes from 20 per cent of the causes.[2] When considering your to-do list, this principle suggests that 80 per cent of the value may come from just 20 per cent of the items you've put down.

The logical part of my brain asks, 'Is this mathematically correct?' But then I remember the two ways of assessing value we touched on in Chapter Seven. One is 'judgement value', which is about whether the numbers add up right. The other is 'movement value', which focuses more on where this idea takes me. If I accept that a big part of the value comes from just a few items, then I want to know which these items are, and give them my full attention. If more is less, I can achieve more by focusing on fewer things. That means some items need crossing out.

When I'm applying this approach, I take a moment to jot down a list of items competing for my attention. Whatever comes into my head, I just put it down. 'Anything else?' I ask myself. I add that too, repeating this until I've emptied out all the pushes and pulls calling me at that time. If I've listed ten things, much of the value may come from just two of these – so what are they? They're my big rocks, and I make sure I focus on them. If I've listed a hundred things to do, the same principle holds – what are the top twenty? I can't do everything, so I need to choose. The 80/20 principle points me to the precious few items I focus on first, and relieves my guilt about not getting around to others.

Insight part two: saying yes means saying no

There's an old story of two donkeys tied together in a stable with straw at each end. The donkeys are in the middle, but they have different ideas on which end to head for. One pulls one way, the other sets off in the opposing direction. That leaves the donkeys stuck in the middle, in a state of conflict (see Fig. 2 below). Do you ever feel caught between choices like this?

Fig. 2: Torn between two choices

Saying no is part of saying yes. My putting myself behind an option is reinforced by turning away from the competition. If I'm thinning plums, selecting one to keep requires me to eliminate those on either side. A strategy that helps me apply this insight to my work and life pressures is commitment cropping.

Strategy: commitment cropping

What different roles do you play in your life? For example, in your work you may have more than one role, particularly if you work in a variety of ways or with a range of people. At home you may play particular roles in your family or household. If you're a member of a club or community group, you'll have roles there too. The commitment-cropping process involves first listing the different roles you play, then asking yourself what obligations and expectations come with each one. Here's an example.

Jill worked as a teacher, sang in a choir, and shared with her partner the tasks of managing their home. She also played a role in supporting her mum, and her sister, who struggled with depression. She wanted to spend time with her friends too. She identified seven main roles in her life.

Jill's main roles:

Teacher
Partner
Householder
Daughter
Sister
Friend
Member of a choir

Each of these roles involved a range of tasks Jill expected of herself, and others expected of her too. Not just tasks, though: there were also expectations about how she presented herself, as well as the manner with which she spoke and behaved. These expectations and obligations included:

Teacher – prepare classes, teach classes, be available to speak with learners, do marking of homework and exams, keep up with professional development, attend staff meetings, go to supervisions/appraisals.

Partner – share cooking, spend time together, go on holiday, listen to them, be interested in their life, remember their birthday and other important occasions.

Householder – pay bills, do shopping, cook food, clean the flat, keep up regular repairs and maintenance.

Daughter – phone several times a week, visit every fortnight, keep in touch by email, send interesting pictures and links, remember their birthday and Mother's Day.

Sister – phone and visit occasionally, remember their birthday.

Friend – phone main friends at least once a month, be available when needed, show up for social occasions, invite them round for meals from time to time.

Member of a choir – show up on a Tuesday evening for practices, practise the pieces between sessions, attend concerts, attend choir social occasions.

For all roles – speak kindly, listen attentively, show up on time, don't lose temper or express frustration.

When Jill wrote all these out, she realised why she'd been feeling so overloaded recently. She had high expectations of herself, and tended to be harshly self-critical if she fell below the bar she'd set. Seeing it all written out on paper, she felt overwhelmed (and she recognised there's much more she could have listed, as she was just giving a broad overview of key expectations).

One important role Jill had missing on her list was that of self-care. Most of her roles involved care for others. In her busyness what got left out was care for herself. If she wanted to add another role in – and she was already overloaded – some items needed to get crossed off. So that was the next stage, to go through the list, item by item, and ask herself three questions: 'What would it be like if I didn't do this? Would I feel more relief or disappointment? Who else would notice?'

For her teaching role, she saw all the items listed as obligatory – there was little room for choice. But she could approach them in slightly different ways. She could, for example, identify burnout prevention as a key learning goal and training need.

For her partner role, she recognised she was showing up, but not making enough use of the support that was on offer. Her partner saw how stressed she was and wanted to help. He also suffered from the same condition of overload, and they shared this as a problem, but often in a way that led to friction between them. What would it be like to address their stress together as a shared project?

When thinking about her time with friends and family, she knew they were important. But the biggest shift Jill wanted to make was to be a better friend to herself – and that meant blocking out time on a regular basis just to have space to recover. Expressive writing was something she'd found valuable in the past – and that was what she made a commitment to build in time for. Going through the list there wasn't any specific item she wanted to say no to; it was more of a case of scaling some down – giving herself an increased sense of permission to say no when asked to do something she didn't want to do.

Try this – commitment cropping

List the different roles you play in your life. For each role, identify the main demands or expectations you associate with that role. What do you expect of yourself? What do others expect of you?

When you look at the list you have, how do you feel? Do you feel overwhelmed? Or pleased with having a good balance? Are there any clashes (for example, being expected in more than one place at the same time?)

Now go through what you've written and, for each item, ask yourself three questions: 'What would it be like if I didn't do this? Would I feel more relief or disappointment? Who else would notice?'

If you feel overloaded, identify roles, tasks or expectations you can resign from, that you can cross off your list and let go of.

Stress comes particularly from frustrated hopes. It is more satisfying to focus your energies on intentions that are achievable. If you've saddled yourself with more than you can cope with, then, like a hedge that keeps growing, your commitments are something you need to trim back. So after identifying roles and reviewing them, the third stage is to identify what to say no to, what items to let go of. This is commitment cropping.

Skill: assertiveness

When course participants and coaching clients do this exercise, they often find it liberating but also difficult. It can be hard to identify items to cross off the list, and even when you do, it may be a challenge to follow through and actually step back from what you're used to doing or others expect of you. Jill recognised that her pattern was to be a 'niceaholic' who hated upsetting people and letting them down. She found herself saying yes to requests and invitations and then feeling regret afterwards. While her kindness was a strength she celebrated, the learning edge for her was to be as kind to herself as she was to others. It was here that learning how to grow the skill of assertiveness led to a breakthrough.

Assertiveness is different from being bossy. It is about clear communication, where you're able to express your needs, preferences and point of view, while at the same time respecting the rights of others to express theirs. Research confirms that learning the skill of assertiveness can help reduce stress, depression and anxiety.[3] It also gives some protection against the risk of being bullied.[4] No surprise, then, that evidence-based resilience training, such as the Penn Resilience Program, tends to feature assertiveness skills as one of its core elements.

Jill's starting point was of not feeling assertive at all. She'd seen that as just the way she was, and not something she'd be able to change. But she liked the growth-mindset idea and saw how it applied here. When you want to learn a skill and you're finding it difficult, a good place to start is to look at what's in the way. When I teach assertiveness, I identify six common obstacles, and Jill recognised them all. Addressing these hurdles involves the following six steps.

a) Work through mixed feelings
b) Recognise your rights
c) Assertiveness scripts
d) Contingency planning
e) Seek win/win outcomes
f) Aim for progress rather than perfection

a) Work through mixed feelings

It is hard to express a view assertively if you're not sure you agree with it. If you've been asked to do something, and part of you wants to, but another part doesn't, or isn't sure you have the time, you can feel both a yes and a no. If your words say yes, but your body language says no, the 'double signal' you give can be confusing for the receiver. Jill recognised this, having recently met up with a friend, but when there found herself looking out of the window thinking about where she'd prefer to be instead.

An important insight from health psychology is that you can work with and through mixed feelings, rather than just being stuck in ambivalence. When addressing behaviours like smoking or heavy drinking, an approach called 'Motivational Interviewing' is widely used to help people become clearer about what they *really* want. William Miller, one of the developers of this approach, once described it as helping someone make their own argument for change.[5]

Rather than trying to persuade somebody, this approach involves listening with interest to the push and pull of competing motives they experience. When they hear themselves describe the values most important to them and the steps they want to take in support of these, they talk themselves into action. It can be highly effective. Motivational interviewing is of proven benefit in helping people give up smoking, tackle problematic drinking or drug use, increase exercise, lose weight and manage diabetes.[6]

If you're feeling ambivalent, you can work with and through this by expressing, and hearing, both sides of your mixed feelings. A decisional balance sheet is a tool you can use to map out the advantages and disadvantages of each of the choices you're caught between.

Choice	Advantages Things I like about this option include . . .	Disadvantages Downsides of this option include . . .
Saying yes		
Saying no		
Third choice – e.g. 'I need some time to think, I'll get back to you'		

Table 1: A decisional balance sheet

Just to bring your own mixed feelings to the surface allows them to come into view where you can see them. When you do this, you're better able to move towards a decision. If you're not ready to make a decision, you can accept that you're at an earlier stage in the process, and still take steps towards clarity by hearing the different sides of how you feel. A useful question to add is: 'What would need to happen to convince me to choose this option?'

b) Recognise your rights

There were times when Jill was clear what she wanted, but found it difficult to follow through and act on it. 'I've already said I'll go – I can't let them down now,' she told me when describing a social event she felt obliged to attend, even though she'd had second thoughts since agreeing to go. One of the basic principles of assertiveness is that we have a set of rights, things we're entitled to do even if we fear other people won't approve. We can think of this as a 'Bill of Rights' – it is for you to decide which rights feel appropriate for you, but common items include the following:

A Bill of Rights
I have a right to express my feelings, preferences and opinions
I have a right to ask for what I want
I have a right to grow and change, including changing my mind
I have a right to make mistakes
I have a right to say 'I don't know' or 'I don't understand'
I have a right to say no if something doesn't feel right
I have a right to set my own priorities
I have a right to make my own decisions and deal with the
    consequences
I have a right to be human and not be perfect
I have a right to my own personal space and time

Jill looked at the list but wasn't convinced. 'What about other people and their rights too?' she asked. When we looked at the matchstick-people diagram, Jill got it. Her concern had been about becoming like people who are over-assertive and pushy, claiming their rights even when it harmed or disrespected others. This is the aggressive position, where someone sees their needs as more important than others. In the diagram, they're the big person, the other people are smaller and of less consequence.

Fig. 3: Aggressive position – your needs
are more important than theirs

Jill hated people like this, but in her determination never to be a bully, she went too far the other way, downsizing the valuing of her own needs to make room for those of others. This is the passive position, of not telling other people what you want, need or prefer, because your needs aren't seen as important enough. But in habitually putting herself second, Jill ended up exhausted.

Fig. 4: Passive position – your needs
are less important than theirs

The passive position increases the risk of burnout. It can also lead to resentments building up, and when these reach toxic levels, just one small thing can tip someone over the edge into an outburst of anger – where they flip into the aggressive position. If someone feels guilty about this afterwards, they can fall back into the passive position, until the resentment builds up again and the process repeats, in a 'passive-explosive cycle' known as 'the exploding doormat syndrome'.

Assertiveness is about recognising that both you and others have needs; they're both important. Other people won't know what your needs are unless you're able to express them. For assertiveness we need both sides of communication – which involves broadcasting (putting out what our needs and preferences are) and receiving (where we listen and notice what's important for others).

Fig. 5: Assertive position – you both
have needs and they are both important

c) Assertiveness scripts

Jill didn't want to burn out or become resentful, and once she'd recognised the insight expressed in the matchstick diagram, she was fully behind the project of developing her assertiveness. But she wasn't sure how to say, 'I've changed my mind: I don't want to come out and see you – I'd prefer to stay at home,' without offending her friend. She also worried her friend would try and persuade her to change her mind.

What you're doing with an assertiveness script is thinking in advance how you're going to say something in a way that is both clear and respectful. While there isn't one universally agreed correct way to speak assertively, some forms of expression are easier to hear and less likely to provoke an argument or defensiveness. Research has shown, for example, that in negotiations on house prices, criticising the house being sold as overpriced is a less effective way of securing agreement at a lower price than acknowledging your own financial limits. The principle here is that attacking or blaming the other side gets people on edge. Owning up to your own vulnerabilities is more likely to evoke a helpful response.

If you feel unfairly criticised, and you'd like to make an assertive response rather than launch a counter-attack, a commonly used form involves a reply in four parts. This is known as the DESC response, the letters standing for **D**escribe, **E**xpress, **S**pecify and **C**onsequences.[7] Here's an example.

Describe what happened. 'When you described what I said as the most stupid thing you've ever heard–'

Express how you felt. '–I felt attacked and also humiliated.'

Specify your preferences for what you'd like to happen. 'I respond much better to encouraging feedback that points out how I can improve.'

Consequences. Identify benefits for them if they respond in a way that respects your preferences or responds favourably to a request you make.

If the full DESC formula seems too long, you can adapt and shorten it. For example, if someone puts you down, just saying

'Ouch!' is a disarming way of expressing your hurt without blaming or attacking. It is an acknowledgement of how you feel.

d) Contingency planning

A common block to assertiveness is fear about what might happen if you take your own needs more seriously and express yourself more clearly. Fear is part of our threat-detection system: it alerts us to danger. That can be a good thing when it leads to appropriate caution, but blocking when being over-cautious stops us in our tracks. The spider diagram questions of 'What's the best, the worst and most likely things to happen?' counterbalance alertness to threat with appreciation of opportunity. And often we don't know how people will respond until we take steps outside our usual response.

What is the worst that can happen if you're assertive? And what is most likely? If you're concerned about difficult consequences, then contingency planning involves asking yourself how you'd respond if the worst did occur. Knowing you've got a coping response up your sleeve can embolden you to take some risks.

e) Seek win/win outcomes

For many people, behind the fear of assertiveness is a concern that expressing yourself will lead to conflict. If conflict is approached in win/lose terms, then expressing yourself might seem the start of a battle to win. If you think this way, it might well seem easier to keep your mouth shut. But does conflict need to end with winners and losers? While each side might want different things, if the needs of both sides can be clearly expressed, there may be room for each party to get their way.

Aiming for win/win outcomes involves a different stance on conflict, where it is seen as an opportunity for something different to happen that might benefit both sides.

f) Aim for progress rather than perfection

There is a journey to learning to become more assertive that will no doubt have bumps along the way. If you ever find yourself thinking, 'I'm not sure I can do this,' remember the growth mindset and add the word 'yet'. If you take a step and it doesn't work out well, remember the skill of failing better. Developing assertiveness is a process that doesn't happen all at once. The bumps are part of how we learn. And if the assertiveness challenge we face brings up fear of what might happen if we voice our side, then our contingency planning needs to involve a crisis drill. This is what we turn to next.

11

Developing a Crisis Drill

'I've still got it,' said John, tapping the breast pocket of his jacket. He pulled out a laminated postcard on which I could see tiny scribbled notes. I could just make out four big letters down the side: S S R I. This was his crisis card.

Two years dry from drinking, John was my guest speaker in the recovery skills programme I ran for people with alcohol dependence. Having ex-clients come back and talk about their recovery provided both a model to follow and useful teaching. The learning I wanted to draw out in this session was of the value of having a crisis drill for difficult situations and how each of us can develop our own.

I'd taught John how to create a crisis card when he was in his early days of stopping drinking. I was keen to find out how he'd used it. As challenging events are common triggers for relapse in addiction, this was important for the group too. As I listened to John, I was struck by how relevant this was not just to people recovering from addiction, but to all of us. We're all likely to experience a shock or trauma that is out of the ordinary at some point, or some points, in our lives. Whether a car crash, someone close to us dying, a physical attack or a disturbing diagnosis, considering in advance how we'd respond to extreme events like these puts us in a stronger position to deal with them if they occur.

If you have a fire drill where you live or work, you already apply this principle of disaster-preparedness. People are paid money to consider the worst that could happen in the event of a fire or other life-threatening emergency. The questions they explore include, 'What's the worst that could happen here? Can we prevent that? And if it did happen, what could be done to make that less awful?' We can apply this same process to our life.

Consider the worst

We're looking here at a different kind of overload, where rather than too many challenges, it is the intensity or dangerousness of what we face that is too much. We've used the term 'red zone' for when we're out of our depth – yet red is a colour that comes in different shades. For more serious crises and traumatic events, we're considering the deeper hues of crimson and beyond.

As part of his space-flight training, the Canadian astronaut Chris Hadfield regularly rehearsed for disaster. 'Truly being ready,' he wrote in his bestselling book *An Astronaut's Guide to Life on Earth*, 'means understanding what could go wrong – and having a plan to deal with it.'[1] So on a daily basis he and his crewmates would face bad-news scenarios in live simulations, sometimes with real smoke for dramatic effect. They confronted computer meltdowns, engine failures and fires on board the International Space Station orbiting Earth, responding as if these disasters were really happening. 'A sim is an opportunity to practise, but frequently it's also a wake-up call,' he said.[2] If they didn't have a way of addressing a problem, they needed to find one.

One of their simulations involved looking at how to respond if any of the crew died. Who would notify family members? And how? Chris's wife, Helene, had planned to go trekking in the Himalayas while he was in space. When they considered the problems they might have reaching her, and how long it might take her to get back home to their children, she decided to go hiking in Utah instead.

Thinking of the challenges you might face in your life, what are the extreme red-zone possibilities for you? Are there people close to you who might get sick or die? Are there medical conditions you worry about sometimes? Are there risks you face in your day-to-day life or when you step outside it (for example on holiday)? A good place to begin developing a crisis drill is with making a list of the main worst-case scenarios you might face.

Addressing concerns involves facing our fears

Don't be surprised if looking at the worst things possible brings up fear or distress. That's a normal reaction to potential threat. When training, I remind people of the Bill of Rights we looked at when discussing assertiveness, particularly the right to say no to something if it doesn't feel right for you. You have that choice with any exercise, including exploring a crisis drill. At the same time, we grow by stretching beyond our comfort zone, and a way to work through resistances is to listen to our concerns then give them some scrutiny. Two fears sometimes arising with crisis drills are, 'What if I find this too upsetting?' and, 'Will focusing on the negative make it more likely to happen?'

If an area – like looking at our death, for example – feels too upsetting, 'Why do this?' is an important question. Asking 'What might happen if I don't do this?' generates a rationale. Over 30 million adults in the UK haven't prepared a will, even though over 90 per cent of people know who they'd like their assets to go to.[3] For Helene, Chris Hadfield's wife, not considering the possibility of her husband being killed in space might only lead to problems if he actually died. But if that happened, a tragedy could be made worse by poor planning.

If you're concerned that facing your worst fears might be too disturbing, it is worth reviewing the emotional first-aid strategies looked at in earlier chapters. Another useful strategy for strengthening our ability to face anxiety is progressive desensitisation, where we make a list of things we find scary, then rank them in order of intensity. To tackle fear, like learning to swim, start at the shallow end. Develop confidence with less threatening topics first, and then build up to those that are more distressing. If the next step feels too much and seems to carry you too far out of your depth, then step back, take a pause, use your self-steadying practices and get help if needed.

Many of the negative scenarios you consider when developing a crisis drill might never happen. Like buying insurance, hopefully you won't need to use it – but if you do, you'll be glad you made the effort.

Pre-traumatic growth revisited

An idea found in some self-help books is that thinking about negative events makes them more likely to happen.[4] This Law of Attraction suggests that like attracts like, so we should keep our thoughts and focus positive if that's what we want to pull towards us. While there are times when thinking this way can be useful, what would it have to say about learning first aid? Flexible thinking involves using ideas when they help us, but not rigidly sticking with them when they stop being useful.

Positive psychologist Martin Seligman recommends aiming for an optimal balance between positive and negative thinking.[5]

Negative thinking is important when it is accurate and when it helps us identify risks. Positive thinking opens our minds to opportunities and constructive responses to difficult situations. A crisis drill brings these two together in recognising the negative aspects of risks we face, while supporting us to be positive in our response. That's what we were doing in the group addressing crisis as a trigger for relapse in alcohol dependence. Looking at how recovery might go wrong seems negative, but identifying risk areas and then exploring coping responses is of proven effectiveness as a treatment approach.

The oil company Royal Dutch Shell took a similar approach in the 1960s when it pioneered the development of 'scenario planning' as a tool for organisations.[6] In considering different ways the future could go, each scenario developed as a story that illustrated possible consequences of a particular condition. The plotline was built around an 'if . . . then . . .' exploration of 'If this happened, then what would that look like?' When the oil crisis of 1973 caused disruption, the directors of Shell were better prepared because they'd already worked through similar scenarios.

As a result of the success of this approach at Shell, this kind of scenario planning for potential disasters is now widely used by organisations. It has also been used at the level of entire countries, playing a significant role, for example, in guiding the transition to democracy in South Africa after the fall of apartheid. Adam Kahane, who helped bring this approach to South Africa, writes: 'The scenario method asks people to talk not about what they predict *will* happen or what they believe *should* happen, but only about what they think *could* happen.'[7]

When looking ahead at a potential crisis acts as a wake-up call, prompting us to prepare by strengthening our capacities, we can think of this as *pre-traumatic growth*. By considering the worst, we might see how to prevent it, or at least stop it from being quite as catastrophic as it might otherwise have been.

How to develop your crisis drill

When I do this in trainings, I pass round blank postcards. I ask people to write the letters SSRI down the side, then to think back to particularly difficult times they've faced and reflect on what helped them get through those, identifying any strategies, strengths, resources or insights that made a difference. We've already looked at this SSRI-toolkit process for helping factors when facing challenges. We're doing it again here, but focusing on what helps us in more extreme events – perhaps rare times when we, or others close to us, have faced life-threatening challenges, or the situations we find most difficult. What are the tools that have helped you in the past? I invite people to write those on their cards. I invite you to try this now.

> *Try this – reviewing what's helped in the past*
>
> What are some of the most difficult situations you've faced so far? Looking back, what helped you through? Particularly identifying:
>
> Strategies, things you did
> Strengths, inner qualities you drew upon
> Resources, sources of help outside yourself you found useful
> Insights, guiding ideas or sayings that made a difference

What we're doing now is adding to that, reviewing and refining our toolkit for life's larger emergencies. But what might they be for you? One clue is what you find yourself worrying about. Do you have situations you fear or dread? What are potential dangers you face or hazards you might encounter?

What might a story of resilience look like for you if you faced one of these situations? If you're facing a situation like this at the moment, ask: 'What would a story of resilience look like here?' Storyboarding is a way of mapping out your answer. Here are the steps.

Try this – storyboarding your crisis drill: the SHIFTS process

1. **S**tarting point – describe the challenge you're facing (either something you're facing at the moment or scenario planning for a situation you might face in the future). What I'm facing is . . .
2. **H**oped-for outcome – think of the spider diagram, and of the preferred potential timelines (or spider legs) from this point. My hopes here are . . .
3. **I**n the way of that, obstacles or difficulties include . . .
4. **F**acing that, what helps is . . .
5. **T**urning point – a turning or shift might happen if I were to . . .
6. **S**pecific achievable steps I can take in the next seven days to make my hoped-for outcomes more likely are . . .

An example from Chris

I use all the strategies I teach. If I have a worry that comes up, I ask myself: 'What would a story of resilience look like if that happened?' A practice simulation is not the same as the real thing, as we never know for sure how we're going to react when faced with an extreme adversity. But, applying the proverb 'Forewarned is forearmed,' here's my storyboard of facing a challenge I worry about sometimes. Doing this as a simulation, I'm putting myself in the situation as if it is actually happening.

1. *Starting point.* What I'm facing is . . . A month ago I coughed up some blood. Knowing this could be a sign of something serious, I went to my doctor, who arranged a chest X-ray. It showed up a cherry-sized shadow in my lung. I had a bronchoscopy, and a biopsy showed I had an aggressive form of lung cancer. A body scan showed this had spread to my lymph nodes and my liver. It looked as if I might only have a few months left to live, though chemotherapy could possibly extend this a bit. (As this is a simulation, I'm imagining how I'd think, feel and respond if this was real.)

2. *My hope* would be some new treatment is invented that cures me, and I have many more satisfying years to live. But if that doesn't happen, if the worst came to the worst, my hopes are that I make the best of the time I have left. I hope I am able to face my predicament and see it as a challenge to rise to, to find strengths in myself I didn't realise were there and to have a creative response. I also have some hope-nots. I'd hate to die and leave my wife Kirsty in trouble financially, not knowing my passwords for my bank account, without any advance planning. Sure, it would be awful if I died, but there are different versions of how awful can go. Recognising this is at the heart of resilience – then taking steps to make the worst less awful and the best more likely.

3. *In the way of my hopes, obstacles or difficulties include*: a sense of powerlessness, that I'm facing a threat I have no control over, something that has already happened, and that has already spread throughout my body. While survival statistics show there are occasional people with this type and stage of cancer who are still alive five years later, they are very rare. I'm not feeling optimistic that I'd be one of them.

4. *Facing all this, what helps me . . .* Strategies – getting my will updated. Making sure I have a list of all the passwords and accounts and policies and contact details for those I'd like to be informed if/when I die.

   Strengths – the strength of courage helps me face something uncomfortable, and not let that discomfort put me off looking. There is also a strength in perspective, where I balance my consideration of the worst that can happen with attention to a range of better possibilities too. Resources – I found out about will writing. I talked it through with Kirsty, my wife, and with my brother and sister. Resources include the beauty in my life right now – which I'm more appreciative of, as I consider it could be a limited resource. So a valuable resource is the life I have left. It is possible to take this for granted. When I consider that it might run out one day, it prompts me to take better care of myself, to also show up for the time I have, to be more present. Insights – the insight of pre-traumatic growth. That's what I'm experiencing here – that by considering a potential trauma before it happens, I can step up in my ability to face it if it were to occur. There is also the insight that we can be strengthened by uncertainty: that one thing we know is that we will die. Some things we don't know are when and how.

5. *A turning or shift might happen if I were to . . .* Firstly, educate myself. I want to find out everything I can about this condition. I want to see if there are examples of people who've survived, and if there was anything they did that helped that happen. I also want to use the time I have in a way that is meaningful.

6. *Specific achievable steps.* In the next seven days, I want to get my will up to date. I want to look at the time I might have and

consider some of the ways I want to spend that. I want to have time with the people I love, and doing the things I love, while also doing everything I can to support my wellbeing and recovery and chances of still being here in a year.

When I finished this process, I took in a breath to appreciate and savour that this was a simulation rather than for real. When you consider losing something precious, it reminds you of the value of it. It did for me; I felt deeply grateful that I'm alive, and more determined to use what time I have left – however long that is, as well as I can.

There were some practical things too. I don't have to wait for a terminal diagnosis before I check that my will and end-of-life planning are up to date. I want to ensure I've got some insurance to give Kirsty a buffer if anything might happen to me. I want to ensure I take the time to tell those I love they matter to me.

Facing our fears, while constructive, can also feel emotionally bruising. If you do this exercise and feel worse afterwards, or have a negative scenario stuck in your mind, you can explore, as a counterbalance, your best hopes for the future in a similar way. In a yoga class, you might stretch to the left and then the right, stretch downward and then up. Think of this next process as an upward stretch. This 'Best possible self' intervention has been shown to improve mood and optimism, helping build a positive buffer that strengthens your capacity to cope with the difficult stuff.[8] Here are the instructions from Laura King, who in 2001 published a study showing how this intervention led not only to improved mood, but also to fewer visits to health centres in the following three months.

Try this – the best possible self-intervention

Think about your life in the future. Imagine that everything has gone as well as it possibly could. You have worked hard and succeeded at accomplishing all your life goals. Think of this as the realisation of all your life dreams. Now write about what you imagined.

When our training is most needed – Lucy's story

In exploring how to develop a crisis drill, we've looked back in time at what has helped us in the past, and forward in time at imagined futures, both for better and for worse. Another important source of learning is to listen to someone who has studied and taught resilience, and then found themselves experiencing the deep distress of severe adversity. One such person is Dr Lucy Hone.

Deciding to develop a new career in her forties, Lucy travelled from her home in New Zealand to study positive psychology with Martin Seligman and Karen Reivich at the University of Pennsylvania. Returning home to teach about resilience and wellbeing, she found her skills in demand when the city where she lived, Christchurch, was struck by a series of earthquakes between 2010 and 2012. A hundred and eighty-five people were killed and 70 per cent of the buildings in the central part of the city were destroyed.

Lucy's work was educating local people and businesses in the strategies of real-time resilience, looking at what might help them keep well when living with the stresses of an earthquake-ravaged city. Something that made this particularly difficult was that the tremors continued for an extended period – with more than fifty aftershocks that were over 5 on the Richter scale. The ground could start shaking at any time, day or night, leaving people feeling permanently on edge.

Lucy had studied with some of the leading resilience trainers in the world. Now she was tasked with passing on what she had learned. When the earthquakes eventually stopped, such prolonged exposure to threat had left many people with symptoms of post-traumatic stress. An important step in recovery was to re-establish routines. This helped people recognise that the scary time was behind them and that their nervous systems no longer needed to be in a constant state of alarm. For Lucy and her family, though, the safe period didn't last long.

In 2014, Lucy and her husband Trevor heard there had been an accident. A policeman called to say he was on his way. When he arrived, he told them their twelve-year-old daughter, Abi, had been killed, together with her best friend Ella and Ella's mother, Sally.

In her book *Resilient Grieving*, Lucy describes her journey of exploring what helps us to live with grief, keep on going and do the best we can.[9] She draws on insights from resilience psychology, as well as her own professional and personal experience in presenting the principles and practices she found most useful. 'Learning to live with grief,' she writes, 'is learning to live in a shattered world, where the familiar components have been scattered into disarray and we are left to rebuild our lives with different pieces.'[10]

One of her chapters identifies six strategies for coping in the immediate aftermath of a death of someone you love.[11] Each of these is a helpful addition to any crisis plan.

a) There are no rules
Normally our lives are governed by a whole string of conventions about what we should or shouldn't do, with a right and wrong way in all matter of things. Even if we're unconventional,

we may still have our own rulebook. Lucy found she needed to let this go, and re-evaluate any hint of obligation by asking, 'Is this likely to help or harm our recovery?'[12]

If you've recently had, or are currently experiencing, an extreme adverse event, it is helpful to follow your own sense of what you need to do to get through the day as best you can. That might mean not answering the phone or engaging in conversation if what you really want to do is run away and cry. This is about permission-giving, granting yourself an entitlement to follow your own sense of rightness, even when this clashes with what's normally expected of you.

When coaching people who are struggling with severe stress, I invite them to apply a similar principle that I call 'the flu test'. If you feel a pressure to do something, but just right now it feels too much, ask yourself, 'Would I do this if I had the flu?' If you're unwell in bed, it is OK to say no to things and prioritise self-care. We can do the same when we're in a crisis state or situation. There might also be times when we do need to push ourselves to reach out, to make contact, to answer the phone. That's why that question, 'Will this help or harm your recovery?' is such an important one.

b) Choose where you focus your attention
When looking at emotional-first-aid strategies, we applied the insight that our attention is like a spotlight, and we have choices about where we point it. How we feel is shaped at least in part by what we focus attention on. If we've only a limited amount of attention each day, then choices about where we place it can make a huge difference.

c) Take your time
While Lucy found people telling her that 'Time will heal' frustrating, a piece of advice she valued was 'Take your time.'[13] She

was comforted to know that she could grieve at her own pace, while also recognising that how she would feel and think would in fact change in time.

When we're facing a time of intensity, whether a bereavement of someone close, news of a disturbing diagnosis, or other event that pushes us far outside our comfort zone, we need time to adjust, to find ourselves and adapt to new circumstances. Allowing ourselves that time can be part of our crisis drill.

d) Feel the pain: walk right in, feel it and weep

Lucy found helpful some words by Pema Chodron, an American Buddhist teacher and author. 'We think that the point is to pass the test or to overcome the problem,' wrote Chodron, 'but the truth is that things don't really get solved. They come together, and they fall apart. Then they come together again and fall apart again. It's just like that.'[14] There was a spaciousness here, an acceptance that this is how life is, and with that an invitation to be with what's there, including the pain.

e) Beware the grief ambush

Don't be surprised if, after a significant loss or difficult events, you have strong feelings that come up at unexpected times and in unpredictable ways. While recognising this as a normal part of bereavement, Lucy found the term 'grief ambush' fitted with her experience of being caught by surprise and overwhelmed by emotion. Having a term to describe what she was going through helped her understand what was happening in these moments. Naming our experiences can help steady us through them.

f) Re-establish routines

As Lucy had found with the recovery from earthquakes, resuming routines and ordinary functions helped her family gradually move to a new normal. Returning to work gave her a focus that was absorbing enough to offer a break from grieving. As with other high-stress situations, finding ways to punctuate the stress, to have temporary refuge from it when focusing our attention on absorbing activities, allowed a space for renewal.

Finding time for regenerative activity and practices can be hard when we're still feeling the shockwaves of recent upheaval. The finding of a new normal is a journey, with obstacles likely on the way. It is here that creative problem-solving approaches can often open up new pathways forward. So this is where we turn next: to our Fifth Way.

Overload Management –

The Fourth Way at a glance

What does it look like when you do this skilfully?

You're able to distinguish between functional and dysfunctional overload, maintaining high levels of performance even during busy times by focusing on priority areas where you can be more effective. You support your capacity for perseverance by engaging in practices for renewal, taking pauses to recharge and saying no to demands that push you too far. You have in place a 'crisis drill' to draw upon in extreme situations. When facing stressful situations and high levels of challenge, you see overload management as an ongoing project requiring continued attention.

What helps you do this?

a) Recognising that when in overload, more is less. Trying to do too much can make you less effective.

b) Knowing where you are on the hill. Apply the coping-under-pressure graph, so that when you're over the hill you can take steps to draw back.

c) Noticing early warning signs. Recognise your personal stress signature: the first signs alerting you that you're in a stressed state.

d) Renewal pauses. Punctuated stress is better tolerated than continuous stress. Taking pauses to catch your breath and recharge improves performance and strengthens your capacity for coping.

e) Commitment Cropping. When you've got too much on, review the roles you play and the obligations or expectations that come with them. What can you let go of? Where might you feel more relief than disappointment if you do?

f) Assertiveness. Being able to express clearly your needs, preferences, and point of view, while at the same time respecting the rights of others to express theirs.

MY CRISIS DRILL

S

S

R

I

g) Crisis drill. Just as a fire drill plans ways to make a disaster less harmful, thinking in advance about how you can respond to risks puts you in a stronger position to deal with them if they happen. The SSRI framework can be used to identify strategies, strengths, resources and insights you can use in the event of emergencies.

The Fifth Way –
Problem Solving

When dealing with challenges, we may at times be brought to a halt by problems we can't see how to solve. We might scratch our heads, feel stuck and consider giving up. But then we apply the P of SETOPSS, the skill of problem solving. This involves drawing upon strategies, strengths, resources and insights that help us work with and through problems we might otherwise feel defeated by.

This way includes:

12

The Strength of Frustration Tolerance

Years ago, I struggled with giving up smoking. I knew I wanted to stop, but there were times I found it so difficult. I'd say to myself, 'I'm not going to smoke, I'm not going to smoke, I'm not going to smoke' – yet within an hour, I'd have a cigarette lit in my hand. I felt defeated.

Looking back on it now, I recognise this was great training for the work I'd later do in the addictions recovery field. I got to understand how something that should be simple, like following through on a decision to stop a harmful behaviour, can feel impossible. More importantly, I experienced the life lesson that just because something feels impossible that doesn't mean it is. Here I am now, more than two decades on since my last cigarette.

The stop-start-stop-start process I went through, and my clients have been through too, went like this: decide to do something (stop smoking for me, stop drinking for my clients); struggle; defeat; struggle; frustration; try again; failure; it seems hopeless, but something changes; a turning occurs; recovery happens. Then another relapse messes things up; failure again; feelings of despair, but somehow stick with it, a day at a time. Recovery returns. This process of committed perseverance in spite of obstacles, resistance and setbacks doesn't just happen with recovery from addiction. There's a much wider pattern here – and a phenomenon called *grit* that we can all benefit from.

What helps us keep going when things get tough?

While being a teacher can be deeply satisfying, stress and other factors cause half of all new recruits to leave the profession within their first five years. The psychologist Angela Duckworth and her colleague Claire Robertson-Kraft wanted to find out what made the difference between those who gave up and those who carried on.[1] They found it wasn't how well new teachers had done in exams or the leadership qualities they expressed at interview. The only factor shown to predict how likely they were to stay in their job was past evidence of grit, a quality defined as 'passion and perseverance for long-range goals'.

The researchers analysed the résumés of nearly 500 new teachers, looking for mentions of any activities stuck with for more than two years, plus any achievements in these. If, for example, someone had played volleyball for three years or been involved in a local theatre group over this time, they'd get a point in a grit-rating scale. If they'd won any awards or been in leadership roles, they'd get another point on the 0 to 6 scale. Similar studies have now been done in a range of other fields too. Scores on grit scales help predict who'll stick with the process when people start military academy, join a sales team, begin college or sign up for a Special Forces selection process.

In any long-term endeavour that stretches us, we're likely to face moments when the challenges seem too much and we can't see the way forward. Grit is not the same as resilience, but is closely related to it, especially at those make-or-break points where we might feel like giving up. While resilience helps us deal with difficult times, grit is more directional: it is linked to our sense of passion and purpose. As Angela Duckworth writes, 'Grit is not just having resilience in the face of failure, but also having deep commitments that you remain loyal to over many years.'[2]

Whether the deep commitment you want to remain loyal to is recovery from addiction, developing your career or making progress in any other challenging long-term project, a learnable skill that helps you deal with roadblocks along the way is problem solving. We're going to be looking at two essential steps to growing this skill.

How to become better at maths

Alan Schoenfeld is a professor of maths and education in California whose work has shed light on how we think when facing difficult problems. Videoing students as they tried to solve difficult maths puzzles offered him a striking finding: how rare it is for anyone to stick with a challenge for more than a few minutes if they can't see how to do it. When he asked high-school students how long they'd keep trying with a homework question they were struggling with, the average response was just two minutes.

Schoenfeld's work was one of the puzzle pieces Malcolm Gladwell identified in his book *Outliers,* which explores factors supporting exceptional performance. 'We sometimes think of being good at mathematics as an innate ability,' he writes, 'but to Schoenfeld it's not so much ability as attitude . . . Success is a function of persistence and doggedness and the willingness to work hard for twenty-two minutes to make sense of something that most people would give up on after thirty seconds.'[3] Albert Einstein came to a similar conclusion when he said, 'It's not that I'm so clever: I just stick with problems longer.'[4]

If you had lost your keys, would you be more likely to find them if you had just two minutes to look, five minutes or twenty-two minutes? How long would you keep searching before you gave up? While your answer might depend on where you thought you'd lost them, whether or not you had other ways of opening doors important to you and any concerns you had about security risks, other factors relevant here are your beliefs about whether you will find them, and your ability to tolerate frustration. These last two factors are relevant more generally when we're searching for solutions to problems. They are both things we can change in ways that strengthen our capacity for problem solving. The first is about challenging disbelief, and the second is about developing the growable strength of frustration tolerance. Let's look at each of these in turn.

1) Challenge disbelief

When I'm struggling to solve a difficult problem but keep failing, a thought that comes up is: 'There's no way you can do this.' When we're disputing unhelpful thoughts, Martin Seligman suggests imagining them as spoken by someone else.[5] I find it helps to give the blocking voice a name, so I call mine Professor No Way. Whatever you want to do, they'll say you can't do it. In my mind, this voice always has convincing reasons why I'm wasting my time.

It could be that on occasions this professor is right. At the same time, it is also possible they're wrong. Have you ever succeeded in doing something that some while previously you thought was impossible for you? I often ask this question to participants on my courses, and there are always some who recognise this. One person told me she'd started running half-marathons in her fifties, after having thought herself incapable of anything like this before. To be able to do this, she first had to challenge her inner 'No Way' voice.

So how do we argue back? One approach we've already looked at is to apply the growth mindset. Interestingly, research shows that growth mindsets are linked with grittiness, and it is easy to see why. When you're stuck with a problem and you have a fixed mindset, it is easy to believe 'I'm not good at this type of thing.' The shift, as Carol Dweck points out, is from 'I can't do this' to 'I can't do this *yet*.' If you've lost your keys, it is the shift from 'I can't find them' to 'I can't find them yet.' If you're facing a difficult situation and can't see a way to deal with it, this shift is the move from 'I can't see a way' to 'I can't see a way yet.' What helps problem solving is to keep looking, rather than giving up. A helpful concept here is that of the 'stage of disbelief'.

In my addictions recovery work, I'd often see clients who didn't believe they could stop drinking. 'I'm a hopeless case,' Peter, in his fifties, said to me. He told me he'd given up giving up because he kept failing and didn't believe he could make it. Yet in the group session, someone else said, 'I felt like that three months ago, and then something changed.' Like a frame in a film, the stage of disbelief is something we can move through.

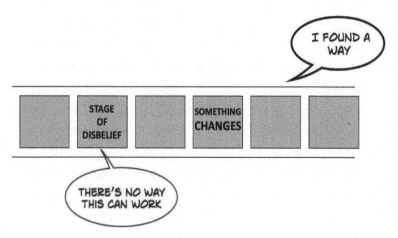

Fig. 1: The stage of disbelief

Remembering times when we've been through this sequence gives us an antidote to the feeling of impossibility that often arises when we dare to step beyond what we know we can do. Another powerful way of challenging Professor No Way (though don't be surprised if at first you think, 'There's no way I can do this') involves time travel.

I had a long train journey recently and felt silly for forgetting my water bottle. 'Darn,' I thought. 'Why didn't I think of that before?' Looking back, it seems obvious that I would need it, but it is easier to see things in hindsight. That principle, of being able to see things more clearly after they've happened, forms the basis of a problem-solving approach. Research has shown this improves decision making and strengthens creative thinking. It is called imaginary hindsight.

There are four steps to this. First you identify something you'd like to happen. You could, for example, storyboard a situation, and identify your hoped-for outcome, along the lines of, 'What I'd like to happen here is . . .' The second stage is to imagine moving forward in time into a version of the future where that has happened. Then, thirdly, from that imagined possible future, you ask yourself how it happened, and identify what you did that made this more likely. Lastly, you return to the present moment, having the benefit of this 'imaginary hindsight' to prepare you, so you can then take the steps needed to make your hoped-for outcome more likely. Here's an example with my train journey, thinking of a different way that day might have gone.

At the start of the day, I did the imaginary hindsight process. Step one is to consider how I'd like the day to go. 'What I'd like to happen is . . . that I get to the station, catch my train, have an enjoyable journey, and get to my destination on time.' Step two is to imagine that happening. I've arrived, I look back on my train journey and feel pleased that I've had some recharge time. It has been a good day. Then I ask myself how that occurred, looking at choices I made and actions I took that made a better day more likely. In my imagination, I see myself looking comfortable and content on the train, reading a book, listening to music, having a picnic and drinking from my water bottle. Returning to the present moment, I have enough time to pack the things I need then before heading off.

A research study asked people to consider how an important social event could be organised.[6] One group was instructed to describe as many reasons as they could that would help the event go well. Another group was told that the event had already happened, that it was a great success, and their task was to list as many reasons as they could for what helped it go smoothly. The second group gave 30 per cent more reasons, with more detailed and action-orientated descriptions. By holding in your mind the thought that potential problems have already been solved, you have a way of challenging Professor No Way's list of reasons it might fail. If you're looking for your keys, and you know you will find them, you're more likely to keep on looking. If you're struggling with a situation, and you know you'll find a way of dealing with it, you're more inclined to stick with it. Imaginary hindsight is a tool that helps you remain open to the possibility that you'll find a way.

Try this – imaginary hindsight letter to yourself

1) Focus your attention on a challenge you face that you'd like to respond to well, dealing with it in the best way you can imagine.

2) Pretend for a moment that you have succeeded in this, addressing the challenge in a way you're proud of. Picture yourself there in that imaginary future, where it has worked out the way you want it to.

3) Now write a letter or card to yourself, where you first describe what has happened, particularly the bits you're most pleased

about, then list any decisions and actions you took that helped this happen.

> Dear . . . (address this to yourself)
> I'm delighted that . . . (describe what worked out well)
> And what I did to help this happen was . . .

4) Now return to the present moment and be guided by this imaginary hindsight.

2) Develop frustration tolerance

Building on Alan Shoenfeld's work that we mentioned earlier in this chapter, Malcolm Gladwell describes how a pivotal factor in solving maths problems is how long we're willing to stick at it when we're struggling.[3] Not just maths, though. It was similar for me with giving up smoking: the longer I could tolerate the frustrated desire to have a cigarette when I had a craving for one, the more likely I was to get through a day without a relapse. Teaching frustration tolerance became an important part of my work when helping others recover from addiction too. And a central insight here was of the tolerance threshold.

When frustration builds up, there's a line we cross where we move from what is tolerable to what is not. Moving over that threshold takes us to a place where we're vulnerable to whatever we reach for to ease tension. For someone who smokes, it is their cigarettes. For someone else it might be Facebook or shopping or comfort eating. We all have different places we turn when things are too much. The more we reach for a particular comfort, the more ingrained, habitual and compulsive that behaviour tends to become. But we can learn to influence where our tolerance threshold is, both by putting up with higher levels of frustration and by finding other ways to reduce the pressure.

One way of tolerating higher levels of frustration is to tell ourselves a different story about what it means. We've looked at this already with the growth mindset. If we see frustration as evidence that we've dared to step outside what is easy, we feel differently than if we see it as proof that the problem is beyond us. With the growth mindset, when we can't see how to do something, that doesn't mean we won't be able to. We're more likely to find a way if we keep looking. Frustration is then viewed as just part of the process. It is a feeling that comes with searching when it matters to us. If it wasn't important, we wouldn't be so bothered.

If we accept that searching longer increases our chances of finding what we're looking for, then strengthening our ability to tolerate frustration can be valued as a useful capacity. What if you see each time you struggle as an opportunity to train in a gym for your mind, where the muscle you're building is the strength of frustration tolerance? With this view, practising experiencing discomfort can be seen as a useful training process, just like lifting weights.

Are you ready to give it a go?

Just as you might do physical training by running on the spot for three minutes, or doing other exercise, we can train our mind by doing the mental equivalent of lifting weights. The key here is to push a bit, then step back. Push a bit and then step back. You build strength by regularly exercising muscles, but not straining them so much that they get fatigued.

Here's the three-minute frustration-tolerance challenge

Your goal here is simply to stick at the task for three minutes. If you complete the task before the time is up, then find another that is more challenging for you, that you know you'll not complete easily.

Try this – the three-minute frustration-tolerance challenge

Your challenge is to keep to the task of solving difficult puzzles for a three-minute time period, and not to give up if you find it too difficult. If you don't solve the puzzle but do keep at it for the full time, then you have succeeded. If you've experienced frustration, and not been put off, then you've done well.

Here are two difficult questions. If you succeed with one, then proceed to the next. If you don't, stick with it until either you find a solution, or the three minutes is up. Set a timer. Then go . . .

1) Your task is to draw a clock that tells the time correctly without any part visibly moving or changing in appearance. How can you do this?

2) Two mothers and two daughters meet for lunch. They have six slices of pizza delivered, which they divide equally between them without cutting or breaking apart any of the pieces. How do they do that?

If you race through both puzzles in less than three minutes, please find an alternative challenge that stretches you. The purpose is to step outside your comfort zone of ease and take on something you find so difficult that its solution evades you, at least initially. If you stick with it for the full three minutes and experience frustration in this time, you have succeeded.

Outcome goals and process goals

We live in a society that divides people into winners and losers, where if you're not succeeding at something it is easy to brand yourself a loser. As that's uncomfortable, the space of trying but not succeeding carries shame. What we're doing with the frustration-tolerance challenge is changing the goalposts. A potent factor blocking problem solving is the discomfort of failure and fear of this shame. If your only goal is to show up, then that takes pressure off. As with mindfulness, there's less room for performance commentary, because you're not needing to act in a particular way. Just show up.

There are two types of goal. One is an outcome goal: this is the destination you'd like to reach. With problem solving, the outcome goal is usually solving the problem. But what we're doing here is making the process the outcome – making the journey of moving in a direction a success in itself. This is a process goal.

Outcome goal – my goal is to reach a particular point
Process goal – my goal is to take specific steps that take me towards that point or that support progress in that direction.

So what are the solutions to these puzzles? Let's find out.

13

The Five-stage Problem-solving Process

Patrick had just lost his job. He felt stunned. He knew some people were going to be laid off but hadn't expected to be one of them. 'My life is falling apart, and I don't know what to do,' he told me when I interviewed him. The challenge facing him was coping with a loss of livelihood. He wanted to rebuild his life but didn't know where to start.

If you crash into a life challenge that leaves you feeling at a loss for what to do, just recognising that recovery and rebuilding don't happen straight away is itself a positive step. It is about acknowledging that there is a process to change, and allowing yourself space to adjust to a shock. This helps prepare you for your next step.

Part of the challenge here is facing uncertainty, of being with the not-knowing. But once you've accepted the need to tolerate this, what next? What helps you find your next steps? We're going to look at an evidence-based problem-solving strategy that has been shown to be as effective as medication in the treatment of depression.[1] You don't need to be depressed in order to benefit, though, as this is a tool we can use whenever we're facing situations where we can't see an easily available solution and the next step isn't clear. That's how it was for Patrick: he felt stuck and unsure what to do.

Although this is called a problem-solving strategy, there is no guarantee that it will solve your problem. What it is good at, though, is helping you identify a next step. Just as when you're walking in thick fog, it is difficult to plot a precise course into the distance. You can only see just the bit in front of you. Taking things a bit at a time, you take that next step, and then the one after that becomes clearer.

What about the puzzles?

Before we come to the problem-solving process, it is worth looking again at the two puzzles from the last chapter, and the solutions to these. What makes each of these difficult (if you found them so) is that they challenge you to think outside the box, as their solutions lie beyond what common assumptions might lead you to expect.

As nearly all the clocks tell the time by visibly showing it, a common assumption is that this is how clocks work. If you can't see a part visibly moving, how can it tell the time? To find the answer we need to shift outside the mainstream-thinking track, to think 'laterally'. So how about a talking clock? There's a speaking-clock service you can phone, and a range of talking clocks you can buy that tell the time with a recorded or synthe-sised voice when you touch a button.

With the second question, how many people did you think there were? The description 'two mothers and two daughters' suggests four people, leading to the impossible challenge of dividing six slices equally four ways without cutting them. But what if there were three women instead, with one of them being both a daughter and a mother? If there were three generations present, with a woman joined by both her mother and her daughter, there would be two mothers and two daughters. They could have two slices of pizza each.

As with the clock puzzle, the answer is easy to see once you've seen it. Before that, however, the mainstream-thinking track takes you the wrong way. To think outside of our normal way of looking, we need to stimulate our creative thinking, by considering a wide range of options, including ones we'd normally dismiss as stupid or impossible. This is what the five-stage problem-solving process does.

Stage one – clearly describe the problem

Working through the five stages, the first stage is to identify, and then clearly describe, the problem you'd like to address. As problems often come in tangles with several connected issues, it is helpful to provide space to unpack the problem, to draw out its aspects and layers, as part of the process of becoming clearer about the issue you face.

If you're doing this problem-solving process with someone else, perhaps a friend or client, your goal with the first step is to understand their problem so well that you can summarise it back to them, and they say, 'That's it!' feeling heard and understood. You can ask them to correct you if you haven't got it quite right – this review process is a way of building a more accurate understanding. If you're doing this by yourself, perhaps in a notebook so you can see what you've put down, you can summarise it yourself, and ask yourself, 'Is that it?' to confirm if you've hit the nail on the head.

I use three steps in this first stage. I ask, 'What's the problem?' and write down whatever comes to mind. Whatever you write, ask yourself, 'Why is that a problem?' There are often layers to difficulties, and exploring why something is difficult helps you get to the nub of what's particularly hard. I asked Patrick, 'What's the problem?'

'I've just lost my job,' he replied.

While it might seem obvious, I went ahead and asked, 'Why is that a problem? – or what about this are you finding particularly difficult?'

He told me he'd never been unemployed before: he'd always, since leaving school, had a job. Now he was in his fifties, and this was new ground for him.

'Why is that a problem?' I asked again.

He didn't feel confident that he'd be able to find another job. He wasn't sure how he'd cope financially.

Once you've described what the problem is, and unpacked it a bit, then summarise, with a problem statement that starts: 'The problem is . . .' This might be the same as you started with, but exploring it in more detail deepens your understanding. Patrick summarised it as: 'The problem is: I've lost my job, and I don't know what I'm going to do next.' He said he had enough money saved to last a year or two, but within that time, he needed to get back into work he could do for another decade or so.

Stage two – creative generation of response options

The next two stages separate the process of generating options from the process of judging them. We'll be applying two different types of thinking here – known as divergent and convergent thinking. With divergent thinking in stage two, we're widening out and considering a range of options. With convergent thinking in stage three, we're choosing between them and narrowing down.

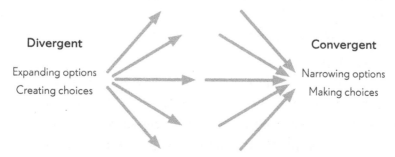

Fig. 1: Divergent and convergent thinking

With stage two, write, 'Response options include . . .' at the top of a page, and then fill the space below with as many options as you can think of. When doing this in groups, I aim for twenty or more options. It can be fun to generate new and wild ideas. At this stage anything goes, because in stage three you'll be able to narrow down by crossing out any options you don't want to consider. But at this stage, you're wanting to explore possibilities, and so giving yourself a free range helps. It is this stage of creative thinking that helps us generate options outside our normal way of looking. It encourages lateral thinking.

If twenty options seem overwhelming, make it easier. You could start with just two or three ideas and build up from there. When using this process in coaching, I suggest that the client and I come up with five options each, taking it in turns until we've got ten between us. Sometimes we continue with more options from there as the process of generating options often opens up a creative flow.

Patrick and I decided to aim for ten options between us. Considering his starting point of, 'Here's me, facing the loss of my job and I don't know what to do next,' we listed possible response options from here. These were:

- Give myself a month of adjustment time, where I don't have to make any major decisions
- Go on holiday and have some recovery time
- Start looking for a new job
- Seek out a careers adviser
- Personal coaching
- View this as a project that might take a while to develop
- Give myself time to rediscover activities I used to enjoy doing
- Explore training options to learn new skills
- Make an inventory of my assets, skills, interests and resources
- Write a novel

Once we'd listed ten, I asked Patrick if he'd like to generate some more options. As he found it easier than he thought it would be, we decided to produce another three options each, which added the following:

- Become a volunteer somewhere with accommodation and rent out my home
- Join a circus
- Move to another country
- Explore a different type of work
- Reduce spending
- Learn practices that help deal with uncomfortable feelings, such as mindfulness

Stage two is purely for generating options, writing them down as they come and not stopping to discuss them. Judging the options is saved for the next stage.

Stage three – delete any options you're not willing to consider

You don't have to do everything that remains on your list, but you should be willing to at least consider it. If there's an option you know is out of the question for you, cross it out. Knowing you can rule out options at this stage makes it easier to be more free-ranging in stage two. The anything-goes attitude encourages creative thinking, or what we've called 'divergent thinking', expanding outwards, beyond what you'd normally think of. Stage three is for convergent thinking, where you're beginning a process of narrowing down by excluding options you want to put a line through.

Patrick crossed off options 11, 12 and 13 – at a time when he faced so much uncertainty, he didn't want to leave his home, as this offered an anchor of stability for him. However, the idea of renting his home made him think he could get a lodger, and that would reduce his financial pressures. So he crossed off three options and added one.

Stage four – pick out the cherries: your favourite options

I asked Patrick to read through the remaining options on the list and mark any he found promising or attractive. I call this picking out the cherries. Patrick picked out options 1 (adjustment time), 4 (careers adviser), 6 (see this as a project), 9 (inventory of assets) and 17 (find a lodger).

Stage five – identify specific achievable steps and then take them

I asked Patrick how he might move his preferred options forward. If he was going to do something for each one in the next week, what could that be, no matter how small a step? He could immediately see how he could do this with some options, but was less sure with others. I asked Patrick how we could become clearer in the areas he was less sure about. Partly it was allowing some thinking time, but there's also a difference between passive thinking time (just leaving it for a while) and active thinking time, where you set aside a period for reflection, perhaps writing in a notebook.

A default option I use when I'm not sure is, 'I'll schedule in thirty minutes of writing time to explore this on paper.' When I do this, I write the item at the top of the page, and then have a sentence starter such as, 'What I feel about this option is . . .' I invite myself to write down whether I feel ready to do this yet, and if not, what steps might be needed in order to become ready. There is a journey to readiness that passes through the phases of finding out more, making a decision, and then preparing by taking steps that strengthen your ability to do this.

When someone moves from a state of being stuck to identifying specific achievable steps they can take, it shifts their mood and energy. They're moving from a 'going nowhere' story of feeling blocked, to a 'going somewhere' narrative. Patrick told me he felt transformed in his outlook and mood after doing this process, previously feeling tired and downhearted, but afterwards he felt energised by having a clearer sense of direction and intentionality.

Try this – the five-stage problem-solving process

Stage one – clearly describe the problem
a) Ask yourself what the issue is and write down your response. Sometimes more than one thing comes tumbling out; let it roll, write whatever comes. Then choose the main problem or aspect of this you want to tackle.
b) Ask yourself, *'Why is that a problem?'* Write down your response. Repeat this process several times to help get to the nub of what bothers you or what you find difficult.
c) Choose the main issue or aspect of this you want to tackle, writing this in the form of 'The problem is . . .' This becomes the working definition you are aiming to respond to.

Stage two – list possible responses
Get a big blank piece of paper and completely fill this with possible responses, aiming to get at least twenty (but don't be put off by numbers. Start with five, then see if you can get another five – any more is a bonus). At this stage you are only generating options and not judging their potential value. This

embargo on judgement is important, as it separates the creative process from editing, which can come later.

Stage three – delete options that are unrealistic or unacceptable
Knowing that you are able to edit out any unacceptable options at this stage can make it easier to be more adventurous and uncensored at stage two. If an option is fine for someone else but isn't for you, cross it out.

Stage four – pick out your preferred options
This is the stage to focus on the options that most interest you. Mark these with a star. Look at the advantages and disadvantages of each option you've marked.

Stage five – identify achievable steps to take in the next seven days
Look at the options you've marked with a star. How could you move any of these forward? Identify specific, achievable steps you could take over the next seven days, and from these choose ones you commit yourself to take. Write these down in the form of 'I will . . .' Book a review time with yourself in a week to see how you've done.

How to make goal setting more effective

Research has shown the power of writing down goals in helping us achieve them. Gail Matthews, professor of psychology at the Dominican University of California, demonstrated that we can make our written goals even more effective by sharing them with an accountability partner who we check in with on progress. In a randomised study, she compared different strategies.[2] Subjects identified a goal they wanted to accomplish in the next four weeks, and were then invited to follow one of five different strategies.

Group one just thought about the goal but didn't write it down

Group two wrote their goal down in an online survey

Group three did as group two, and also identified specific action steps

Group four did as group three, and then sent these by email to a friend

Group five did as group four, but in addition also sent their friend weekly progress reports

At the end of four weeks, participants rated to what extent they'd accomplished their goals or made progress towards them. All four groups who had written down their goals reported more progress than the first group. Group four did better than group three, suggesting that having your commitment witnessed by someone else strengthens its impact. Group five did better than all the other groups and were twice as likely (70 per cent rather than 35 per cent) to make good progress as those in the first group.

Building in a review time and an accountability partner

This study suggests that when you're doing this problem-solving process, you increase your chances of making it effective if you write down the steps you're planning to take and find someone else to act as an accountability support partner.

In my work with staff teams, I've found this problem-solving tool and the storyboarding process are strategies people like doing together in support partnerships. Asking a friend or colleague to go through the process with you, and taking it in turns so you both have opportunities to give and receive support, means you're building in a support structure using proven tools. This is moving into our next pathway of building resilience – strengthening support.

Problem Solving –

The Fifth Way at a glance

What does it look like when you do this skilfully?

When you're confronted with an issue you find difficult, you're aware of the spider diagram. The best legs suggest you'll find a way through; the worst legs suggest you won't. While you won't yet know which way things will go, there are things you can do that make the better legs more likely. You can take a moment to reflect on your motivation – is this problem important to you? If so why? Remembering good reasons makes it worth the effort of applying yourself. You can also check your state – are you in the resilience zone? Are there steps you can take that help you bring your full attention and focus to the challenge you face? Then you can draw upon tools that strengthen your problem-solving capacity.

What helps you do this?

 **a) Frustration tolerance.** What is the meaning you give to frustration? Seeing it as evidence that you've dared step out of the comfort zone helps you value frustration tolerance as a strength. As with building muscles by lifting weights, your strength of frustration tolerance grows through practice and training.

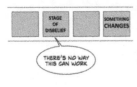

b) Challenging disbelief. Can you remember times you've succeeded in doing something you previously thought was impossible? If you see the state of 'not believing something can happen' as a stage you may pass through, it helps you challenge disbelief.

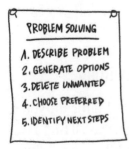

c) The Five-stage Problem-solving Process. This takes you through a structured process where you start by clearly describing the problem you face. Then you list possible response options. You leave judging these till the third stage, when you go through the list and cross off any you don't want to consider. Then pick out the best and identify specific achievable steps for taking them forward.

d) Imaginary hindsight. First identify what you'd like to happen. Then imagine that you've succeeded in arriving at this point. Looking back from that preferred future, can you identify the steps you took and choices you made that helped this happen? Write them down, perhaps as a letter to your earlier self. Then come back to the present moment and start the process of taking those steps.

The Sixth Way – Strengthening Support

You're facing a challenge, and you need reinforcements. Where do you turn? This pathway to building resilience invites you to widen your network of support, drawing in resources both from others and from deeper within yourself.

This way includes:

14

Supporting Ourselves

'Chris – you've got to hear this!'

My friend Nicola was excited. She'd just listened to a radio programme about resilience, and was keen to fill me in. I tracked down the link on the BBC website. It was here I heard the remarkable story of Peter Shaw.

Peter was a banker from Wales who'd been working in Georgia, Eastern Europe, for eight years. He was coming to the end of his time there and was looking forward to return-ing home. Just days before he was due to leave, he was out driving when a police officer stepped onto the road and signalled for him to stop. Almost as soon as he'd parked, three other men in uniforms appeared out of nowhere and dragged him out of his car, bundling him into a van waiting nearby. Driving off into the distance, they travelled for days, first by van and then by foot. Eventually they reached a tiny farmhouse.

Peter was taken to a small room, where they opened up a trapdoor. There was a small ladder leading into a hole in the ground. He was told to go down into it. They attached a thick metal chain round his neck and fixed this to a bolt on the wall. He was given a small candle and some matches. Lighting the candle, he could see a tiny space with a dirty bed and a small table. It smelt. It was damp and dark and cold.

While his kidnappers tried to secure a million-dollar ransom for his release, Peter was imprisoned in this hole in the ground for months. The small candles they gave him allowed about an hour of light each day. His company was an army of slugs and a dead rat. Sensory and social isolation are known forms of torture, and it wasn't long before Peter was reduced to a state of such desperation that he considered ways to kill himself.

Reflecting on his ordeal, he came to a decision: he was going to do what he could to keep going. 'There was no blinding light or flash of inspiration which led me into taking the decision to try and survive,' he later wrote in his book *Hole*.[1] 'Rather it was a gradual process ... I was going to be here for some time, possibly for the rest of my life, however long or short that would be. The only thing to do was to get on with it as best I could.'

Doing the best he could was an active process. He saw that there were tasks involved in his survival. He had to keep himself fit. So he exercised every day. Not just fit physically, though – psychologically fit too. He had to learn ways to fill his time and to counter the extremes of despair he'd sometimes feel.

One of his discoveries was of the power of memories. 'Memories are wonderful companions,' he wrote. Though not always. He found that recent good memories were pleasing while he was thinking them, but left him painfully sad afterwards. It was heartbreaking to be away from his partner, his children, his family and friends. Yet older memories were comforting. Even more than that – he could, through combining recall with imagination, reinhabit his history and spend time with people fondly remembered from the past.

What impresses me about Peter's story is the way he so intentionally engaged in practices to protect his wellbeing. Knowing that the lack of social and sensory stimulation was psychologically harmful, he set himself the task each day of identifying someone who'd been important to him, and composing a speech to them, reminiscing on times together. There were times they spoke back to him too. Out of isolation and an unbearable loneliness, Peter had used the power of his memory and imagination to import supportive company into the darkness of his hole.

The challenge of loneliness

While we're unlikely to face extreme isolation like Peter Shaw, loneliness has been described as a modern epidemic. Surveys show half of all older people see television or pets as their main form of company, and almost half a million people in the UK might go five or six days each week without seeing or speaking to anyone.[2,3] While isolation contributes to loneliness, it isn't the only factor. Changing patterns of relationship also play a part in making the uncomfortable feeling of aloneness more common. In the USA, the General Social Survey showed that the number of people without anyone they could discuss important matters with has tripled in recent decades.[4] If loneliness is a challenge you face, how might resilience help?

The advice of John Cacioppo, one of the world's leading researchers on loneliness, is to ease your way back into social connections, the letters EASE pointing you towards four steps.[5] The first E is for *Extending yourself* – reaching out a little at a time to build or rebuild relationships. The A is for an *Action plan*, where, recognising that it might not be easy, you identify practical steps you can take. The S is for *Seek collectives*, where you search out ways of connecting with people having similar interests. And the final E is for *Expect the best*, understanding that the fear of it not working out well can block people from even trying, while optimism can become a self-fulfilling prophecy. Confidence helps us take the first steps in building connections with others.

Strengthening our network of support can be one of the most important ways of building resilience. As John Cacioppo's four-step sequence recognises, this is an active process. It doesn't just happen by itself, particularly if your starting point is of feeling more alone than you'd like to be. A useful principle for any support network is not to rely too much on just one source. I think of a spider's web that is stronger for having different strands. For that reason, each of the next four chapters explores a different category of support.

Fig. 1: Support is like a spider's web –
it needs many different strands

Even if we have strong networks, there will also be times when we want, or need, to cope by ourselves. That's why the first type of strand we look at is self-support. There will be lots of ways you already do this well. Like any capacity, though, the ability to support ourselves is something we can develop. Whatever our starting point, this is an area we can learn to approach more skilfully. The insight of the spider's web is the first part of that skilfulness, reminding us not to rely on ourselves so much that we don't feel any need to reach out. The danger of being too self-sufficient is that it can leave us lonelier. An image we touched on earlier was that of the bridge whose weight-bearing ability depends on strong foundations and support structures. A bridge has two sides. In this chapter we look at how we develop strong foundations and supporting structures on our side of the bridge. Then we will look at strengthening support from the other side.

How do you support someone?

In exploring what support is and how it is given, I invite you to reflect on some of the different ways you might support some-one else.

Try this – an enquiry about support, part one

Imagine visiting a friend who is facing a difficult situation. You'd love to support them. How can you do that? List as many ways as you can of how to offer and give support.

When we explored this together on a recent training course, answers that came up included: spend time with them; listen; ask how things are and also what kind of support they'd find helpful; bring a cake to share; go for a walk together; take them on an outing; talk kindly and be encouraging; notice what they're doing well and appreciate that; tell a joke and be playful; avoid being critical or judgemental; give them a present and sing. I then asked the group to look at the list we'd generated and consider how many of them they could also offer to themselves if they wanted to give themselves support.

Try this – an enquiry about support, part two

Of the items you've listed and also those described above, how many of these could you also apply to yourself if you wanted to offer self-support? Which ones work best? Why not try some out and see?

Each day over the next two weeks, take a moment to pause and say to yourself: 'I support myself by . . .', reflecting either on something you're already doing, or something you intend to try out.

Seven strands of self-support

Much of what we've been looking at so far involves different ways to support ourselves when facing difficult times. When we ask, 'What does a story of resilience look like here?', as with Peter Shaw's example, it involves taking active and conscious steps to support ourselves. Yet even if we know about resilience, and have well-developed tools to respond to challenges, we might not always use these. Developing the skill of self-support involves not just knowledge of what to do, but also having ways to nudge ourselves to do it. It is here that the framework of the seven strands can help, with the acronym SUPPORT.

Fig. 2: Seven strands of self-support

Self-talk

Daniel, a teacher attending a recent course, was struck by the difference between the way he spoke to other people and the way he spoke to himself. His familiar pattern when he was struggling was to be harshly critical of himself. He recognised that the voice saying, 'You're such an idiot' was an echo of what his dad used to say to him when he was growing up. Recognising the choice point of being able to change his style of 'self-talk' was his biggest take-home from the course.

Self-talk is the way we talk, or think, to ourselves. When you speak to yourself, either out loud or in your mind, is the tone and content of what's said encouraging and supportive? Research, particularly from sports psychology, shows supportive self-talk brings proven benefits to performance and learning.[6] It may help you keep to a path you've chosen, and remind you of techniques you find helpful. Research has shown that teaching children encouraging self-talk can help them cope with anxiety in situations they find frightening, like going into hospital.[7] When we face something scary or difficult, we can draw on our memory and creativity to have an imaginary supporter alongside us, cheering us on in a way that sustains us.

Try this – three alternative self-talk perspectives

When you face a challenge, consider what the following three people might say to you if they were alongside you and wanting to offer support. Imagine these are people who know you well, care about you and respect you.

- A supportive friend
- An encouraging coach
- An inspiring manager

What you're doing here is inviting in a supportive channel of self-talk. You can include here phrases you find comforting or insights you'd like to remind yourself of, such as, 'I know this is temporary,' 'Don't take this personally,' or, 'One day I'll look back on this as my advanced resilience training.' I use this technique to remind myself to use resilience tools I know help me, such as, 'Remember the spider diagram,' 'How's my water level?' and, 'There's what happens, and then there's what happens next.'

Understanding

How can you help someone if you don't know what direction they'd like to move in or what difficulties they're experiencing? The RAPID psychological first-aid model we looked at as part of the Second Way began with Rapport, built through listening. It is by tuning in that we develop empathy. It is the same with giving yourself support – we need to listen to ourselves so that we can understand what we need.

When people are too busy it can be hard to find time to listen to themselves. So a way of supporting yourself is to build in protected time and structures to help you hear yourself. Two of the practices we've already looked at, mindfulness and expressive writing, are both ways of structuring in listening time. Both have been shown to bring proven benefits.

Try this – self-listening

How do you listen to yourself? How do you get to know more about how you feel and think about issues that matter to you? Take time to consider how you reflect and identify your favourite practices for tuning in.

Personal strengths

Imagine if there was a hidden force that could come to your aid when needed, and that you could learn ways to access this more easily. Does this sound like something out of *Star Wars*? I'm referring here to your inner strengths.

There are three main ways to identify your strengths. One is by looking back at times when you've used them. These might be the times you've felt at your best, or where you've been pleased with how you've conducted yourself. They could be times you've faced a challenge and got through. Looking back at your best and your worst times, what strengths helped you to step up and cope?

A second way is to ask those who know you well to describe strengths they recognise in you. A '360-degree review' is where you intentionally seek feedback from many sources around you.

A third way is through strength-identifying questionnaires. While the American Psychiatric Association and World Health Organization both have thick manuals describing all the things that can go wrong with us, positive classification systems have been developed to give counterbalancing attention to what can go right with us. Linked to these systems, questionnaires are available for free online that help us hunt the good stuff within ourselves.[8]

Once you've identified your strengths, how do you use them to support yourself? One approach is just to practise using them. In a randomised controlled trial of a strength-based intervention, participants identified their main strengths, and then were invited to use these in new and different ways each day over the next week.[9] Follow-up showed significant rises in happiness and falls in depression in those who did this.

Positive process

Have you ever been to a lecture or course that was incredibly boring, yet at another time experienced someone teaching the same content in a way that was engaging and enjoyable? What we're looking at here is the difference between content and process. Content refers to what you do; process is about how you do it. In a similar way, we can do the same task, with identical content, but engage with the task in different ways, where our process of going about things is different. I can do the washing-up in a way where I hate it. Or I can put music on and also give attention to the sensation of warm water in a way that makes it more enjoyable.

When we use a positive process to support ourselves, we're applying the spider diagram to what we do. We're recognising that we can do the same task in many different ways. We can support ourselves by reflecting on different pathways available and choosing a preferred version for how we do it.

Try this – positive process

Take a task or activity you do often and, using the spider diagram, consider some of the many different ways of doing this. Ask yourself: 'Is there a better version than what I normally do?' If there is, give it a try.

Offer self-forgiveness

While encouraging self-talk has proven benefits in both well-being and performance, not everyone finds it easy. If there is guilt and shame linked to past events, these can be expressed in a self-punishing way. In my work in the addictions field, I'd often see this, with people who felt awful about things they'd done when drinking. Shame and self-hate could make relapses more likely, creating a vicious cycle. An important part of my work was helping people make a fresh start.

Forgiveness is a process involving a number of steps; it is quite different from just forgetting or ignoring the past. As regret tells us what we don't want to repeat, there can be a valuable side to guilt. So the first step in forgiving – whether yourself or another – is to identify the action you feel regret about. The psychologist Everett Worthington, a leading authority on forgiveness, identifies empathy as the next important step: understanding some of the background that led to the action. Explaining something doesn't make it OK, but deepening understanding can help us access our compassion.[10]

Guilt is about a gap between our values and our actions, and when we listen to and respond to that by coming back to our values, then we don't need to hang on to the guilt. We can move on from it. The next step is to recommit to the value we want to live by. Self-forgiveness doesn't happen straight away. The more we are realigned with our values, the more we can experience self-forgiveness and move on from past mistakes. So the sequence for self-forgiveness – which we can offer ourselves as a way of supporting ourselves – is:

a) Identify the action we regret

b) Empathy/understanding about why it happened

c) Recommit to the value that has been violated

d) Go forward in strengthened realignment with our values

Regenerative habits

A habit is a behaviour that has become part of our routine: something we do without even thinking about it. Once a habit is installed, it has a momentum all of its own, which is why unwelcome habits can be so difficult to shake off. When we let go of a behaviour, it is often easier to replace it with something else rather than just stop. So, for example, if someone turns to a cigarette habitually when they want to take a moment for themselves, finding another way of taking a moment, such as going for a walk or drawing or writing, can make it easier to give up.

Regenerative habits are ones that restore you. For some people, this might involve spending time in a garden; for someone else, it might be taking up a new hobby. The challenge is to find a range of regenerative practices that you can get into the habit of doing, so that you have regular upward arrows nudging up your resilience and wellbeing.

Treat myself well

One side of self-support is how we speak to ourselves. Another is how we behave towards ourselves. If actions speak louder than words, do we treat ourselves in a way that supports us?

A woman I worked with who was recovering from alcohol dependence had a breakthrough when she allowed herself to stay in a warm bath for longer than she needed just to get clean. She was being kind to herself by making room for a positive experience of enjoying the bath. Whenever we're enjoying something, we have a choice point: do we give ourselves permission to stay a little while with the experience and savour it, or rush on to the next thing? What we're doing when we treat ourselves well is acting with self-compassion.

Returning to the hole

If we're in a difficult situation that we can't easily change, supporting ourselves well can help us find a better version of how that adversity might go. The nightmare of Peter Shaw's captivity wasn't fixed by his imaginary conversations, but it was improved by them. Self-care is about more than just comforting ourselves, though. It also puts us in a better place to spot and make the most of opportunities. Peter's efforts to maintain his psychological fitness helped him remain open to the possibility of escape. He was on the look-out for potential pathways to freedom. Eventually his moment came.

After four months underground, Peter was to be moved. His captors unlocked the padlock securing the chain around his neck and helped him climb the ladder out of his hole. It was wonderful to breathe fresh air again. They took him to a nearby car, drove for fifteen minutes, then continued by foot. With few stars visible, there was just enough light to make out the shapes of his guards. He heard them talking, then the sound of a gun bolt being drawn. Peter thought this was it: he was going to be killed. While talking, his guard momentarily loosened his grip on Peter's arm. Sensing his moment, Peter lurched towards some nearby bushes, dived into the undergrowth, and lay hidden in the dark. He heard gunfire and waited for the bullets to hit him. They didn't.

In the darkness, the kidnappers couldn't see him, and eventually moved on. Peter crawled out of the gorse bush and followed a small track up a nearby hill. After more than an hour of stumbling, he saw some lights in the distance, a few cars on a road and a small building. He aimed for the road. Soon after this he heard voices and crouched down to hide. But they'd seen him. One of the voices called in English, 'Who are you?'

Peter yelled back, 'Peter Shaw, Peter Shaw.'

A group of seven or eight men approached out of the darkness. They were soldiers from the Georgian army. 'You are Peter Shaw,' said one of them, who spoke English. 'You are famous – we look for you for many months.'

He was free, at last.

15

Nourishing Relationships

What happens to your heart rate and blood pressure when you have an argument? To find out, researchers at Cornell University in New York wired up volunteers so they could be monitored, asked for their view on a topic, and then strongly disagreed with them.[1] As the research participants were verbally attacked, their hearts pounded faster and their blood pressure rose.

To look at the impact of social support, they repeated the experiment, but this time with someone else in the room who said they agreed with the person under attack and showed they were on their side. They nodded from time to time and looked on in a supportive way. Having an ally doesn't just feel better. It also settles your physiology. The heart rate and blood pressure rose a little when the researchers were being disagreeable, but not nearly as much.

This is just one of a wealth of studies showing how important our relationships are – not just to our ability to cope with difficult times, but also to our wellbeing, life satisfaction and general health. The Harvard psychiatrist George Vaillant, reporting on a study that followed up a group of men over a seventy-year period, summed up the results by identifying the most powerful factor influencing life satisfaction as 'warmth of relationships throughout life'.[2]

We are going to look at two different meanings of the phrase 'nourishing relationships'. First, we'll look at how supportive relationships nourish us and strengthen our resilience, introducing practical strategies for developing and maintaining the social networks that sustain us. Then we will look at how we can nourish our relationships, so that we can strengthen resilience in our connections with the people we value most.

Water-level mapping with relationships: version one

When exploring the link between resilience and relationships, a good place to start is with the boat-and-water mapping tool. Who are the upward arrows in your life? Are there particular people who add to your buoyancy and afloatness at times when you might otherwise feel sunk? At the same time, relationships are not always positive. Are there those that have a downward arrow impact? Consider them too. Some people might, in different ways, have both nourishing and draining effects. You can draw them in with both upward and downward arrows (see Fig. 1 below).

> *Try this – water-level mapping with relationships: version one*
>
> Draw a horizontal line to represent your water level of resilience. Identify people who you feel nourished or supported by, in ways that act as upward arrows for your resilience. Draw them in, with the size of the arrows reflecting the size of the effect. Then use downward arrows to represent those having an undermining or depleting influence on your resilience.

When looking at the impact of relationships on our resilience and wellbeing, the psychologist Sheldon Cohen distinguishes between 'stress-buffer' effects and 'social-connectedness' effects.[3]

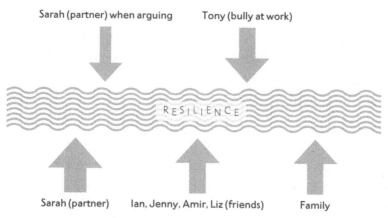

Fig. 1: Mapping influence of relationships on resilience

When turning to friends helps us get through difficult times, that's the stress-buffer effect. While Cohen's research showed people reported higher levels of depression and physical ailments when stressed, the more social support stressed people had, the less depression and fewer physical ailments they reported. Stress buffering from our social support networks can also save lives. A study in Sweden showed that while highly stressed men were significantly more likely to die over a seven-year follow-up period than those less stressed, the higher death rate was particularly apparent in those who had less emotional support.[4]

While the stress-buffer relationships are with people you might reach out to when you're struggling, the social-connectedness effect Cohen refers to is when there's a protective effect on our wellbeing even when there isn't stress around. The health benefits of well-developed social networks are striking, with lower mortality, improved immune function, higher survival rates from heart attacks, less depression and anxiety as well as less severe cognitive decline with ageing.[3]

Our social networks don't just protect us from disease, though: they also increase the positives too. As mentioned earlier, Gallup poll surveys have asked more than 15 million people about their wellbeing and friendships at work. The 30 per cent of employees who reported having a best friend at work were seven times as likely to find their work engaging, had higher levels of wellbeing and produced better-quality work. Reviewing what these surveys tell us about engagement and wellbeing in the workplace, Tom Rath and Jim Harter reported: 'We discovered that the single best predictor is not *what* people are doing – but *who* they are with.'[5]

The growth mindset applied to nourishing relationships

'I totally get it that having friends is good for you,' said Joanne, on one of my courses, 'but what if you're not a people person and struggle to make friendships that last?'

While some people might have greater social ease than others, this is another capacity we can apply the growth mindset to. A great starting point is recognising our relationships as important enough to give our attention to. Then, as with other areas we've looked at, we can explore how to grow the skills and intelligences that make a difference. Here are five steps to cultivate stronger social networks:

1) See this as a project

2) Support-network mapping

3) Water-level mapping with relationships: version two

4) Be guided by the Gottmans

5) Active Constructive responses to good news

1) See this as a project

Some people think friendships should happen naturally, and that if we put too much effort into our socialising it might appear contrived. At the same time, taking a gardening analogy, if you want to grow things, you need to choose what you plant and give attention to. What you're doing with seeing your social network as a project is applying the spider diagram, recognising that your social life can develop in different ways, and that choices you make influence how things go. So, what's the best that could happen? How do you make that more likely? What's the worst? How do you make that less likely? Storyboarding is a useful tool here.

Try this – storyboarding your social network

Try these sentence starters and see where they take you.

a) Starting point – Here's me, facing the challenge of developing and maintaining a strong social network.
b) Hopes if I succeed here include . . .
c) In the way of this, obstacles and difficulties include . . .
d) Facing these, what helps me is . . .
e) Turnings or shifts might happen if I were to . . .
f) Specific achievable steps I can take in the next seven days include . . .

This storyboarding process can start you thinking about how you can develop your social network. For more support pointers on where to act, a useful tool is a social network map.

2) Support-network mapping

Support-network mapping is a way of visually representing important relationships in your life, together with the flows of support both towards and from you. To start, get a blank piece of paper and draw your name in the middle. Around this, name the key people in your life, your most important relationships. Draw an arrow from them to you to represent support you gain from them. The more support you receive, the thicker you draw the arrow. For support from you to others, draw arrows from you to them. Here's an example (see Fig. 2 below).

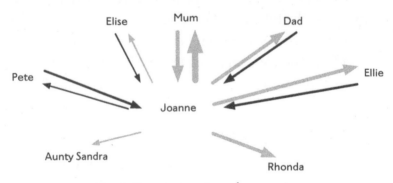

Fig. 2: Support-network mapping

Once you've drawn your support network, ask yourself how you feel. Do you feel well supported? If not, where are the gaps? What would you change? This is what you take on as a project. The support-network-mapping process is something you can revisit to see how your network is developing, and what your next steps might be.

When you're developing an area, it is useful to identify specific growth edges. For example, Joanne noticed she was grateful to Pete and Ellie, for the ways they had supported her, but she hadn't expressed this yet. Expressing gratitude is a way of setting off positive loops in your network, as the more you express gratitude by giving back, the more people are likely to reciprocate.

You can also give forward – where if you're grateful to someone you've received from, you don't necessarily need to give back to that specific person. If, for example, they have died or moved far away, you can give forward to someone else.

3) Water-level mapping with relationships: version two
If you've identified a particular relationship you'd like to nourish, a helpful tool here is the boat-and-water level, but applied to the relationship as a whole rather than just you. The water level here represents the level of wellbeing and resilience in the relationship, the boat containing not just you but the other person too. So, what nourishes trust and satisfaction with the relationship? How can you feed this?

While you and the other person involved might see this water level differently, thinking of the joint water level rather than just your personal one can change the way you think about giving and receiving in the relationship. When you look at things purely in individual terms, giving can seem like a loss from one side to offer a gain to the other. But when you give to a relationship, and also when you receive from it, you strengthen the relationship in ways that both sides benefit from. Rather than running an internal balance sheet of who's given what when, you're both playing roles in nourishing a larger entity that you can draw from. It is similar with families, teams and communities: you can do the boat-and-water level looking at collective wellbeing. When we play a role as an upward arrow in a collection of people we belong to, we both gain and receive at the same time. Interestingly, research shows that people who give in relationships have health benefits linked to this, including extending their life spans.[6]

A question remains, though: how do you give in relationships? If you've chosen a relationship you'd like to nourish, what types of upward arrows are most effective? It is here that it is worth turning to the work of John and Julie Gottman.

4) Be guided by the Gottmans

John Gottman and his team at the University of Washington spent decades studying couple interactions to see what made the difference between relationship success and failure. By identifying key warning signs, they could interview newly wed couples and predict with 87.4 per cent accuracy which ones would still be together five years later and which would divorce.[7] Further studies reported over 90 per cent accuracy in divorce predictions just from analysing a fifteen-minute video of couples discussing an area of disagreement.[8]

Four particular warning signs, which Gottman and his team refer to as 'the Four Horsemen of the Apocalypse', were found to predict most of the divorces. We can think of each of these as a powerful downward arrow reducing relationship resilience. Relevant to friendships and work relationships as well as marriage, these horsemen are:

Destructive criticism – negative statements about the partner's personality or behaviour.

Contempt – name-calling or other ways of putting their partner down. Expressions of contempt were the strongest predictor of divorce.

Defensiveness – when issues are raised, responding with blame and counter-attack rather than curiosity and understanding.

Stonewalling – switching off to or turning away from the relationship, shutting the partner out.

An important upward arrow that protected couples, even in the presence of these horsemen, was the ability to repair the relationship after a clash. When a partner recognised a wrong turning and apologised, or took a step to make up, and this was received well, that helped get the relationship back on track.

Building on their understanding of how things can go wrong, as well as how things can go right, John Gottman and his wife Julie developed a framework for building and maintaining satisfying relationships that last. They called it the Sound Relationships House Theory. Just as houses are built with supporting structures, so our relationships can be supported by key behaviours and guiding principles. Like the horsemen, these apply not just to romantic relationships, but to friendships and working relationships too. Here are nine guiding principles the Gottmans recommend.[9]

1. *Understand what they love and like.* If you know what's important to them, their fondnesses as well as what they don't like, you're better able to offer the sort of support that is a good fit and appreciated.

2. *Share fondness and admiration.* How do they know you like them unless you have ways of showing that?

3. *Turn towards instead of away.* There are moments in a relationship where they ask us for something, make a bid for our attention or express a need. Turning towards them, showing your interest and responding with care, strengthens the relationship. For example, when they make a joke, you listen, smile and laugh. You're with them rather than looking away.

4. *The positive perspective* – taking a constructive approach to problem solving, responding positively to their attempts to repair after clashes.

5. *Manage conflict.* All relationships with depth have bumpy times. Having ways to work constructively with conflict

(especially when these are hard to resolve) is a keystone to relationship resilience.

6. *Support their dreams.* Encourage each other to talk about heartfelt hopes, values and dreams, and support each other in pursuing these.

7. *Create shared meaning.* Are there purposes and plans you share? If so, when you're able to be allies in these, your common direction can bring you closer together.

8. *Trust.* A sense of knowing the other person is for you, and acts with your best interests at heart. You being for them in the same way.

9. *Commitment.* This is about valuing the relationship, treasuring it as something special that you want to maintain and keep in good shape. It includes recognising what's good here and feeling grateful for that, while also taking a long-term view that is resilient to periodic bumpiness.

Try this - being guided by the Gottmans

Think of a relationship you'd like to nourish. Reflect on the downward arrows of the four horsemen of destructive criticism, contempt, defensiveness and stonewalling. Do any of these happen between you and the other person? If so, there's what's happened, and then there's what happens next. See if you can move away from these.

To nourish the relationship, go through each of the nine upward arrow points, and ask yourself: 'How much do I do this? Are there ways I can do this more, or develop this more?' Consider steps you can take, and then take them.

Review this process periodically and try it with different relationships. While you'll experience a different depth of commitment with very close relationships, each of these nine upward arrows can be relevant to any relationship you'd like to nourish.

5) Active Constructive responses to good news

The positive psychologist Shelly Gable videotaped dating couples discussing recent events in their lives. She found that the way people responded to their partner sharing good news played a pivotal role in relationship wellbeing.[10] She identified three types of response that had damaging effects: ignoring the good news; acknowledging it but with dampened enthusiasm; or, worst of all, pointing out reasons why the good news might really be bad news. Each of these dropped the water level of resilience in the relationship. If the partner showed what Shelley Gable called an 'Active Constructive response', with interest and delight in the good news, this had the opposite effect. Couples with this response not only reported higher levels of satisfaction with their relationship, they were also more likely to still be together nine months later.

Try this – nourishing relationships in your response to good news

Be on special alert for times when people share good news with you. Recognise these times as crucial moments in your relationship with them, where your response can raise or lower the shared water level of satisfaction between you. Can you be as pleased as they are? How would you respond if you were delighted and interested to hear more?

Research from Shelley Gable and the Gottmans alerts us to ways we can nourish the relationships that nourish us. When things go well, savouring and celebrating this is good for both sides.

When things go wrong between you, resilience isn't just about endurance and putting up with this. We can play a role in relationship repair and improving conditions. This same principle can be applied not only to people, but also to our larger social and physical environment. That's where we turn next.

16

Improving Conditions

More than three decades ago, I went to a lecture by the surgeon Denis Burkitt, a pioneer of research linking diet and disease. He drew a picture of doctors in a boat, busily saving people's lives by rescuing them as they struggled to swim in a big river they'd fallen into.

Fig. 1: Doctors rescuing people in the river

He then posed the question: isn't prevention better than cure? The next picture showed people further upstream falling from a cliff into the river.

If people are at risk from harmful conditions, one approach is to train them in resilience skills that might protect them and

Fig. 2: A preventable cause upstream

make better outcomes more likely. Our focus so far has been on pathways to doing this. Something we haven't touched on so much yet are *upstream interventions* that reduce the risk of harm people are exposed to by improving conditions.

To develop Denis Burkitt's metaphor, personal resilience training is like teaching people to swim, so that if they're in the river, they can make their way to safety more easily. An upstream intervention would involve looking at how people are falling into the river and doing something to prevent that. It might be that there's a slippery path by the river, or someone pushing people in. This approach would tackle these causes.

I've been fortunate to be involved in a number of upstream interventions to promote wellbeing. They have contributed to building resilience not just in individuals but also in the larger systems they are part of, for example in their teams, communities and organisations. Here is an example.

The anti-bullying project

My friend Nicola Banning and I were asked by a local council to design an anti-bullying training intervention for their staff. Our aims were firstly to strengthen people's ability to tackle bullying if they were exposed to it, and secondly to promote a more positive working environment where bullying was less likely to occur.[1] Two of our starting questions were: 'What's the opposite of a bully? And how can we help people become more like that?' The opposite of a bully is not a victim. It is someone who is respectful both to others and themselves.

One of the exercises we asked people to do was to think about the difference between a workplace from heaven and a workplace from hell. Imagine the sort of workplace you'd look forward to going to. What would that be like? Compare that with one you hated, where you dreaded going to work. People immediately knew what we were talking about, and most had some experience of both ends of the spectrum.

Looking at the differences between more desirable and less desirable workplaces, we then focused on features people could readily influence. 'I'd know I'd arrived at the right place, because I felt welcome,' said a participant, telling us that in the jobs she'd loved the most, she felt part of a team and knew there was support around if needed. Factors like trust, being treated fairly, and clear, honest communication were seen as among the most important. We looked at how the culture of teams and organisations is influenced by contributions from everyone present. A team or office can get stuck in a difficult mood or atmosphere, just as people can. In a similar way, shifts of collective recovery are also possible.

Any team or organisational culture has norms, the ways of doing things that are accepted as normal. These include the way people speak to each other, whether we ask for help and how we respond if others ask us. By becoming more conscious of the norms that have developed, and then being able to review these, deciding to keep some and agreeing to change others, staff could shape the way the team culture developed. Having agreements around what is OK and not OK help establish more supportive and respectful norms, thus acting as an upstream intervention to make bullying less likely.

The technology firm Google has been on a similar quest to find out what makes a workplace work well, particularly in the way teams are organised. In 2012, the company started its Project Aristotle initiative, which looked at hundreds of teams, and also reviewed what research had shown.[2] Factors like teams having clear goals and a culture of dependability strengthened the chances of performing well. But above these two, more important for a team's success was the degree of psychological safety within it. If people believed they could voice their opinion without feeling shouted down, and be listened to and respected, the team was likely to function better.

Where is resilience located?

While personal resilience involves factors within people, and resilience in relationships is based on what happens between people, with resilience in teams, communities and organisations, there is something else happening too. Each of these larger collections of people is a whole that is more than the sum of its parts, a system that has its own properties and story. We can apply many of the tools we've looked at so far, like storyboarding, the boat-and-water level and the resilience zone, to these larger collective levels too.

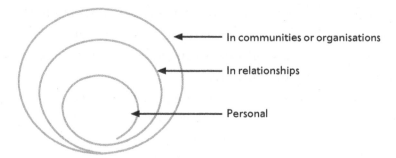

Fig. 3: Different levels of resilience

When thinking about a community, the two-part storyboard looks like this:

1) Here's us, a community facing the challenge of . . .

2) What helps us here is . . .

Can you think of examples of teams, communities or organisations expressing resilience in response to difficult conditions? Just as we can learn from inspiring personal stories, situations where people act together to address shared challenges also offer us models to follow. I was interested therefore to read about how a community in Somerset was tackling an issue threatening to both personal and collective wellbeing – that of loneliness.

The Compassionate Frome project

A vicious cycle common when people develop long-term health problems is that unwellness can lead to social isolation, and loneliness can undermine good health. Recognising the limits of what mainstream medicine could offer, Dr Helen Kingston, a GP in the Somerset town of Frome, began thinking about a community-level response.[3] She teamed up with Jenny Hartnoll, a community development specialist, to set up Compassionate Frome, a project to cultivate stronger networks of support in the town and surrounding area.

A first step was to map the resources already available in the area. They produced a directory of over 400 groups and organisations offering support, advice, companionship and creative activity. Then they trained volunteer 'community connectors' who'd help people find and make use of services, projects and other resources in the town. They also set up groups to address areas of need identified by people in the community.

One of the groups they set up was a 'Talking Café', a time each week when people living in the town were invited to meet each other, make new friends, and find out more about resources available. Their goal was to make it easier for people to take that first step in connecting with others. It worked so well that soon the idea spread to other nearby towns too. 'If it weren't for this Talking Café,' said one participant, 'I would have a lonely experience. They have helped me look forward to getting up on a Monday morning.'[4]

One approach to loneliness is to develop strategies to cope with it, such as finding ways to more enjoyably spend time alone. This is an example of *adaptive resilience*, where we deal with difficult situations by getting used to them and finding ways of bouncing with them. The Frome project illustrates a different approach, that of *transformative resilience*, where they addressed the difficulty by changing the situation and bouncing forward to something new. In this case, transformative resilience brought important changes both at the level of individual people and with the community as a whole.

At an individual level, people became more confident about approaching others, something made easier by supportive contexts that encouraged them to take the first steps. As people got more involved, a positive cycle was set off, where the more people engaged, the better they felt, and the better they felt, the more they engaged. A positive cycle was also set off at a community level, where the more people developed mutually supportive relationships, the more they were likely to become involved in community events and projects, making these more likely to succeed.

Social capital is a term used to describe the wealth of relationships within a community; research shows communities rich in social capital not only have lower rates of depression and suicide, they also have fewer strokes and heart attacks.[5] In the first few years of the project, the county of Somerset saw emergency hospital admissions rise by 29 per cent, while admissions from Frome (which lies within Somerset) fell by 17 per cent, saving 5 per cent of the local health budget.[3] While the Compassionate Frome project can't claim to be the only cause of this, it is likely to be a contributing factor.

Upstream interventions in the workplace

The UK Department of Work and Pensions (DWP) commissioned a review looking at wellbeing in the workplace. This reported that organisations spending money on wellbeing recouped their investment and made savings.[6] Staff sickness rates were reduced; staff turnover was lower, and productivity was higher.

Two of the main causes of staff sickness are musculoskeletal problems (particularly back pain) and stress-related problems, including anxiety and depression. Significant advances in tackling musculoskeletal problems have come from taking an ergonomic approach.

Ergonomics is a science looking at the impact of work environments on people's comfort and performance. It addresses design factors in furniture, room layout and working routines. When someone suffers from back problems made worse by sitting on an uncomfortable chair, an ergonomic approach would look at how improving the chair, office design or way of working might help. In a case study quoted in the DWP report, a manufacturing company was able to save more than four times as much as it spent on investing in ergonomic improvements to its workplace.

By improving conditions, ergonomic interventions strengthen resilience at an organisational level. Could we apply this approach to stress-related problems?

There's growing awareness that resilience in the workplace isn't purely a personal skill set. While individual capacities play a vital role, there also needs to be a valuing of resilience thinking and design at an organisational level. With toxic levels of stress a common experience, there is a long way to go in promoting the cultural shift needed to make ergonomic working the norm. Each of us can play a role in this shift – as with tackling bullying, an important step involves changing the norms of what we see as acceptable.

That's all very well, but . . .

When doing the heaven-and-hell exercise with local-government staff, an issue that often came up was resource shortages. Many staff had experienced reorganisations, with teams being merged, staff made redundant and budgets cut. Feeling overburdened and under-resourced, with a 'more for less' expectation, many people didn't feel supported in or by their working environment. They also often felt powerless to do much about it. What does a story of resilience look like in a situation like this? Is there anything we can do? I faced a situation like this too.

Diary of a doctor

In the late 1980s, my contract required me to be available for work for an average of 88 hours a week, though some weeks I'd work much more than this. I'd be up on my feet from early morning till the small hours of the night. I might get to bed for a brief snatch of sleep before being called out again. The rationale for these long working hours was that outside the standard working day we were 'on call' for emergencies, but not working all the time. However, many of the jobs I did were so busy we'd be on the go throughout the day, in the evening, through much of the night, and then work the next day too. To give an example, here's a diary of a fairly ordinary day and night at work in my job in an Obstetrics (child delivery) unit.

8.25 a.m.	Start work with ward round, followed by work on the ward, then assisting with a Caesarean section delivery, followed by seeing more patients on the ward.
12.43 p.m.	Stop for lunch, respond to three phone calls while eating.
1.30 p.m.	Back on the ward working.
3 p.m.	Pause for coffee.
3.20 p.m.	Admitting new patients.
5.11 p.m.	Called to emergencies: one of my patients may miscarry. I discuss this with her and her partner. Then see two other patients who are seriously unwell.
7.15 p.m.	Supper, followed by catching up on paperwork.
8.26 p.m.	Called to the labour ward: very busy there. Seeing new patients, putting in drips, attending to emergencies.
10 p.m.	Called to assist with emergency Caesarean section.
10.45 p.m.	Called to see patient with heavy vaginal bleeding.

11.04 p.m.	Meet with more senior doctor to discuss patients.
11.20 p.m.	Seeing another new patient on the ward. Called to assess abnormal foetal heart trace.
12.20 a.m.	Go round the wards I'm covering to check all is OK.
1.01 a.m.	Get to bed, but difficult to sleep because I know I'm likely to be called, as one of my patients may need an emergency operation.
2.17 a.m.	Called back to the ward to see a new patient.
3.30 a.m.	Called to assist a colleague with emergency forceps delivery, and to be ready for emergency Caesarean section if this is unsuccessful.
4.15 a.m.	Baby delivered by forceps. Go to review another patient.
5.20 a.m.	Another new patient waiting to be seen, arrange for foetal trace to be done.
6.25 a.m.	Sit down, feel sick from exhaustion, retch twice.
6.35 a.m.	Get to bed.
7.40 a.m.	Alarm goes. Get ready for work again.
8 a.m.	Morning medical meeting.
9.10 a.m.	Seeing antenatal patients on the ward, including one who is likely to miscarry. She is very upset, but I feel like a zombie and am not able to offer much support.
11 a.m.	Pause for coffee.
11.30 a.m.	Seeing more patients, writing up notes.
1 p.m.	Pause for lunch. Finish writing notes.
1.40 p.m.	Finish 29-hour shift and go home.

This sort of round-the-clock working was not unusual for junior hospital doctors. In previous jobs, I'd worked 104 hours in a single shift when on call at weekends, and over 135 hours in a week. To explore what might help us, a group of us organised a resilience workshop, which we called Coping Without Sleep. We concluded that attempting to strengthen adaptive resilience through improved personal coping strategies, while helpful, wasn't going to be enough. We also needed transformative resilience, through improving our working conditions. So, we started campaigning.

We wrote a letter to the hospital management describing our concerns, and had this signed by most of the junior doctors in the department. When this didn't lead to any changes, we became whistle-blowers, speaking to the press about the conditions in which we worked.

Even though we got good press coverage, our conditions still didn't improve. So, we considered other ways to influence our situation. A friend who was a lawyer as well as a doctor suggested it might be against the law to be working under such conditions, as employers had legal obligations to protect safety at work. Together we went and saw a leading lawyer who'd taken on several high-profile cases. His opinion was that a legal challenge to our contract wouldn't stand a chance, and that we might even be laughed out of court. Undeterred, we sought a second opinion, but he had the same view, saying our case was unwinnable because there wasn't a legal precedent to support it.

Then another friend, also a lawyer, said she saw things differently. She agreed to take the case on free of charge. Issuing a writ created massive publicity, putting me on the front page of newspapers and on the television news. The court process was long and frustrating, with ten hearings over a six-year period. Initially the case was thrown out, but we appealed, and this led to a more encouraging result. Eventually, a victory at the Court of Appeal came with a judgement that, whatever I'd signed in my contract, employers were still bound by their legal obligation to provide a safe system of work. Winning the case set an important legal precedent that has been quoted in other cases.[7]

Thinking differently about collective resilience

In the storyline of bouncing forward, crisis moments can be turning points when they provoke a response that leads to improvements later on. For example, someone responding to a heart attack by shifting to a healthier lifestyle can significantly reduce their risk of a second coronary.[8] In the story of team or organisational resilience, several people going off sick with stress might be the wake-up call that prompts a review of working conditions. Whether this happens or not depends on how much decision-makers consider the ergonomic impact of the working environment. If stress is seen in purely individual terms, the danger is that the victim gets blamed. This would be like criticising people for having back pain when they sit on poorly designed chairs. As personal and situational factors both play a role, collective resilience involves a both/and approach that addresses both personal skills and situational factors.

A common problem faced here is that situational factors are often seen as beyond people's control. When I spoke to my doctor colleagues about our hours of work, everyone agreed it was an appalling situation, but most didn't believe there was anything we could do. 'We don't have the power here,' I was told. 'We just have to put up with it.' I couldn't accept that. What helped me respond in a different way were some of the resilience tools we've been looking at, particularly the practice of identifying inspiring examples, the narrative feature of turning points, the flexible thinking of challenging disbelief and the water-level mapping tool.

Inspiring examples of turning

In 1785, the buying and selling of people as slaves was an accepted norm in many parts of the world. Writing an essay about the transatlantic slave trade while a student at Cambridge, Thomas Clarkson was horrified. Two years later, he and eleven others held a meeting in London to set up a campaign against the slave trade. At the time, they were a tiny minority pushing against an established way of doing things. Yet twenty years later, a law was passed abolishing the slave trade in the British Empire. It took until 1833 for another law to be passed abolishing slavery.

You can track the process of other important historical shifts, such as women getting the vote in much of the world, or the dismantling of apartheid in South Africa, and see a similar sequence of events. At one point in time, the change seems unlikely: the order of the day is against it. Yet a small group of determined people don't accept this, and begin working together for something different to happen. Other people join them, a tipping point is reached, a new norm is established.

I took comfort from recognising that important changes might seem impossible before they happen. A feature found both in adventure stories and inspiring real-life examples is that of a turning point, which tends to appear in ways that couldn't be predicted earlier on. At the start of the story, there's no guarantee such a shift will occur, but if we know one might, we can look for ways to make that more likely.

When I started the court case, we knew the odds were against us. We believed that launching the case was itself a success, as it helped raise awareness and focus attention on our hours of work. After several rounds of court cases, though, I was getting despondent and wondered about giving up. I heard the Professor No Way voice inside me saying, 'There's no way this is going to work out.' That voice was echoed in the national press by leading legal figures like the former top judge Lord Denning, who said I didn't have much chance.

Several factors acted together to tip the balance towards a turning. The first was the overwhelming and sustained support I got from so many people who backed my cause. When we started the case, we didn't have the money to take on a high-profile and expensive legal challenge. After a newspaper article mentioned this, people started sending in money with letters of support. Thousands of pounds were raised, enough to get the case off the ground until the BMA, the doctors' union, agreed to back it. I found the letters deeply moving, including several from doctors who said that they, like me, had considered suicide when struggling with burnout and severe exhaustion.

Then, around that time, a young doctor the same age as I was, and working in a similar job, collapsed and died after an 86-hour working week. Another doctor, whom I'd worked with and knew, ended up in intensive care after a serious suicide attempt. For both of these, I thought, that could have been me. This strengthened my resolve to continue.

Challenging disbelief and water-level mapping

We have looked already at how we can apply the boat-and-water mapping tool to many kinds of change. I tried it out in relation to improving my working conditions. If a lower water level represented worsening conditions, then the more this fell, the more likely I'd be to crash into the rocks of depression, burnout and stress-related harm. I mapped out downward arrows that made conditions worse, and upward arrows that improved things. A big downward arrow was the fact that I got paid much less per hour for overtime, making it cheaper for health authorities to work doctors longer hours. That gave employers a financial incentive to maintain the status quo. Another powerful downward arrow was the widespread belief that there wasn't much we could do, leading to a resigned acceptance of conditions that had been getting steadily worse over many years.

A powerful upward arrow was increasing awareness of the health risks to patients and doctors from excessive hours of work. The court case was succeeding in drawing attention to these. Another upward arrow was the legal obligation of employers to provide a safe system of work.

In a story of change, the turning point depends on a shift in the balance between downward and upward arrows. Until you reach that tipping point, it can seem that any action you take isn't enough and might even seem futile. But if you persevere, the context changes and becomes more supportive of change. In the end, it might be one more small thing that subtly alters the mix so that people turn one way rather than another.

The way we think about cause and effect is one of these downward or upward arrows, and so influences the balance of change. When my doctor friends said, 'We don't have the power here,' they were thinking of power in terms of control. If A (a person) controls B (an event), then A has the power and can cause B to happen. This way of thinking led us to feel like victims.

With flexible thinking, we can take a different approach to power, viewing it in terms of influence instead of control. Rather than 'A causes B' in a direct controlling way, another way of thinking is, 'A adds to a context that makes B more likely.' All the publicity from campaigning was adding to a context that made change more likely. Each letter of support I received added to a context that made it more likely that I'd continue with the case. The court case victory helped create a shift by establishing a new norm in how employment law was interpreted.

When we're looking at the impact of context, each little change subtly alters the mix. Since each of us is part of the background for everything else that happens in the world, our choices and actions add to a context that can make changes we'd like to see happen either more or less likely.

Two sides of VUCA realities

In the first year of the twenty-first century, supermarket executives warned the UK government that their shops had only three days' worth of food left.[9] The fuel protests, where big lorries from road hauliers had blockaded British oil refineries, had brought much of the country to a halt. Imagine what might have happened if we had run out of food. Were we just nine meals away from anarchy? Our lives depend on complex interrelated systems running smoothly, whether in supplying our food, water and energy or addressing our needs for communication, transport and waste disposal. Because disruptions can happen in any of these areas in unexpected ways, the term 'VUCA' is being increasingly used to describe our modern world: **V**olatile, **U**ncertain, **C**omplex and **A**mbiguous.

Uncertainties in our larger economic, political and environmental landscape are added to by climate change. According to NASA, each decade over the last fifty years has been warmer than the last, with the hottest years on record happening since 2010.[10] Climate disturbance is bringing an increase in extreme weather events throughout the world, with more severe heatwaves, wildfires, droughts and floods. In a two-part story of resilience, our part one might start with, 'Here's us, facing Volatile, Uncertain, Complex and Ambiguous conditions.'

When looking at the second part of this story, a different view of VUCA is offered by Bill George from Harvard Business School. He suggests that four qualities needed in our time are **V**ision,

Understanding, Courage and Adaptability.[11] Vision grows out of having a clear sense of our values, so that we know which direction and purpose call to us most strongly. To develop understanding in rapidly changing circumstances, we need to be open to new information, even if this clashes with our previous view. Courage is needed to step up to the challenges our times present us with, making bold moves to innovate and tread new paths rather than just playing it safe by sticking with what's familiar. Adaptability is about being responsive to changing conditions with a willingness to alter the route by which we express our vision.

With these qualities, we can apply the spider diagram to the bigger challenges we face. We don't know what is going to happen, but those three questions of 'What's the best? What's the worst? And what's most likely?' help us consider a range of possibilities. When considering the worst that can happen, it is easy to feel overwhelmed. Yet at the same time inspiring examples remind us that a narrative with a difficult beginning, even to the extent that things seem hopeless, can change in unexpected ways. When thinking about the best that can happen, we're giving room for our hopes. What the skills of resilience help us with is playing an active role to support those hopes, to make them more likely. Following the Seven Ways sequence of Storyboarding, Emotional First Aid, Thinking Flexibly, Overload Management Problem Solving, Strengthening Support and Stickability (SETOPSS), we can apply the six ways we've looked at so far to address the challenge of improving conditions.

Storyboarding

A storyboard follows the 'journey approach to change', recognising that if you can't see a way to improve conditions that trouble you, you can add the word 'yet' and begin the process of looking. The way to begin is to start from where you are, with

'Here's me (or us), facing this.' Are there conditions around you, whether in your home, workplace, community or world, that you'd like to improve? If so, I invite you to use the process described over the next few pages.

> *Try this – storyboarding the challenge of improving conditions*
>
> **S**tarting point: Considering the conditions in my . . . (identify an area you'd like to apply this to), challenges I face include . . .
> **H**ope: What I'd like to happen here is . . .
> **I**n the way of that, obstacles or challenges include . . .
> **F**acing these, what helps is . . .
> **A T**urning or shift is more likely if I were to . . .
> **S**pecific achievable steps I can take in the next week towards this include . . .

When looking at conditions in the larger context around us, turnings or shifts tend to need the input of many people. That's why the wording of the fifth story element has been changed to 'a turning or shift is more likely if I were to . . .' We can contribute to larger shifts and turnings. We can make them more likely by finding and playing our part in them.

Emotional First Aid
Our emotional reactions play an essential role in rousing us to safeguard or improve conditions around us. We're more likely to protect or maintain what we love and appreciate. Anger, sadness and anxiety are important motivators too. Yet extreme conditions can push us outside the resilience zone when distressing events leave us feeling overwhelmed, sunk or frozen. By valuing, listening to and understanding our emotional responses, while also drawing on self-steadying practices where needed,

we strengthen our capacity to face disturbing realities and respond with resilience to them.

Try this – emotional resilience

1. Emotional awareness: when I look at conditions in . . . (name the area you're addressing), I feel . . .
2. Emotional coping: I deal with these feelings by . . .
3. Emotional intelligence: what I gain from these feelings is . . .

Thinking Flexibly

When you think about the larger context of your life, taking in the conditions around you, what sort of thoughts do you have? And what is the effect of thinking that way?

A survey about people's experiences of world problems found feelings of powerlessness to be a common response.[12] Yet, as with the example of tackling my working conditions as a junior doctor, our view of what's within or beyond our power to influence is shaped by the way we think about it. The thinking track, 'We don't have the power here; there's nothing we can do,' blocks people from even trying to make a difference.

Try this – inspiring thought experiments

1) Notice thoughts you have about addressing your conditions. Where does this sort of thinking take you?

    For example, 'When I think like this . . . (describe the thinking track) 'I'm more likely to . . . (describe the sort of response you might have).'
2) What sort of thoughts inspire you? Try them out as thinking experiments.

    For example, 'If I think like this, what might that lead me to do?'

An idea I find inspiring is that of the Butterfly Effect, where tiny influences can lead to unexpected large changes. The concept is linked to the work of the meteorologist Edward Lorenz, who in 1979 presented a paper to the American Association for the Advancement of Science with the title, 'Does the flap of a butterfly's wings in Brazil set off a tornado in Texas?'[13] A common idea rooted in classical physics is that the impact of an action is proportional to its size. So, if you want a big effect, then you need big resources to produce that. The science of complexity, which the Butterfly Effect is rooted in, suggests something different. Lorenz was looking at the development of weather systems, and showed that tiny changes in initial conditions, even as small as a butterfly flapping its wings, can set off a sequence of events that amplifies over time to create bigger impacts.

When I think of the Butterfly Effect, I'm more likely to see the power of small steps, and believe it is worth the effort. I'm more likely to show up and play my part in efforts to improve conditions, even when I hear the Professor No Way voice within me saying there's no point.

Overload Management

A recent UK survey showed 74 per cent of people had reached the point of being so stressed in the last year that they'd felt overwhelmed and unable to cope.[14] To address the epidemic of overload we need to recognise it isn't just a personal issue, but also a collective one. Simply doing that can subtly alter conditions, because rather than feeling personally at fault if we're struggling, we can instead look for allies in addressing the issue.

While being motivated to improve conditions is good for collective resilience, when so many aspects of our context call for attention, it is easy to feel overloaded. With economic conditions, environmental conditions, the disturbance in our climate, pressures at work or issues in our community, it might be hard to know where to act. Yet the lesson of the people spinning plates in our Fourth Way is that more can be less. Trying to do more when you're already doing too much risks making you less effective. The other side of this is that less can be more, as focusing well on fewer things can help you make more impact.

Problem Solving

When we try and improve conditions but don't see change occur, we might come to believe the challenge is beyond us. Yet if we apply the growth mindset to our capacity to deal with obstacles, then every time we bump into difficulty, we can see this as an opportunity to practise our problem-solving skills. What might happen if we used the tools and strengths we explored when looking at the Fifth Way? If we saw frustration tolerance as a growable strength, and experimented with the five-stage problem-solving process, would we open up new pathways for constructive change?

Strengthening Support

Self-help addictions recovery groups have a motto of 'I can't; we can.' They recognise that some challenges are bigger than us, and we can't address them alone. We need to shift a level in the story, so that we're looking at how we play a part in something larger.

While looking for the support we need can help us, another route to becoming more effective is to see who's already addressing conditions that concern us, and then look at how we can support them. Rather than taking the lead, sometimes we can play a more strategic role by stepping in alongside or behind someone else.

17

Deepening Rootedness

In dry regions, the roots of trees grow longer and stronger.[1] When we're struggling, could we learn from nature and do something similar? When we look at a tree, it is easy to forget there is almost as much growing below the ground as above it. Root systems anchor the tree and draw in nutrients. I invite you to explore what lies below the surface for you, and how deepening your sense of rootedness might anchor, sustain and nourish you in difficult times. We're going to be looking at rootedness in three areas: purpose, community and spirituality.

Purpose

Viktor Frankl was an Austrian psychiatrist imprisoned in Auschwitz and other concentration camps during the Second World War. From his Jewish family, his first wife, parents and brother were killed in the Holocaust. Enduring appalling conditions, he drew strength from having a sense of purpose that gave him something to live for. One time when he was almost in tears from pain, limping with terrible sores on his feet while marching for miles in the bitter cold, he pictured himself in a possible future. 'I saw myself standing on the platform of a well-lit, warm and pleasant lecture room. In front of me sat an attentive audience on comfortable upholstered seats. I was giving a lecture on the psychology of the concentration camp!'[2]

What Dr Frankl did here is similar to the treatment for recurrent nightmares we looked at in Chapter Two. He imagined a better way his living nightmare could end. That gave him something to aim for and a framework of meaning that helped him make more sense of his experience. If he was to give this lecture well, he'd need to pay attention to what was happening around him. So he took on the project of growing his understanding of the psychology behind the grim realities he faced. After the Second World War ended, he went on to give that lecture many times, writing influential books and developing an approach to psychotherapy based on deepening our rootedness in purpose.

Having a strong sense of purpose is good for our wellbeing in a number of ways, improving our recovery after stressful experiences and even helping us live longer.[3,4] Amy Wrzesniewski, a Professor of Organisational Psychology at Yale University, has shown that it is possible to strengthen people's sense of purpose in their work through supporting them to 'recraft' their jobs so that these become more meaningful.[5] Doing this improves satisfaction and performance. Hospital cleaners, for example, when given more choice about how they approached their work, were able to craft their role so that they saw it as not just about cleaning, but also as contributing to the healing environment of the hospital.

When I worked in hospital emergency departments, I'd witness tragedies often. I saw people lose their loved ones as victims of violence, accidents or disease. Even though it was stressful and sometimes very sad, it was also deeply satisfying. I had a role that was clear and compelling. I was part of a team that worked together well. Some years earlier, as a medical student in the same hospital departments, I'd been exposed to scenes just as harrowing. But as a bystander, I had often felt useless and in the way. Being able to make a difference changes our relationship with adversity, in a way that nourishes our sense of meaning.

In their book *Career Burnout - Causes and Cures*, psychologists Ayala Pines and Elliot Aronson warn that we're most at risk of burnout when we lose the sense that what we do serves a worthwhile purpose. 'Stress, in and of itself, does not cause burnout,' they write. 'People are often able to flourish in stressful, demanding careers if they feel valuable and appreciated and that their work has significance. They burn out when their work has no meaning and stress continuously outweighs support and rewards.'[6]

When we're struggling, a question that helps exploration of purpose is, 'What good can come from this?' This is finding a better ending to the nightmare. When we're in the depths of difficulty, it can be hard to see. But later we might recognise ways we can help people facing something similar, or play a role in preventing the same hardship happening to others. Distress might also become the starting point of creative expression – a piece of writing, a poem, a song or an image. Like a fern that unfolds, purpose has the potential to take us somewhere different.

The tool I most use to draw out purposefulness is storyboarding, though with a different first sentence. I follow the same SHIFTS framework, with the starting-point sentence beginning as: 'Something I'd like to move forward with is . . .' We can apply this storyline at different levels, ranging from the big-P purposes that give guiding direction to our lives, down to the small-p purposes we might give attention to over the next few minutes, hours or days.

Try this – storyboarding a purpose that calls you

Either through talking to a friend or writing down in a notebook, see where these sentence starters take you:

1) **Starting point:** Something I'd like to move forward with is . . .
2) **Hoped-for outcome.** If I succeeded with this, my hopes are that . . .
3) **In the way,** obstacles or difficulties include . . .
4) **Facing that,** what helps me is . . .
5) **A Turning point** or shift might happen if I were to . . .
6) **Specific achievable steps** I can take in the next seven days include . . .

Community

Excited to start her new job, Luisa had been headhunted as Chief Operating Officer for a consultancy firm.[7] On her first day, her heart sank when her CEO tasked her with making 70 per cent of the staff redundant. Shortly after she'd completed her first work assignment, the CEO resigned, leaving her to pick up the pieces. The remaining staff felt demoralised and uncertain about their future. They also had an understandable mistrust of senior management. Luisa faced an uphill challenge as the new CEO.

Facing that, what helped her was reading Patrick Lencioni's book *The Five Dysfunctions of a Team*. The first dysfunction he identifies is absence of trust. 'In the context of building a team,' he writes, 'trust is the confidence among team members that their peers' intentions are good, and that there is no reason to be protective or careful around the group. In essence, team-mates must get comfortable being vulnerable with one another.'[8]

When people feel threatened, they can become guarded and defensive. If the threat of redundancy hangs over their heads, it may seem unsafe to reveal areas of difficulty or own up to mistakes. Luisa's task was to cultivate the sort of psychological safety that Google's Project Aristotle initiative found to be so nourishing for team effectiveness. Working hard to improve conditions, her team experienced a recovery in morale, performance and levels of trust. After eighteen months it seemed that they had turned a corner, with a clearer vision and more sustainable financial foundation. Then, in a single day, it all seemed to fall apart.

Losing a major client, the board of directors decided to close the business down. Luisa now had to tell everyone, including herself, that their jobs were coming to an end. What happened next was extraordinary, and Luisa still regards it as one of the most profound experiences of her life. Over the previous year and a half, the staff had built such a strong sense of a community that they all pulled together as a team behind a new vision. They committed to wind the company up in a professional way, while finishing the projects they were involved in and leaving their clients feeling well looked after.

I asked Luisa what helped her and her team through this. A key factor was that they'd built such a strong feeling of team spirit that they felt loyal to each other. 'I didn't feel alone: we had each other's back,' Luisa explained. 'I couldn't abandon them, because they hadn't abandoned me.' Their rootedness in the community they had created at work was a pivotal factor in transforming what could have been an awful time into one they look back on with fondness. The team, now moved on to other jobs and roles, still meet up and keep in touch.

American author and activist Joanna Macy describes two main ways that people respond to collective suffering. 'The suffering of a people can bring forth from them new strengths and solidarity,' she writes, 'or it can breed isolation and conflict, turning them against each other.'[9] We can see this happening at so many levels. In marriages, families, teams, communities, organisations and societies as a whole, times of hardship can draw out our best responses and deepen bonds of mutual care. 'We cannot welcome disaster,' writes Rebecca Solnit in her study of deepened community experiences among survivors of disasters, 'but we can value the responses, both practical and psychological.'[10] The best that can happen is inspiring, and happens more often than many might think. Yet the worst, when people turn against each other, can also be seen in all corners of our world.

A central question for resilience is what makes the difference – what helps us bring out our best responses rather than turn against each other? For Luisa's team, one crucial factor seemed to be preparation. The difficult time they'd been through, and the work they'd done building trust and community together, put them in a more committed and resourced state to bring their organisation to a good ending. Are there ways we can deepen our rootedness in community so that we, collectively, are better prepared to deal with difficult times if they arise? There are several inspiring models of community initiatives already doing this.

We looked in Chapter Twelve at 'imaginary hindsight', where we identify what we'd like to happen, imagine that it has happened already, then look back from that imaginary preferred version of the future and ask, 'How did we get here?' Addressing concerns about our over-reliance on fossil fuels, with risks from climate change in a VUCA world, the Transition Movement has spread internationally, based on the idea of 'back-casting' from a more resilient and community-rich future.[11] Rather than waiting for a disaster and then developing resilience, the transition model is that we start the process of preparing ourselves now.

Another community-building initiative that strengthens social capital and resilience while also promoting sustainable living is the Cool Block program.[12] In this, neighbours living on the same city block follow a group-based programme to improve local conditions and reduce carbon emissions. Piloted in 2016 in forty-five areas from three US cities, it led to a 32 per cent reduction in household carbon footprints, while also improving neighbour-to-neighbour support.[13] 'Cool Block has changed things in our neighbourhood,' said Lori Castellano from Pal Alto. 'Not only have we lowered our carbon footprints and prepared our block for any emergency, but we actually talk to each other.'[14]

What we're doing by strengthening the community we belong to, and our rootedness in it, is reinforcing a buffer that protects us, and those around us. A starting point for this is recognising the types of community we already feel connected with, and then taking steps to nourish those connections.

Try this - nourishing rootedness in community

Here are some sentence starters to explore. See how many different responses you can make for each one.

1) I refer to 'us' and 'we' when I'm talking about . . .
2) I am part of . . .
3) I can contribute to communities I feel part of by . . .

Spirituality

When I've interviewed people about what's helped them when they've been at their most broken or defeated, an important dimension of support many referred to was spiritual. Yet while this is a rich area to explore, when the spiritual side of resilience comes up in my workshops, there's often a mixed response.

Some people light up with enthusiasm, while others feel sceptical or suspicious.

In my work in the addictions recovery field, where self-help groups like Alcoholics Anonymous have an explicitly spiritual side to them, I experienced a similar mixed vote of confidence in my clients. A number of people I'd worked with closely described spiritual experiences as turning points in their recovery, while others said they found references to religion and spirituality in self-help group meetings had put them off. Research findings are changing the picture, though.

Practices drawn from spiritual and religious traditions, such as mindfulness meditation, yoga and prayer, now have convincing studies showing their positive impact on wellbeing.[15] For example, a study of women who'd broken their hips found that those identifying religious faith as a source of strength were less likely to become depressed and recovered their mobility more quickly.[16] Another study reported that elderly people who drew strength and comfort from their spiritual beliefs were nearly three times as likely to survive cardiac surgery.[17] Reviewing the studies, resilience researchers Steven Southwick and Dennis Charney reported that 'recent meta-analyses have concluded that practising religion is associated with physical and emotional well-being among healthy individuals and with better coping among people who are suffering with medical illnesses.'[18]

Reviewing research in a report for the US military, the RAND Corporation concluded that spirituality can act as a buffer against stress, and that spiritual interventions are an effective pathway to building resilience.[19] The US Army includes spiritual fitness as a core theme in the resilience training it developed. As mentioned previously, outcome studies show their programme has been effective in reducing depression, anxiety, post-traumatic stress and substance misuse problems.[20]

The US army programme is interesting because the army didn't want to be seen as pushing a particular set of spiritual or religious beliefs. They wanted training to benefit people from a range of different religious and non-religious backgrounds, including atheists and agnostics as well as those from established faith traditions. With a similar intention, when I'm training I invite people to try out practices and perspectives, to see what fits, and what works, for them.

What is spirituality?

While someone who is courageous, determined and energised might be described as having a strong spirit, the term spiritual implies they're drawing from a deeper well than just their own personal strength. Spirituality is about our relationship with a bigger story than just that of our own life and the people around us. This larger narrative gives our lives a framework of meaning and purpose, motivating us and also connecting us with a wider network of resources and support.

The terms religion and spirituality are sometimes used interchangeably. While they're closely related, they have different meanings. Spirituality is more personal, and linked to experience, while religion tends to refer to established systems of belief and institutions that support these. While the words, practices and beliefs of different religions vary, the spiritual experience of people connecting with something larger than themselves may have much in common. For some, this larger presence may be God, Allah or the Great Spirit. But it is possible to have a strong faith or belief in something larger than yourself even if you're an atheist. For some that might be the power of nature or loyalty to a group; for others, it might be a principle or cause they hold dear.

Kenneth Pargament and Patrick Sweeney, two of the people behind the human spirit education programme for the US forces, aimed to use language that can span this range of perspectives. Here's an example:

> we define *spirit* as the essential core of the individual, the deepest part of the self, and one's evolving human essence . . . But the human spirit is not synonymous with personal identity. It has a deeper dimension to it . . . it is an animating impulse – a vital, motivating force that is directed to realising higher-order goals, dreams, and aspirations that grow out of the essential self. In this sense, the human spirit organises people's lives and propels people forward. [21]

Do you have a sense of a part of yourself that is deeper than your personal identity? Do you sometimes feel a motivating force within you tugging you towards goals of a higher order than just personal gain? Deepening spiritual rootedness is about strengthening this side of ourselves, and three elements in the journey of doing this are spiritual practices, spiritual beliefs and spiritual experience. It is useful to consider each in turn.

Spiritual practices

Since a key part of spirituality is about deepening connection with a higher power or bigger picture, spiritual practices can be thought of as 'connecting practices' that strengthen this relationship. Like growing a stronger root system, either to deeper places within ourselves, or to something that extends or transcends beyond ourselves, practices involve a stretch beyond our normal everyday reality. Here are some examples:

- Taking 'soul time' – a quiet time where we can reflect and listen. Particularly if a feature of a spiritual path is being open to guidance, in order to be guided, we need to stop and listen. Journaling may be a way of doing this, or walking in nature, or just sitting quietly

- Mindfulness – which we have touched on previously

- Prayer – about a speaking out, or calling in, expressing gratitude, or worship. Research has shown that prayer leads to measurable health benefits[22]

Try this – soul time / special place

Do you have a time and place for connecting to your root system, however you see that? For some people this might be a place of worship such as a church, mosque, temple or synagogue. Or it might involve going out to nature and finding a 'sit spot', a special place you get to know well. Or it might be to have a corner in your home that you set up in a way you choose, perhaps with a candle. Or it could be that in your week you set aside time where you open up space for something different to happen, non-ordinary moments where you recharge. What is soul time for you?

One form of spiritual practice is the use of personal or shared rituals. In a research study at Harvard by Michael Norton and Francesca Gino, 247 grieving people were invited into their laboratory to write about their loss and the emotions and thoughts they had at the time of the loss.[23] One group was also invited to write about rituals they'd performed in relation to the loss, while a comparison group had no mention of the role of ritual in their writing instructions. Both groups were sad, but the group who wrote about the rituals were less sad. 'Although the specific rituals in which people engage after losses vary widely by culture and religion – and among our participants,' wrote Norton and Gino, 'our results suggest a common psychological mechanism underlying their effectiveness.' The rituals could include practices like taking special moments of silence to remember the person they had lost, lighting a candle or performing a ceremony with a faith group. Whatever it was, the common psychological mechanism the authors found was regaining some feeling of control.

Try this – marking remembrances

How do you honour or mark losses in your life?
Are there rituals, ceremonies or soul-time processes that help you grieve?

Spiritual beliefs

Spiritual perspectives have been strongly associated with optimism, as they often involve a belief in helping agencies, whether angels, other spiritual forces, or God. But not all religious beliefs support resilience, as the resilience researchers Southwick and Charney point out: 'Individuals who see God as punitive and judgemental may feel that they "deserve" their troubles, and that their fate is controlled by an unsympathetic all-powerful being.'[24]

In a study of 1,610 cancer patients, the psychologist Marianne Brady and colleagues found that having a sense of spirituality was a strong predictor of quality of life and the ability to enjoy life.[25] If we *believe* we're on the right path, we can put up with more bumpiness along the way. As a spiritual worldview includes beliefs in a transcendent meaning and purpose, it strengthens the sense that our lives matter and that there is a point to them. Spiritual contentedness comes from feeling aligned with a deeper purpose, even if what we're facing is difficult.

In my addictions recovery work, a spiritual belief many clients found helpful was the idea of 'handing over' problems that felt too big and overwhelming. Rather than fret about a difficulty and ruminate, the process of handing over left people feeling a greater sense of acceptance: that things are as they are, and we do what we can while also trusting in the larger unfolding process of life.

Spiritual experience

If a new drug had been invented which in two minutes or less completely changed people's outlook on life in ways that left them more contented, optimistic and satisfied, we'd be hearing about this on the front page of newspapers. For some people, their spiritual experiences have been every bit as powerful. Here's a description.

> I was going through a period of doubt and disillusion with life and torn by conflict . . . Quite suddenly I felt lifted beyond all the turmoil and conflict. There was no visual image, and I knew I was sitting on a bench in the park, but I felt as if I was lifted above the world and looking down on it. The disillusion and cynicism were gone, and I felt compassion suffusing my whole being, compassion for all people on earth. I was possessed by a peace that I have never felt before or since.[26]

What's interesting, and of relevance to resilience, is that one of the most common and potent triggers for experiences like this is extreme adversity. In a recent study, the psychologist Stephen Taylor interviewed twenty-five people who had significantly transformative spiritual experiences.[27] Of these, twenty-three identified traumatic circumstances as a contributory or main causative trigger factor. These are examples of post-traumatic growth.

If you ever find yourself in an extreme situation, where you're desperate and don't know where to turn, consider a spiritual response. What might that involve? Perhaps just being open to a different kind of listening and being willing to receive a different kind of support.

Strengthening Support –

The Sixth Way at a glance

What does it look like when you do this skilfully?

You know you're not alone. You're able to identify where you need support and have a range of ways of sourcing it. You're not shy about asking for help and you've built up a strong network of allies. And even if you're by yourself, without any means to contact others, you're able, creatively, to access rich seams of support that weren't previously visible.

What helps you do this?

a) Positive Self-Talk. How would a good friend or encouraging coach talk to us when giving support in difficult times? We can speak like that to ourselves. This doesn't have to be in front of a mirror, but if it is, that can sometimes help.

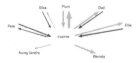

b) Support-Network Mapping. This is a way of visually representing important relationships in your life, as well as flows of support you receive and give out. Reviewing your network helps you recognise the important supporters in your life and also shows where the gaps are.

c) Celebrate good news. The way you respond to people sharing their good news has a powerful impact on your relationship with them. When you show pleasure and interest in what they're pleased about, it strengthens the bond between you.

d) Recognise resilience at different levels. When the relationships, communities and environment around you are in good shape, these all provide important supports for you and your resilience. Playing a role in looking after these aspects of our context is therefore an important part of the story of building resilience.

e) Remember your root system. Having a sense of rootedness in something larger than yourself helps anchor you in turbulent times. So where do you turn, and what do you turn to, when you're feeling at a loss?

The Seventh Way – Stickability

Stickability is the ability to stick with practices and principles you've found useful, so that you're still able to benefit from them in years to come. It involves both remembering tools and keeping to a commitment to use them.

This way includes:

18

How to Make Gains Last Longer

Have you had the experience of going on a course, or reading a book, appreciating it at the time, but then some while later struggling to remember what it covered? We're looking here at the challenge of memory resilience, and we're going to be exploring how to make our memories last longer. But not all our memories. If you never forgot anything, your head might become so stuffed with information that it could be hard to find specific details when you need them. As well as improving memory, it helps to first choose what you want to hang on to.

Remembering is just one aspect of stickability. When you're looking at strengthening skills and improving capacities, as well as more generally changing the way you do things, it is one thing to take a step forward. It is another to maintain and build on that improvement over time. There is a natural tendency to slide back to familiar old ways. A great example of this is with addictions recovery, where the most likely outcome when someone gives up a habit like smoking is that they will start again.[1] That's why we need to give attention to the skill of making changes stick, in what health psychologists call the *maintenance stage of change.*[2]

Smoking is a good example of a sticky behaviour. Once it becomes established, it can be difficult to shake off. Can we learn from unwanted stickiness and apply that learning to the behaviours we'd like to maintain? The challenge here is to find ways to embed resilience practices and thinking as habits in our lives so that they become easier to hang on to. A good place to start is with mapping out a storyline of how to succeed in this.

Storyboarding stickability

We can apply the six-part storyboarding process looked at in the First Way to the challenge of more deeply embedding resilience practices. Here's one version of how the story might go (see Fig. 1 opposite).

Now try this yourself and see what comes up. As this chapter focuses on practices and insights to support resilience stickability, it is worth coming back to this storyboard process after you finish reading it.

Try this – storyboarding stickability

1) **S**tarting point: here's me facing the challenge of . . .
2) **H**oped-for outcome: what I'd like to happen here is . . .
3) **I**n the way of this, obstacles and challenges include . . .
4) **F**acing all that, what helps is . . .
5) **A** Turning or shift might happen if I were to . . .
6) **S**pecific achievable steps I can take in the next seven days include . . .

Acronyms and rhymes as memory tools

What's useful about the storyboarding structure is that once you remember the framework, you've got a pattern to follow where you just fill in the gaps. The acronym SHIFTS (see above) helps you remember that overall structure. In a similar way, the

1) **STARTING POINT –** HERE'S ME FACING THE CHALLENGE OF ...	2) **HOPED-FOR OUTCOME –** WHAT I'D LIKE TO HAPPEN HERE IS ...
wanting to remember what I learn about resilience so that I'm still benefitting from applying useful practices and principles in years to come.	that when facing difficulties in the future, I remember what I've learned and have a well-developed toolkit of skills available to me that feel natural and fluent because I'm well practised in them.

3) **IN THE WAY OF THIS,** OBSTACLES OR DIFFICULTIES INCLUDE...	4) **FACING ALL THAT, WHAT** HELPS ME IS ...
I get busy with other things that fill my attention, and there's a natural tendency to forget, or not nudge myself to use the practices enough to become familiar with them.	storyboarding, aiming for progress rather than perfection, reading this chapter and using the practices described. Sticking with it and encouraging myself.

5) A **TURNING OR SHIFT** MIGHT HAPPEN IF I WERE TO...	6) **SPECIFIC ACHIEVABLE STEPS** I CAN TAKE IN THE NEXT SEVEN DAYS TO MOVE FORWARD ARE...
find someone else who's interested in this too, so that we can support each other in learning more about resilience. Continue the journey, doing more reading and training.	finish this chapter, think about who else might be interested in this, make some notes.

Fig. 1: Six-part storyboard of resilience stickability

letters SETOPSS can remind you of the seven-pathways-to-resilience framework we've been following with each section of the book. These are:

Storyboarding

Emotional First Aid

Thinking Flexibly

Overload Management

Problem Solving

Strengthening Support

Stickability

I use the phrase, 'SETOPSS rhymes with Treetops,' where the E is pronounced 'ee' as in the words Detoxification or Detox. When I teach, I have this on a slide with a picture of treetops (see Fig. 2 below). Rhymes, images and associations reinforce our memory.

Fig. 2: A memory device for
remembering the SETOPSS framework

But how do we remember what the letters stand for? Several strategies are supported by memory research.

Tips from Hermann Ebbinghaus on memory improvement

In nineteenth-century Germany, one of the first psychologists to study memory systematically was Hermann Ebbinghaus.[3] Known for coining the term 'learning curve', he also developed a forgetting curve, which showed how quickly he forgot strings of short words he'd tried to remember. The first time he tried to remember something, he'd forget it fairly quickly, with a steep forgetting curve. But each time he revisited the material, he'd remember it for longer (see Fig. 3 below).

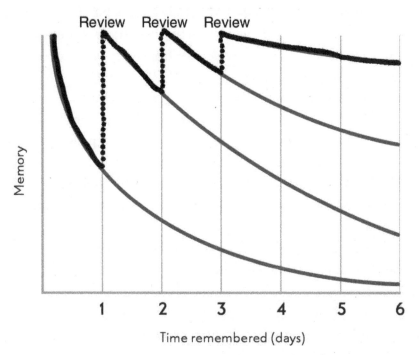

Fig. 3: The forgetting curve of Herman Ebbinghaus[3]

The insight here is that if you want to remember something well in the long term, come back to it several times. This is known as 'spaced repetition'. More recent research by the psychologist Robert Bjork shows you can strengthen the muscle of your memory by practising using it.[4] Each time you revisit material, first test your recall, then look again at what you wanted to remember, reminding yourself of key details.

Towards the end of courses I run, I introduce this memory-strengthening process of practising recall and revisiting the material by asking participants, 'Are you ready for the exam now?' Then I introduce the one-minute memory stretch, and I invite you to try this too.

Try this – the one-minute memory stretch

Set a timer for one minute. Have ready a blank bit of paper or page in a notebook and a pen. When the timer starts, write down as many things as you can remember from what we've covered so far in the previous chapters.

Pause after a minute. Ask yourself, 'Anything else?'

Start the timer for another minute and add anything else you can remember, going through each of the seven pathways to building resilience that we've described, following the SETOPSS framework of storyboarding, emotional first aid, thinking flexibly, overload management, problem solving, strengthening support and stickability.

If you've still got more to write after the second minute, go for another minute too. Keep going until you can't think of anything else to write.

After you've finished writing, look back through the book or your notes and remind yourself of anything else we've covered.

There are different levels of knowing. You can know something at the level of, 'Yes, I've heard of that.' You can go a stage deeper and know it well enough to explain it to someone else. There is a level deeper still when you know something well enough not just to remember it, but also to do it. The second question in the exam (see 'Try this' below) refers to this.

Try this – memory stretch about doing

Set a timer for one minute. Have ready a blank bit of paper or page in a notebook and a pen. When the timer starts, write down as many things as you can remember from what we've covered so far that you've tried out in practice.

What strategies have you used? What insights or principles have you found useful?

Pause after a minute. Ask yourself, 'Anything else?'

Start the timer for another minute and add anything else you can remember doing, going through each of the seven pathways to building resilience.

For many people, the word *exam* has negative associations that include pressure to succeed and the threat of failure. We're applying flexible thinking here in reframing 'exam' as a memory-strengthening device that you can come back to from time to time as a way of exercising your power of recall. In their book *Make It Stick*, the cognitive scientists Mark McDaniel and Henry Roedigger, together with Peter Brown, write: 'Recalling facts or concepts or events from memory is a more effective learning strategy than review by re-reading.'[5]

Whenever you take a piece of information from the back of your mind to the front of your conscious awareness, you reinforce the memory pathway. Like walking the same path through an overgrown field, the first few times doesn't leave much of a trail. But as a pathway becomes more well worn, it becomes easier to follow. It is like this with memories too. And it is much easier to remember something we've done rather than just heard about, so doing the practices, trying them out, again and again, reinforces your remembering even more.

There is a third question too – which is more about moving forward.

Try this – the third question

What would you like still to remember and be doing in five years' time?
What can you do to make this more likely?

Linear and spiral learning

With linear learning, there is a structured progression from one stage to another, where you start at the beginning and become more advanced as you proceed. A common assumption with this type of learning is that moving forward involves learning new material, while repetition is seen as a backward step. Repeating a class can imply you haven't done it well enough the first time, so there may be a sense of failure associated with going back.

Compare this with a course in mindfulness, where you may come back to the same core practices repeatedly. Each time you revisit, you do it from a slightly different place, having more experience and a closer relationship with the practice. I think of this as *spiral learning*: there is progression, but more through deepening familiarity and developing fluency than learning something new. This approach is essential when learning to play a tune, recite a poem or speak in a different language. It is similar with resilience skills and practices: by doing the same thing from a more familiar position, it can come from a deeper place within you.

Linear – progress through knowing more
Spiral – progress through knowing at a deeper level

A term used in meditation teaching is *beginner's mind*, where you approach the familiar as if it were new, with openness, curiosity and freshness of seeing. This way of looking helps you notice subtle details you might have missed first time round, strengthening the impact of spiral learning.

Tracking progress

The journey of learning about and building resilience is lifelong. It is likely that we'll have times where we move forward and times where we slide back. A way of keeping ourselves on track is to find a way of monitoring how we are doing, so we can get feedback that helps us notice when we're making progress.

I use a six-point rating scale from 0 to 5, with the following measures to reflect our level of knowing:

0 – No, I don't know what that is.

1 – Yes, I've heard of that: I sort of know what it is.

2 – Yes, I know what that is, in theory at least.

3 – Yes, I know that because it is something I use or do.

4 – Yes, I know that well, and do it fluently and naturally.

5 – I've taken this in at a deep level; it is a practice I'm so familiar with, I could teach it to others.

You can look at each of the items you identified in the one-minute stretch test and rate yourself on this scale. The purpose of this is to see where you are on a journey of development, and also to recognise if there are steps still to take. If you were to take twenty items, the maximum score would be a hundred. So here are twenty key practices we've covered so far. How would you rate yourself for each of these?

1) Spider diagram and asking, 'What's the best, worst and most likely to happen?'

2) Boat-and-water-level mapping process

3) Resilience SSRI toolkit review

4) Applying the growth mindset

5) Six-part storyboard process

6) The resilience zone and ability to recognise when you're out of it

7) Emotional first aid self-steadying strategies

8) Cognitive reappraisal

9) The ABC thinking check

10) Sentence-starter psychological self-defence prompts

11) Know where you are on the hill, recognising stress signature signs

12) Commitment-cropping process

13) Assertiveness

14) Exercising muscle of frustration tolerance

15) Five-stage problem-solving process

16) Self-support through encouraging self-talk

17) Support-network mapping

18) Active Constructive responses to good news

19) Applying boat and water level to context

20) Spaced repetition of recall for memory strengthening

A guiding principle with the growth mindset is, 'Focus on getting better, rather than being good.'[6] In other words, wherever you are, whatever your score, what would a next step of progress look like from there? And how could you move that way? With spiral learning, progress isn't always moving forward. It might also be about maintaining what you already do, perhaps finding ways to deepen further or to pass on what you know. If you are familiar with the twenty items listed here, are there other items you'd add to the list, or perhaps a different twenty items you'd have in your core practices list?

Becoming a resilience practitioner

A practitioner is someone who practises: a yoga practitioner is someone who practises yoga, and a medical practitioner is someone who practices medicine. The first of these refers to a wellbeing practice you do yourself; the second refers to a way of helping other people. With resilience, we can apply the meaning of practitioner both ways, referring to practices we do to support our own resilience, and also practising in a role that supports resilience in others.

A way of making a behaviour more sticky is to link it to our sense of identity. For example, if we identify with the role of 'yoga practitioner', and that sense of who we are is attractive to us, we're more likely to do yoga. Seeing ourselves as a resilience practitioner has much in common. There may be a spectrum of engagement, depending on the degree to which we identify with this role/label. Engagement with an identity has an 'in', where we're strongly engaged, and an 'out' where we don't relate to the term (see Fig. 4 below).

OUT

That's someone else

How much do you identify with the role of resilience practitioner?

IN

Yes, that's me

Fig. 4: Engagement with identity of resilience practitioner

Support group, network or partner

A way of strengthening a social identity is to join a group with others who share the same interest. Are there people you know or work with who, like you, are interested in resilience? As we saw when looking at support, the research on accountability partnerships suggests we can strengthen our chances of reaching a goal by involving someone else as a support partner and sending them progress reports. Taking on a challenge together and keeping each other updated of your progress is a way of doing this.

The power of habits

Much of our behaviour happens without us needing to think consciously about it because it has been semi-automated. A habit is a behavioural routine that has become semi-automated like this. It is described as *semi* because we have some control over the behaviour – but it has also become implanted as one of those things we do without having to consciously push ourselves. It just seems to happen. For example, if you have a habit of brushing your teeth, you may find yourself walking into the bathroom to do this without having to put it on your to-do list.

How can we establish resilience practices as habits that just happen without us having to consciously plan and make effort each time? A key here is repetition. If we keep doing something enough times, the behaviour builds up a momentum that establishes it as one of our routines. A step towards planting habits is to take them on as a thirty-day challenge.

In a much-watched TED talk, Matt Cutts describes the impact of thirty-day challenges on his life, where he commits to take a particular action every day for the next thirty days.[7] 'It turns out,' he says, 'that thirty days is just about the right amount of time to add a new habit, or subtract a habit, from your life.' He adds that 'I learned that when I made small, sustainable changes they were more likely to stick.' Could you take a resilience practice or a shortlist of your favourite practices, and commit to do one of these each day for the next thirty days? I invite you to try.

Try this – the thirty-day resilience practice challenge

Identify four or five of your favourite resilience strategies and commit to do at least one of these every day for the next thirty days. You could do the same practice each day, or select a different one from your shortlist each day. Find a way of recording whether you've done it or not – for example, ticking on a calendar or in a diary. Then you'll be able to look back after thirty days and see whether you've succeeded here or not. At the end of your thirty days you can also decide whether you'd like to do this process for another thirty days or not.

You can get habit-tracking apps for smartphones to track daily commitments – where you tick each day to record that you've kept to your commitment. Examples of these apps include Don't Break the Chain, Way of Life and HabitBull.

A closing pearl

At the age of seven, Boris Cyrulnik had to disappear in order to stay alive. A Jewish child in Nazi-controlled France in the early 1940s, he hid on farms to avoid the fate of his parents, who were both taken to Auschwitz and killed. After the war, he was taken into care, and later trained as a doctor in Paris.

Something he encountered in medicine, and reacted against, was the tendency to dismiss people as 'damaged goods' if they'd had a very troubled background. He'd hear colleagues say things like, 'No point in bothering with him – he's lost.'[8] He knew from his own experience that it is possible to find an upslope from the deepest of pits.

Boris went on to work with orphans in Romania, child soldiers in Colombia and survivors of genocide in Rwanda. He made the study of resilience his life's work. In looking at what helps us deal with, and recover from, traumatic events, he writes:

The pearl inside the oyster might be the emblem of resilience. When a grain of sand gets into an oyster and is so irritating that, in order to defend itself, the oyster has to secrete a nacreous substance, the defensive reaction produces a material that is hard, shiny and precious.[9]

Resilience is like a pearl. It is something precious we generate in response to adversity. What we've been looking at is how we can consciously cultivate it, with tools we can use and insights that can guide us. Perhaps the most important insight is that pearl-making is something we have a role in. It is linked to skills we can learn, practise and improve.

Every time you come across something frustrating, annoying, difficult or challenging, you can see this as the sand that provokes you to deepen and reinforce your skills. Through practising resilience, life trains you.

I think back to my car crash all those years ago. It was a moment when I could have easily been killed, a time when I was so tormented and ground down. Yet without that, I might not have followed the path that led me here. When we face adversity, we can never know where that will take us or how it will work out. Just because a beginning is difficult, that doesn't mean the end will be too. Whatever our starting point, whatever we face, the skills of resilience help us create a better version of what comes next.

Stickability –

The Seventh Way at a glance

What does it look like when you do this skilfully?

What makes stickability a skill is that you don't leave it to chance, but instead see it as an active process you can get better at through learning and conscious attention. This is the skill that helps the other skills we've looked at be effective in a sustainable way. When you're good at this, you see continuing the path of developing resilience as a project you give regular time to, reviewing progress, ideally drawing in support from others sharing a commitment to this same intention.

What helps you do this?

Practise remembering. Spaced repetition of recall has been shown to strengthen memory and improve learning. You can do this to support your resilience by periodically testing yourself, recalling what you remember that might be useful to you.

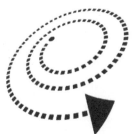

b) Do what you want to remember. It is easier to remember something you've done than something you've only heard or read about. If you set yourself the challenge of doing a resilience practice every day, then you become so familiar with it that you remember it with greater ease, and it may even become a new habit.

c) Spiral learning. You learn skills through repetition, coming back to the same core practices again and again until you have fluency in them.

d) Identify steps and recognise progress. In learning new skills, or improving old ones, it helps morale to see yourself making progress. What are the milestones you identify and reach? Breaking complex learning into smaller steps and noticing when you've taken these helps keep you going.

e) Seeing resilience as like a pearl. It is something precious generated in response to adversity. Each difficult situation you encounter can act like the grain of sand in an oyster, provoking you to practise, deepen and reinforce the skills that build resilience.

Notes

All websites accessed in February and March 2018 unless otherwise stated.

Introduction

1. *Daily Express* (28 August 2016): see https://www.express.co.uk/news/uk/704180/Richard-Branson-accident
2. A. L. Leppin et al., 'The Efficacy of Resiliency Training Programs: A Systematic Review and Meta-Analysis of Randomized Trials', *PLoS ONE* 9: 10 (2014): e111420. https://doi.org/10.1371/journal.pone.0111420
3. Jane E. Gillham, Karen J. Reivich, Lisa H. Jaycox and Martin E. P. Seligman, 'Prevention of Depressive Symptoms in Schoolchildren: Two-Year Follow-Up', *Psychological Science*, vol. 6, no. 6 (November 1995), pp. 343–351.
4. Martin E.P. Seligman, Peter Schulman, Alyssa M. Tryon, 'Group prevention of depression and anxiety symptoms', *Behaviour Research and Therapy*, 45 (2007), pp. 1111–1126.
5. See Martin Seligman, *Flourish* (London, Nicholas Brealey, 2011), p. 127.
6. P. Harms, M. Herian, D. Krasikova, A. Vanhove and P. Lester, 'Report #4: Evaluation of Resilience Training and Mental and Behavioral Outcomes', *The Comprehensive Soldier and Family Fitness Program Evaluation*, 4: 19 (2013). Retrieved from https://digitalcommons.unl.edu/cgi/viewcontent.cgi?article=1009&context=pdharms
7. I. Robertson, C. Cooper, M. Sarkar and T. Curran, 'Resilience training in the workplace from 2003 to 2014: A systematic review', *Journal of Occupational and Organizational Psychology*, vol. 88, issue 3 (2015), p. 533–562.
8. For a good short introduction to this concept, see Miriam Akhtar, *What is Post-Traumatic Growth*, (London, Watkins, 2017).
9. A. Bell and T. D'Zurilla, 'Problem-solving therapy for depression: A meta-analysis', *Clinical Psychology Review*, Volume 29, Issue 4, June 2009, p. 348–353.

Chapter One

1. See Giles Duley, *One Second of Light* (London, Benway Publishing, 2015).
2. Described by Giles Duley in his TEDx talk at https://www.youtube.com/watch?v=5qdZybH-LnI
3. https://en.wikipedia.org/wiki/2015_Rohingya_refugee_crisis, accessed 5 January 2017.
4. *Concise Oxford Dictionary*, 12th edition (Oxford, Oxford University Press, 2011).
5. Giles Duley, 'I lost three limbs in Afghanistan but had to go back,' *Observer*, 10 February 2013, https://www.theguardian.com/artanddesign/2013/feb/10/gilehiss-duley-photography-amputee-afghanistan
6. Andrew Zolli and Ann Marie Healy, *Resilience* (London, Headline Business Plus, 2012).
7. Stephen's story is told at http://stephensstory.co.uk
8. Stephen Sutton, *Stephen's Story* (Kindle book Magic Future, 2014).

Chapter Two

1. Carol Dweck, *Mindset,* 2nd edition (London, Robinson, 2017).
2. For review see Christie Blazer, 'How students' beliefs about their intelligence influence their academic performance', Information Capsule Research Services, vol. 1012 (June 2011): http://files.eric.ed.gov/fulltext/ED536502.pdf
3. Adapted from Dweck, *Mindset,* op. cit.
4. Maguire, Woollett, & Spiers, 'London taxi drivers and bus drivers: a structural MRI and neuropsychological analysis', *Hippocampus*, 16: 12 (2006); pp. 1091–101.
5. Janina Boyke, Joenna Driemeyer, Christian Gaser, Christian Büchel and Arne May, 'Training-Induced Brain Structure Changes in the Elderly', *Journal of Neuroscience*, 28: 28 (9 July 2008), pp. 7031–7035; DOI: https://doi.org/10.1523/JNEUROSCI.0742-08.2008
6. Quoted in 'Can you grow new brain cells?', *Harvard Men's Health Watch* (September 2016), https://www.health.harvard.edu/mind-and-mood/can-you-grow-new-brain-cells
7. Alvaro Fernandez and Elkhonon Goldberg, 'Neuroplasticity', https://sharpbrains.com/resources/1-brain-fitness-fundamentals/neuroplasticity-the-potential-for-lifelong-brain-development/
8. Lee, Yeager and Jamieson, 'How to Improve Adolescent Stress Responses', *Psychological Science*, 27: 8 (August 2016), pp. 1078–91.
9. Discussed by Jan Hoffman in 'Teaching Teenagers to Cope with Social

Stress', *New York Times* (29 September 2016), https://www.nytimes.com/2016/09/30/health/teenagers-stress-coping-skills.html

10. See Chris Johnstone, *Find Your Power*, 2nd Edition (East Meon, Permanent Publications, 2010).

11. Gabrielle Oetingen, 'Future Thought and Behaviour Change', *European Review of Social Psychology*, 23 (2012), pp. 1–63.

12. Heidi Grant Halvorson, *Succeed* (New York, Plume, 2012), p. 24.

Chapter Three

1. http://www.nhs.uk/Livewell/coldsandflu/Pages/Preventionandcure.aspx, accessed November 2017, and widely quoted by other health websites. Page taken down when revisited February 2018.

2. Sheldon Cohen, 'The Pittsburgh Common Cold Studies: Psychosocial Predictors of Susceptibility to Respiratory Infectious Illness', *International Journal of Behavioral Medicine*, vol. 12, no. 3 (2005), pp. 123–131.

3. Sheldon Cohen et al., 'Positive emotional style predicts resistance to illness after experimental exposure to rhinovirus or influenza A virus', *Psychosomatic Medicine*, 68 (2006), pp. 809–815.

4. D. C. Nieman, D. A. Henson, M. D. Austin et al., 'Upper respiratory tract infection is reduced in physically fit and active adults', *British Journal of Sports Medicine*, 45 (2011), pp. 987–992.

5. Sheldon Cohen et al., 'Sleep Habits and Susceptibility to the Common Cold', *Archives of Internal Medicine*, 169: 1 (12 January 2009), pp. 62–67.

6. Martin Seligman, *Authentic Happiness* (London, Nicholas Brealey, 2003), p.45.

7. Seligman, *Authentic Happiness*, op. cit., p. 47.

8. See https://www.genome.gov/19016904/faq-about-genetic-and-genomic-science/

9. Emmy Werner and Ruth Smith, 'Resilience and Recovery: Findings from the Kauai Longitudinal Study', *FOCAL POiNT: Research, Policy, and Practice in Children's Mental Health*, vol. 19, no. 1 (Summer 2005), pp. 11–14.

10. 'Even mild dehydration affects mood, energy level and ability to think clearly' (18 February 2012), at https://www.news-medical.net/news/20120218/Even-mild-dehydration-affects-mood-energy-level-and-ability-to-think-clearly.aspx

11 Quoted by Denis Campbell, 'Half of fizzy drinks have more sugar in one can than adult daily limit,' *Guardian* (15 November 2016): https://www.theguardian.com/news/datablog/2014/jun/12/how-much-sugar-is-in-your-fizzy-drink

12. Dr Mehmet Oz, at https://www.sharecare.com/health/energy-boosters /how-sugar-affect-energy-level
13. S. J. Schoenthaler, 'The Northern California diet-behavior program: An empirical examination of 3,000 incarcerated juveniles in Stanislaus County Juvenile Hall', *International Journal of Biosocial Research,* 5: 2 (1983), pp. 99–106.
14. C. B. Gesch et al., 'Influence of supplementary vitamins, minerals and essential fatty acids on the antisocial behaviour of young adult prisoners. Randomised, placebo-controlled trial', *British Journal of Psychiatry,* 181: 1 (July 2002), pp. 22-28.
15. Tasnime N. Akbaraly et al., 'Dietary pattern and depressive symptoms in middle age', *British Journal of Psychiatry,* 195: 5 (October 2009), pp.408-413.
16. Dr Mike Evans, '23½ hours: What is the single best thing we can do for our health?' https://www.youtube.com/watch?v=aUaInS6HIGo
17. Jim Loe and Tony Schwartz, *On Form* (London, Nicholas Brealey, 2003), p.175.
18. Quoted in Sarah Klein, '13 All-Natural Ways To Fall Asleep Faster', *Huffington Post,* https://www.huffingtonpost.co.uk/entry/natural-sleep-aids_n_3882229

Chapter Four

1. Jonathan Rottenberg, 'The Depression Epidemic will not be televised,' *Huffington Post* (22 May 2014), https://www.huffingtonpost.com/jonathan-rottenberg/the-depression-epidemic-will-not-be-televised_b_5367479.html
2. Interview with Allan Horwitz and Jerome Wakefield, 'Is there really an epidemic of depression?,' *Scientific American,* https://www.scientificamerican.com/article/really-an-epidemic-of-depression/
3. Clare Wilson, 'High antidepressant use could lead to UK public health disaster,' *New Scientist* (12 May 2016), https://www.newscientist.com/article/2087949-high-antidepressant-use-could-lead-to-uk-public-health-disaster/
4. Matt Haig, *Reasons to Stay Alive* (Edinburgh, Canongate, 2015). p.3.
5. World Health Organization, Problem Management Plus (PM+), http://www.who.int/mental_health/emergencies/problem_management_plus/en/
6. C.S. Lewis, quoted at http://www.quotationspage.com/quote/25736.html

Chapter Five

1. Daniel Goleman, *Emotional Intelligence* (London, Bloomsbury, 1996), p. 53.
2. See Dr Laurie Leitch, 'The Nervous System and Resilience', at https://www.thresholdglobalworks.com/pdfs/nervous-system-and-resilience.pdf
3. Dr Laurie Leitch, described in personal communication when interviewed by author.
4. Images adapted from Leitch, 'The Nervous System and Resilience', op. cit.
5. Goleman, *Emotional Intelligence*, op. cit., p.18.
6. A. R. Damasio et al., 'Subcortical and cortical brain activity during the feeling of self-generated emotions', *Nature Neuroscience*, 3, pp. 1049–1056.
7. Stephen Joseph, *What Makes Us Stronger* (London, Piatkus, 2013).
8. Martin Seligman, *Flourish*, op. cit., p. 127.
9. Dr Clay Cook, EdX Course 'Becoming a resilient person': https://www.edx.org/course/becoming-resilient-person-science-stress-uwashingtonx-ecfs311x-0
10. K. Kircanski, M. Lieberman and M. Craske, 'Feelings Into Words: Contributions of Language to Exposure Therapy', *Psychological Science*, 23: 10 (1 October 2012), pp. 1086–1091.
11. Joanna Macy and Chris Johnstone, *Active Hope* (Novato, California, New World Library, 2012).
12. For a good introduction, see Russ Harris, *ACT Made Simple* (Oakland, California, New Harbinger, 2009).
13. George A. Bonanno et al., 'What Predicts Psychological Resilience After Disaster? The Role of Demographics, Resources, and Life Stress,' *Journal of Consulting and Clinical Psychology*, Vol. 75, No. 5 (2007), pp. 671–682.
14. George Everly and Jeffrey Lating, *The Johns Hopkins Guide to Psychological First Aid* (Baltimore, Johns Hopkins University Press, 2017).
15. ibid.

Chapter Six

1. J. A. Russell, 'A circumplex model of affect', *Journal of Personality and Social Psychology*, 39 (1980), pp. 1161–1178.
2. John Kabat-Zinn, 'What is mindfulness?': https://www.psychalive.org/what-is-mindfulness/
3. Daphne David and Jeffrey Hayes, 'What are the benefits of Mindfulness?' *Monitor on Psychology*, vol. 43, no. 7 (July/August 2012), http://www.apa.org/monitor/2012/07-08/ce-corner.aspx

4. Stacy Lu, 'Mindfulness holds promise for treating depression,' *Monitor on Psychology*, vol. 46, no.3 (2015), p.50, http://www.apa.org/monitor/2015/03/cover-mindfulness.aspx

5. Denise Williams, 'Rumination: The danger of dwelling,' *BBC News Magazine* (17 October 2013), http://www.bbc.co.uk/news/magazine-24444431

6. Mark Williams and Danny Penman, *Mindfulness* (London, Piatkus, 2011), p.5.

7. ibid, p.4.

8. Shawn Achor, 'The Happiness Dividend', *Harvard Business Review* (23 June 2011), https://hbr.org/2011/06/the-happiness-dividend

9. J. Ö. Schäfer, E. Naumann, E. A. Holmes, B. Tuschen-Caffier, A. C. Samson, 'Emotion Regulation Strategies in Depressive and Anxiety Symptoms in Youth: A Meta-Analytic Review', *Journal of Youth and Adolescence*, 46: 2 (2017), pp. 261–276.

10. J. W. Pennebaker and R. C. O'Heeron, 'Confiding in others and illness rate among spouses of suicide and accidental-death victims', *Journal of Abnormal Psychology*, 93: 4 (1984), pp. 473–476.

11. J. W. Pennebaker and S. K. Beall, 'Confronting a traumatic event: toward an understanding of inhibition and disease,' *Journal of Abnormal Psychology*, 95: 3 (1986), pp. 274–281.

12. Karen A. Baikie and Kay Wilhelm, 'Emotional and physical health benefits of expressive writing', *Advances in Psychiatric Treatment*, 11: 5 (August 2005), pp. 338–346.

13. James W. Pennebaker, 'Writing about Emotional Experiences as a Therapeutic Process', *Psychological Science*, vol. 8, no. 3 (May 1997), pp. 162–166.

14. For example, see G. Ramirez and S. L. Beilock, 'Writing about testing worries boosts exam performance in the classroom,' *Science*, 331 (2011), pp. 211–213.

15. Daeun Park et al., 'The Role of Expressive Writing in Math Anxiety', *Journal of Experimental Psychology: Applied*, vol. 20, no. 2 (2014), pp. 103–111.

16. Martin Wolgast and Lars-Gunnar Lundh, 'Is Distraction an Adaptive or Maladaptive Strategy for Emotion Regulation? A Person-Oriented Approach', *Journal of Psychopathology and Behavioral Assessment*, vol. 39, issue 1 (March 2017), pp. 117–127.

17. Karen Reivich, 'How to raise an optimistic child' (4 August 2009), https://www.todaysparent.com/family/parenting/how-to-raise-an-optimistic-child/

18. Barbara L. Fredrickson, 'The Broaden-and-Build Theory of Positive Emotions', *Philosophical Transactions: Biological Sciences*, vol. 359, no. 1449 (29 September 2004), pp. 1367–1378.

19. Martin Seligman et al., 'Positive Psychology Progress, Empirical Validation of Interventions', *American Psychologist*, vol. 60, no. 5 (2005), pp. 410–421.
20. Jo Barton and Jules Pretty, 'What is the Best Dose of Nature and Green Exercise for Improving Mental Health? A Multi-Study Analysis,' *Environmental Science Technology*, 44: 10 (2010), pp 3947–3955.
21. R. S. Ulrich, 'View through a window may influence recovery from surgery', *Science*, 224: 4647 (27 April 1984), pp. 420-1.
22. Stephanie Pappas, 'Oxytocin: Facts About the "Cuddle Hormone"', *Live Science* (4 June 2015), https://www.livescience.com/42198-what-is-oxytocin.html
23. Alexandra Sifferlin, 'Our Brains Immediately Judge People,' *Time Health* (6 August 2014), http://time.com/3083667/brain-trustworthiness/

Chapter Seven

1. Thomas J. Watson, https://en.wikiquote.org/wiki/Thomas_J._Watson
2. Quoted by Sean Billings, 'The Importance of Failure' (14 March 2017), https://www.linkedin.com/pulse/importance-failure-why-we-should-afraid-anyone-whos-never-billings/
3. Anthony Robbins, *Awaken the Giant Within* (London, Simon and Schuster, 1992), p. 78.
4. Edward de Bono, *De Bono's Thinking Course* (Harlow, BBC Active, Pearson Education, 2006), p. 58.
5. C. R. Brewin and J. Firth-Cozens, 'Dependency and self-criticism as predicting depression in young doctors', *Journal of Occupational Health* (APA), 2: 3 (1997), pp. 242–6.
6. T. Vandevala et al., 'Psychological rumination and recovery from work in intensive care professionals: associations with stress, burnout, depression and health', *Journal of Intensive Care*, 5: 16 (2 February 2017).
7. Karen Reivich and Andrew Shatté, *The Resilience Factor*, (New York, Broadway Books, 2002), p. 65.
8. Seligman, *Authentic Happiness*, op. cit., p.288.

Chapter Eight

1. Jack Kornfield, interviewed in Lucinda Watson, *How They Achieved* (New York, John Wiley, 2001).
2. Necker Cube, see https://en.wikipedia.org/wiki/Necker_cube
3. These are from the Life Orientation Test: see M. F. Scheier, C. S. Carver and M. W. Bridges, 'Distinguishing optimism from neuroticism (and trait

anxiety, self-mastery, and self-esteem): A re-evaluation of the Life Orientation Test', *Journal of Personality and Social Psychology*, 67 (1994), pp. 1063–1078.

4. E. M. Kleiman et al., 'Optimism and well-being: a prospective multi-method and multi-dimensional examination of optimism as a resilience factor following the occurrence of stressful life events, *Cognition and Emotion*, 31: 2 (February 2017), pp. 269–283.

5. Seligman, *Authentic Happiness*, op. cit., p. 88.

6. ibid, p. 93.

7. ibid, p. 95.

8. Karen Reivich, described in her excellent online course 'Positive Psychology: Resilience Skills', https://www.coursera.org/learn/positive-psychology-resilience

Chapter Nine

1. Wikipedia. List of Bridge Failures. https://en.wikipedia. org/wiki/List of _bridge_failures

2. Chartered Institute of Personnel and Development, *Are We Working Harder Than Ever?* (London, CIPD, 2014).

3. The Radicati Group, *Email Statistics Report 2015-2019*, https://www.radicati.com/wp/wp-content/uploads/2015/02/Email-Statistics-Report-2015-2019-Executive-Summary.pdf

4. With thanks to Patricia Ezechie, https://www.patriciaezechie.com

5. E. M. Hunter and C. Wu, 'Give me a better break: Choosing workday break activities to maximize resource recovery', *Journal of Applied Psychology*, 101: 2 (2016), pp. 302-311.

6. Atsunori Ariga and Alejandro Lleras, 'Brief and rare mental "breaks" keep you focused: Deactivation and reactivation of task goals pre-empt vigilance decrements,' *Cognition*, vol. 118, issue 3 (March 2011), pp. 439-443.

7. Alejandro Lleras, quoted in 'Brief diversions vastly improve focus, researchers find,' *Science Daily* (8 February 2011), https://www.sciencedaily.com/releases/2011/02/110208131529.htm

8. See https://www.startstanding.org/sitting-new-smoking/

9. Hannah Steinberg et al., 'Exercise enhances creativity independently of mood,' *British Journal of Sports Medicine*, 31 (1997), pp. 240–245.

10. H. Budde et al., 'Acute coordinative exercise improves attentional performance in adolescents,' *Neuroscience Letters*, 22: 441(2) (August 2008), pp. 219–23.

11. M. Berman, J. Jonides and S. Kaplan. 'The Cognitive Benefits of Interacting With Nature', *Psychological Science*, vol. 19, issue 12 (2008), pp. 1207-1212.

12. V. Gladwell et al., 'The great outdoors: how a green exercise environment can benefit all,' *Extreme Physiology & Medicine*, 2:3 (2013).

13. Tom Rath and Jim Harter, *Wellbeing: The Five Essential Elements* (New York, Gallup Press, 2010).

14. N. Lovato and L. Lack, 'The effects of napping on cognitive functioning', *Progress in Brain Research*, 185 (2010), pp. 155–66.

15. Leslie Perlow and Jessica Porter, 'Making Time Off Predictable – and Required', *Harvard Business Review* (October 2009), https://hbr.org/2009/10/making-time-off-predictable-and-required

Chapter Ten

1. See https://www.youtube.com/watch?v=zV3gMTOEWt8

2. See 'The Pareto Principle', Wikipedia, https://en.wikipedia.org/wiki/Pareto_principle

3. A. Eslam et al., 'The Effectiveness of Assertiveness Training on the Levels of Stress, Anxiety, and Depression of High School Students', *Iran Red Crescent Medical Journal*, 18: 1 (January 2016).

4. S. A. Karakaş and A. Okanli, 'The Effect of Assertiveness Training on the Mobbing That Nurses Experience', *Workplace Health Safety*, 63: 10 (October 2015), pp. 446-51.

5. 'This Month's Expert: Motivational Interviewing by William Miller, PhD.', https://pro.psychcentral.com/this-months-expert-motivational-interviewing-by-william-miller-phd/

6. S. Rubak, A. Sandbæk, T. Lauritzen and B. Christensen, 'Motivational interviewing: A systematic review and meta-analysis', *British Journal of General Practice*, 55 (2005), pp. 305–312.

7. See https://www2.fgcu.edu/studentservices/StudentConduct/files/D.E.S.C._Script.pdf

Chapter Eleven

1. Chris Hadfield, *An Astronaut's Guide to Life on Earth* (London, Pan Books, 2015), p. 54.

2. ibid, p. 61.

3. Mark King, '30 million UK adults have not made a will', *Guardian* (23 October 2010), https://www.theguardian.com/money/2010/oct/23/making-will-dying-intestate

4. A well-known example is Rhonda Byrne, *The Secret* (London, Simon and Schuster, 2008).

5. Seligman, *Authentic Happiness*, op. cit., p.288.
6. A. Wilkinson and R. Kupers, 'Living in the futures', *Harvard Business Review* (May 2013).
7. Adam Kahane, *Transformative Scenario Planning* (San Francisco, Berrett-Koehler Publishers, 2012), p. 5.
8. Laura King, 'The Health Benefits of Writing about Life Goals', *Personality and Social Psychology Bulletin*, 27: 7 (July 2001), pp. 798–807.
9. Lucy Hone, *Resilience Grieving* (New York, The Experiment Publishing, 2017).
10. ibid, p. 228.
11. ibid, p. 19.
12. ibid, p.21.
13. Lucy Hone, personal communication, 16 Sept 2018.
14. Pema Chodron, *When Things Fall Apart: Heart Advice for Difficult Times* (Boston, MA, Shambhala Publications, 2005), p.10.

Chapter Twelve

1. Claire Robertson-Kraft and Angela Lee Duckworth, 'True Grit: Trait-Level Perseverance and Passion for Long-Term Goals Predicts Effectiveness and Retention Among Novice Teachers,' *Teachers College Record*, vol. 116 (March 2014).
2. Deborah Perkins-Gough, 'The Significance of Grit: A Conversation with Angela Lee Duckworth', *Educational Leadership*, vol. 71, no. 1 (September 2013), p. 14–20.
3. Malcolm Gladwell, *Outliers* (London, Penguin, 2009), p. 246.
4. http://www.twoquotes.org/einstein-all.html
5. Seligman, *Authentic Happiness*, op. cit., p. 88.
6. Deborah J. Mitchell, J. Edward Russo and Nancy Pennington, 'Back to the Future: Temporal Perspective in the Explanation of Events', *Journal of Behavioral Decision Making*, 2 (1989), pp. 25–38.

Chapter Thirteen

1. A. Bell and T.D'Zurilla, 'Problem-solving therapy for depression: A meta-analysis', *Clinical Psychology Review*, vol. 29, issue 4 (June 2009), pp. 348–353.
2. Gail Matthews, see https://www.dominican.edu/dominicannews/study-highlights-strategies-for-achieving-goals

Chapter Fourteen

1. See Peter Shaw, *Hole: Kidnapped in Georgia* (Pembroke Dock, Accent Press, 2006), p. 167.
2. Susan Davidson and Phil Rossall, *Age UK Loneliness Evidence Review* (July 2015), https://www.ageuk.org.uk/globalassets/age-uk/documents/reports-and-publications/reports-and-briefings/health--wellbeing/rb_june15_lonelines_in_later_life_evidence_review.pdf
3. Haroon Siddique, 'Half a million older people spend every day alone, poll shows,' *Guardian* (6 January 2017), https://www.theguardian.com/society/2017/jan/06/half-a-million-older-people-spend-every-day-alone-poll-shows
4. Miller Mcpherson et al., 'Social Isolation in America: Changes in Core Discussion Networks over Two Decades', *American Sociological Review*, 71: 3 (June 2006), pp. 353–375.
5. John Cacioppo, *Psychology Today* (12 December 2008), https://www.psychologytoday.com/us/blog/connections/200812/easing-your-way-out-loneliness
6. Antonis Hatzigeorgiadis et al., 'Self-Talk and Sports Performance: A Meta-Analysis', *Perspectives on Psychological Science*, 6: 4 (2011), pp. 348–356.
7. T. R. Zastowny, D. S. Kirschenbaum and A. L. Meng, 'Coping skills training for children: Effects on distress before, during, and after hospitalization for surgery', *Health Psychology*, 5: 3 (1986), pp. 231–247.
8. See http://www.viacharacter.org
9. Martin Seligman et al., 'Positive Psychology Progress, Empirical Validation of Interventions', *American Psychologist*, vol. 60, no. 5 (2005), pp. 410–421.
10. See http://www.evworthington-forgiveness.com/reach-forgiveness-of-others/

Chapter Fifteen

1. W. Gerin, C. Pieper, R. Levy and T. G. Pickering, 'Social support in social interaction: a moderator of cardiovascular reactivity', *Psychosomatic Medicine* (May/June 1992).
2. Vaillant study, https://en.wikipedia.org/wiki/Grant_Study
3. Sheldon Cohen, 'Social Relationships and Health', *American Psychologist* (November 2004), pp. 676–684.
4. A. Rosengren, K. Orth-Gomer, H. Wedel and L. Wilhelmsen, 'Stressful life events, social support, and mortality in men born in 1933', *British Medical Journal*, 307 (1993), pp. 1102–1105.

5. Tom Rath and Jim Harter, *Wellbeing* (New York, Gallup Press, 2010), p. 41.
6. Stephanie L. Brown, Randolph M. Nesse, Amiram D. Vinokur and Dylan M. Smith, 'Providing Social Support May Be More Beneficial Than Receiving It: Results From a Prospective Study of Mortality,' *Psychological Science*, vol. 14, issue 4 (2003), pp. 320–327.
7. Sybil Carrère, Kim T. Buehlman, John M. Gottman, James A. Coan and Lionel Ruckstuhl, 'Predicting marital stability and divorce in newlywed couples', *Journal of Family Psychology*, vol. 14: 1 (March 2000), pp. 42-58.
8. J. Gottman and R. Levenson, 'A Two-Factor Model for Predicting When a Couple Will Divorce: Exploratory Analyses Using 14-Year Longitudinal Data,' *Family Process*, 41 (2002), pp. 83–96.
9. See https://www.gottman.com/about/the-gottman-method/. I also recommend the video 'How to Make Relationships Work', available to buy at the Gottmans' website at https://www.gottman.com/product/how-to-make-relationships-work/
10. Shelly L. Gable, Gian C. Gonzaga and Amy Strachman, 'Will You Be There for Me When Things Go Right? Supportive Responses to Positive Event Disclosures,' *Journal of Personality and Social Psychology*, vol. 91, no. 5 (2006), pp. 904–917.

Chapter Sixteen

1. Nicola Banning and Chris Johnstone, 'From counselling room to training room', *Counselling at Work* (Autumn 2010), pp. 2–8.
2. Charles Duhigg, 'What Google Learned From Its Quest to Build the Perfect Team', *New York Times Magazine* (25 February 2016), https://www.nytimes.com/2016/02/28/magazine/what-google-learned-from-its-quest-to-build-the-perfect-team.html
3. George Monbiot, 'The town that's found a potent cure for illness – community', *Guardian* (21 February 2018), https://www.theguardian.com/commentisfree/2018/feb/21/town-cure-illness-community-frome-somerset-isolation
4. Quoted in Health Connections Mendip, Annual Report 2016, https://healthconnectionsmendip.org/wp-content/uploads/2016/12/hcm-annual-report-2016.pdf, p.11.
5. R. D. Putnam, *Better Together* (Report of the Saguaro Seminar on Civic Engagement in America, 2000).
6. PricewaterhouseCoopers, 'Building the case for wellness' (2008), https://www.gov.uk/government/uploads/system/uploads/attachment_data/file/209547/hwwb-dwp-wellness-report-public.pdf
7. See https://en.wikipedia.org/wiki/Johnstone_v_Bloomsbury_HA

8. Katherine R. Tuttle et al., 'Comparison of Low-Fat Versus Mediterranean-Style Dietary Intervention After First Myocardial Infarction', *American Journal of Cardiology*, vol. 101, issue 11 (2008), pp. 1523–1530.
9. Andrew Simms, 'Nine meals from anarchy', *Guardian* (11 Jan 2010), https://www.theguardian.com/commentisfree/2010/jan/11/nine-meals-anarchy-sustainable-system
10. See https://en.wikipedia.org/wiki/Instrumental_temperature_record and https://www.nasa.gov/press-release/long-term-warming-trend-continued-in-2017-nasa-noaa
11. Bill George, *Forbes* (17 February 2017), https://www.forbes.com/sites/hbsworkingknowledge/2017/02/17/vuca-2-0-a-strategy-for-steady-leadership-in-an-unsteady-world/#624217e013d8
12. 'World troubles affect parenthood', BBC News (8 October 2007), http://news.bbc.co.uk/1/hi/uk/7033102.stm
13. James Gleick, *Chaos* (New York, Penguin, 1987).
14. 'Stressed Nation: 74% of UK "overwhelmed or unable to cope" at some point in the past year', Mental Health Foundation (14 May 2018), https://www.mentalhealth.org.uk/news/stressed-nation-74-uk-overwhelmed-or-unable-cope-some-point-past-year

Chapter Seventeen

1. I. Brunner et al., 'How tree roots respond to drought', *Frontiers in Plant Science*, 6: 546 (August 2015), pp. 547.
2. Viktor Frankl, *Man's Search for Meaning* (New York, Pocket Books, 1985), p. 95.
3. Stacey M. Schaefer et al., 'Purpose in Life Predicts Better Emotional Recovery from Negative Stimuli,' *PLoS One*, 13: 8: 11 (November 2013), e80329.
4. P. A. Boyle, L. L. Barnes, A. S. Buchman and D. A. Bennett, 'Purpose in life is associated with mortality among community-dwelling older persons', *Psychosomatic Medicine*, 71 (2009), pp. 574–579.
5. Amy Wrzesniewski, 'Job Crafting and Cultivating Positive Meaning and Identity in Work', *Advances in Positive Organizational Psychology*, vol. 1 (2013), pp. 281–302.
6. A. Pines and E. Aronson, *Career Burnout Causes and Cures* (New York, Free Press, 1988), p. 11.
7. With thanks to Luisa Wing, personal communication, 9 January 2018. See www.Vermelho.com.au
8. Patrick Lencioni, *The Five Dysfunctions of a Team* (San Francisco, Jossey-Bass, 2002), p. 43.

9. Joanna Macy and Norbert Gahbler, *Pass it On* (Berkeley, CA, Parallax Press, 2010), p. 38.
10. Rebecca Solnit, *A Paradise Built in Hell* (London, Viking, 2009), p. 5.
11. See https://transitionnetwork.org
12. See https://coolblock.org
13. See https://meetingoftheminds.org/changing-game-around-climate-action-one-block-time-24091
14. Quoted at https://coolblock.org/cool-block-pilot-results
15. See, for example, A. Bussing et al., 'Effects of Yoga on Mental and Physical Health: A Short Summary of Reviews', *Evidence-Based Complementary Alternative Medicine* (2012), http://dx.doi.org/10.1155/2012/165410
16. P. Pressman, J. S. Lyons, D. B. Larson & J. J. Strain, 'Religious belief, depression, and ambulation status in elderly women with broken hips', *American Journal of Psychiatry*, 147 (1990), pp. 758–60.
17. T. E. Oxman, D. H. Freeman Jr and E. D. Manheimer 'Lack of social participation or religious strength and comfort as risk factors for death after cardiac surgery in the elderly', *Psychosomatic Medicine*, 57 (1995), pp. 5–15.
18. Steven Southwick and Dennis Charney, *Resilience - The Science of Mastering Life's Greatest Challenges* (New York, Cambridge University Press, 2012), p. 78.
19. Douglas Yeung and Margaret Martin, *Spiritual Fitness and Resilience* (Santa Monica, RAND Corporation, 2013).
20. P. Harms, M. Herian, D. Krasikova, A. Vanhove and P. Lester, 'Report #4: Evaluation of Resilience Training and Mental and Behavioral Outcomes', *The Comprehensive Soldier and Family Fitness Program Evaluation*, 4: 19 (2013). Retrieved from https://digitalcommons.unl.edu/cgi/viewcontent.cgi?article=1009&context=pdharms
21. Kenneth Pargament and Patrick Sweeney, 'Building Spiritual Fitness in the Army', *American Psychologist* (January 2011), p. 58.
22. P. Boelens et al., 'A randomized trial of the effect of prayer on depression and anxiety,' *International Journal of Psychiatry in Medicine*, 39: 4 (2009), pp. 377–92.
23. M. I. Norton and F. Gino, 'Rituals alleviate grieving for loved ones, lovers, and lotteries,' *Journal of Experimental Psychology: General*, 143: 1 (2014), pp. 266–272.
24. Southwick and Charney, *Resilience*, op. cit., p. 79.
25. M. Brady et al., 'A case for including spirituality in quality of life measurement in oncology', *Psycho Oncology*, 8: 5 (September/October 1999), pp. 417–28.
26. Quoted in A. Hardy, *The Spiritual Nature of Man* (Oxford, The Clarendon Press, 1979).
27. Steven Taylor, quoted at https://www.stevenmtaylor.com/academic-articles/temporary-permanent-awakening-primary-secondary-shift/

Chapter Eighteen

1. Hughes et al., 'Shape of the relapse curve and long-term abstinence among untreated smokers', *Addiction*, 99: 1 (January 2004), pp. 29–38.
2. James O. Prochaska and Carlo C. DiClemente, 'The transtheoretical approach', in John C. Norcross and Marvin R. Goldfried, *Handbook of Psychotherapy Integration*, Oxford Series in Clinical Psychology, 2nd edition (New York, Oxford University Press, 2005), pp. 147–171.
3. See https://en.wikipedia.org/wiki/Hermann_Ebbinghaus
4. Nicholas C. Soderstrom, Tyson K. Kerr and Robert A. Bjork, 'The Critical Importance of Retrieval – and Spacing – for Learning', *Psychological Science*, vol. 27: 2 (2016), pp. 223–230.
5. Mark McDaniel et al., 'Make it Stick: Six Tips for Students', *Psychology Today* (11 June 2014), https://www.psychologytoday.com/blog/make-it -stick/201406/make-it-stick-six-tips-students
6. This is one of Heidi Grant Halvorson's Nine Things in her book *Nine Things Successful People Do Differently* (Boston, Harvard Business Review Press, 2011).
7. Matt Cutts, 'Try something new for 30 days', https://www.ted.com/ talks/matt_cutts_try_something_new_for_30_days
8. Viv Groskop, 'Escape from the past', *Guardian* (18 April 2009), https:// www.theguardian.com/lifeandstyle/2009/apr/18/boris-cyrulnik-chil- dren-trauma
9. Boris Cyrulnik, *Resilience: How Your Inner Strength Can Set You Free from the Past* (New York, Penguin, 2009), pp. 286.

Resources for Further Reading and Training

The author, Chris Johnstone, has set up an online listing of resilience resources at http://collegeofwellbeing.com/resilience-resources that includes:

- A copy of this reference section with clickable links for online sources
- Recommendations for further training in Resilience Skills
- Chris's recommended favourite five books on resilience
- Links to other resilience resources available on the web

Acknowledgements

A motto of many self-help recovery groups is 'I can't, we can'. In the resilience challenge of writing this book and bringing it to publication, that's so true as well. Thank you to everyone who's played a role in supporting, encouraging, inspiring and guiding this process.

I had a home team of people close to me and this project, particularly Kirsty Reid my wife, my agent Suresh Ariaratnam, my graphic facilitator friend Carlotta Cataldi, who drew most of the illustrations, my writer friend Roz Chissick, who went through all the chapters coaching me on writing style, and my first-draft editor Emily Cox, who helped me get the book in a presentable state for the publishers. I appreciate also the support of my brother Dave Johnstone plus friends Chris Macleod and Ariane Burgess.

Then I'm so glad to have Andrew McAleer as my publisher at Little, Brown Book Group, who together with Amanda Keats (editor), Graham Coster (editor), Rebecca Sheppard (editor), Kim Bishop (proofreader), Aimee Kitson (marketing), Clara Diaz (publicity), John Fairweather (production), Liane Payne (illustrator) and Tracey Winwood (design) have worked with me to transform my manuscript, create this book and bring it out to the world.

I'm grateful to my important teachers and those I've quoted from, particularly Martin Seligman, Karen Reivich, Andrew Zolli and Anne Marie Healey, Angela Duckworth, Lucy Hone, Laurie Leitch, Stephen Joseph, Patrick Pietroni, Joanna Macy, Heinz Woolf, David Gershon, Rob Hopkins, Daniel Goleman, John Gottman, Julie Gottman and Ray Ward. I'm lucky also to be part of a community of resilience trainers that includes Professor David Peters, Justin Haroun, Kate Fismer, Paul Anthony, Miriam Akhtar, Jane Sanders and Alan Heeks, among others.

Some of my most significant teachers are those whose stories I've referred to and been inspired by, especially Giles Duley, Stephen Sutton, Sheri Hendricks, Peter Shaw, Luisa Wing and Patricia Ezechie. Thank you also everyone I've interviewed or spoken with, whose stories I have referred to or been informed by, changing your names and identifying details where appropriate to protect confidentiality.

I'm grateful to my test reader panel and those who've endorsed this book, including Professor David Peters, Mark Williamson, Miriam Akhtar, Kathy Sipple, Nicola Banning, Lisa Rossetti, Lissie Michelsen, Deidre Murray, Joanna Macy, Alan Kellas, Sarah Pugh and Heather Thompson.

Lastly, to everyone else who's played a role. If you're not mentioned but should be, know that I'm grateful and thank you, too.

Index

Index